Internet Security for Your Macintosh

A Guide for the Rest of Us

Alan B. Oppenheimer and
Charles H. Whitaker

Peachpit Press • Berkeley, California

Internet Security for Your Macintosh:
A Guide for the Rest of Us

Alan B. Oppenheimer and Charles H. Whitaker

Peachpit Press

1249 Eighth Street
Berkeley, CA 94710
(510) 524-2178
(800) 283-9444
(510) 524-2221 (fax)

Find us on the World Wide Web at: www.peachpit.com
Peachpit Press is a division of Pearson Education

Copyright ©2001 Alan B. Oppenheimer and Charles H. Whitaker

Editor: Clifford Colby
Copy Editor: Kathy Simpson
Production Coordinator: Connie Jeung-Mills
Compositor: Owen Wolfson
Cover Design: TMA Ted Mader + Associates
Cover Compositor: Mimi Heft
Cover Illustration: John Grimes
Indexer: James Minkin

ISBN 0-201-74969-6

9 8 7 6 5 4 3 2 1

Printed and bound in the United States of America.

To: Macintosh users everywhere

From: Alan and Charles

Subject: Keep thinking different!

Thank You

Writing this book took place in two stages. The first stage lasted either seventeen or six years, depending on what you count. For the seventeen part, we'd like to thank all the people at Apple who helped to create and bring the Macintosh to market, helped to create a network (AppleTalk) for it, and helped to bring another one (the Internet) to it. Without you, this book would have been impossible on many levels.

For the six part, we'd like to thank the entire Open Door family, who provided the experience and insights we needed to write this book—along with a whole lot of fun.

The second writing stage was much shorter and more concentrated. It often felt like we were compressing those seventeen years into about six months.

For that stage, we'd like to thank all the people at Peachpit Press and in particular our editor, Cliff Colby. Without you, all the knowledge we've accumulated during the first stage would still be unwritten and unavailable.

Finally, we'd like to thank our wives, families, and friends. This book is your accomplishment as well as ours.

Alan B. Oppenheimer
Charles H. Whitaker
June 2001

Table of Contents

PART TWO: SECURING INTERNET SERVICES   93

Chapter 13 Analyzing and Responding to
Security Threats   215

Getting Started

Since 1984, the Macintosh has been the computer "for the rest of us." By "the rest of us," Apple meant—and continues to mean—those of us who want to use the immense power of the personal computer in the simplest, most intuitive manner possible. Those of us who want it to be easy! Apple has done a great job of building and evolving this computer for the rest of us, even in the face of constant and significant change. That first 128KB, black-and-white, closed-box Macintosh got the Mac religion off to a really good start, and Apple has been true to that religion ever since. Changes such as the advent of desktop publishing, the addition of color, the transition from the 68000 processor line to the PowerPC, and most recently, the transition from the Classic Mac OS to Unix-based Mac OS X have all been managed with "the rest of us" as Apple's primary focus.

Of all the changes involving the Macintosh, though, one stands out above the rest in significance: the Internet. Apple was instrumental in the early growth of the Internet with its inclusion of AppleTalk networking hardware and software in every Macintosh and later with the addition of the Internet's native TCP/IP language to the Mac OS. But it wasn't until the late 1990s that Apple began to realize that the Macintosh could easily be made into the Internet machine for the rest of us.

When Apple gets going, though, watch out! The iMac and the iBook were runaway best sellers for many reasons, but principal among these was that they could be taken out of the box and put on the Internet, by the rest of us, in pretty much no time at all. It was (and is) easier to get a Mac online than to get a VCR connected to your TV!

With its easy-on Internet, Apple has once again done an excellent job of taking difficult concepts and making them simple. The personal computer was hard to use; now it's not. Desktop publishing was hard to do; now it's not. The Internet was hard to get on; now it's not.

Certain aspects of the Internet, however, remain a little scary for the rest of us. And the scariest aspect of them all probably is security. It's so easy to get online, can we really be sure that we're safe while doing it? Especially those of us who are used to Apple's pretty much handling everything for us?

As you'll see, Apple has addressed many issues associated with Internet security while shielding the complexities of those issues from the rest of us. The Mac OS probably is the most secure OS around. But security is one of those areas in which we all have to take some measure of personal responsibility. After all, do you really want to put 100 percent of your faith in Apple's (or this book's authors') saying, "Trust us"? The Mac and the Internet have become far too valuable for the rest of us to do that, no?

This book is a guide to Internet security for the rest of us. It focuses on Mac users, but much of it applies to the rest of the rest of us who don't use Macs. Its goal is to present online-security issues in ways that can be understood by a wide range of users, from those who just bought their first iMac and got it online to those who run computer networks either at work or at home. It proceeds from the simple to the (somewhat) complex and, to a large extent, from the most critical to (somewhat) less important. So if nothing else, definitely read the first few chapters. We think all our chapters are important, and we've tried to make them easy to understand, but we do realize that you may have a limited amount of time on your hands, so we've tried to put first things first.

That being said, let's get started!

About This Book

This book is intended for a wide range of Internet users. It assumes that you are familiar with the basic aspects of using both your computer and the Internet. You should be able to send and receive e-mail and to surf the Net with a Web browser, for example. Beyond that, no additional experience is required. Even if you're an expert Internet user, however, we hope you'll be able to get a good deal out of this book as a whole.

This book is especially important if you're one of the many new broadband Internet users. Broadband connections, such as cable and DSL, are high-speed, permanent links to the Internet. Because your computer is potentially online 24 hours a day, the security risks associated with a broadband Internet connection are heightened significantly. But even if you're connected for only a few minutes once or twice a week, this book has a lot to say that you'll find helpful.

This book definitely focuses on Macintosh users, but the first section and most of the concepts throughout apply to Internet users in general. It also focuses more on the home user than anyone else, although the advanced section looks at security in a work environment as well. As far as specific versions of the Mac OS go, this book tries to address security issues holistically and in a version-independent manner. What it says should apply to any recent Mac OS, including Mac OS 8, 9, and X. If a particular issue is OS-version specific, we'll say so. Because Mac OS X's Unix base presents a whole new set of security issues, we've included a chapter in the advanced section on Mac OS X security.

We've divided the book into four main sections:

General Security Principles is must reading for anyone who's interested in getting online safely, regardless of the type of computer you're using or your skill level.

Securing Internet Services tells you how to use the built-in security features of the Mac OS and third-party applications to create a safe online experience. Advanced users may be familiar with much of this material.

Enhancing Overall Security discusses products that you can add to your Macintosh to supplement the built-in security features.

Advanced Topics dives into issues that may not apply to "the rest of us" as a whole but that apply in many situations. Users can read those chapters that apply to their environments.

For up-to-date information on security and on Mac OS X, check out our book's companion website, *www.peachpit.com/macsecurity/*.

Finally, a word about privacy. Although the subject is related to security in many ways, online privacy is distinctly different. This book does not specifically attempt to address online-privacy issues, such as how to surf the Web anonymously, how to prevent junk mail (also known as spam), or how to ensure that Web sites don't track your buying habits. Securing your Mac will help you secure your online privacy, but you may want to take other steps as well. Those steps are topics for another book.

About the Authors

The authors, Alan Oppenheimer and Charles Whitaker, work for Open Door Networks, Inc. Open Door Networks is a long-time Macintosh Internet company, most recently specializing in Macintosh Internet security products. Open Door was founded by Alan, who serves as its president. Previous to founding Open Door, Alan worked on Macintosh networking at Apple Computer for more than eleven years. Charles has been working with Macs for almost as long.

Open Door has created several popular Macintosh Internet products. Open Door's ShareWay IP product line is included by Apple as Mac OS 9's popular Internet file sharing feature. Open Door's DoorStop Personal Firewall was licensed by Symantec Corp. and is used as the basis for their Norton Personal Firewall. And Open Door's Who's There? Firewall Advisor assists with end-user security analysis.

In addition to creating great Macintosh products, Open Door Networks is also a Macintosh-specific Internet Service Provider (ISP) for its home town of Ashland, Oregon. Working at what is both a Mac ISP and a Mac Internet security company has furnished us with a unique and in-depth perspective on issues of Macintosh Internet security. We hope with this book that we're able to convey this perspective to as many readers as possible.

part i

General Security Principles

What, Me Worry?

Before we dive into the general principles you need to know about online security, we think it's best to start by answering a couple of questions that you may have.

The first is, "Do I really need to worry about Internet security?" In these days of intense media hype, it's easy to look at the never-ending parade of stories about hacked Web sites, denial-of-service attacks, and viruses and to wonder how much to believe. What's real, and what's made up? The second, related question is, "Why would anyone want to attack *my* machine?"

The answers to these two questions are simply, "Yes, you really do need to worry about online security" and "People want to attack your machine simply because it's there." We realize, of course, that you might not want to take our word for these answers. So consider some statistics.

More People on the Net More Often

Although the Internet has existed, in one form or another, since the 1960s, it was not until 1995 or so that it really started growing. Statistics on the total number of Internet users are, as you might expect, hard to come by, but the number of Internet hosts is much easier to ascertain.

An Internet host is a specific computer directly connected to the Internet, with its own specific Internet address (as opposed to one assigned from a pool).

The number of Internet hosts can be determined through what is pretty much a computer-driven census. Between 1995 and early 2001, this number grew from 5 million to more than 100 million. That's a growth rate of nearly 20 times in six years, or more than 50 percent a year (**Figure 2.1**).

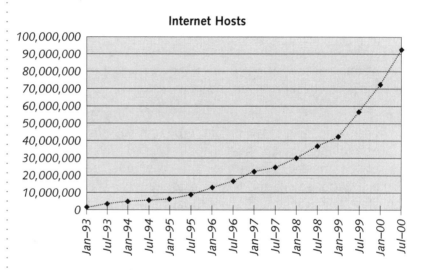

Figure 2.1 A look at the number of Internet hosts per year.

If you're interested in a more people-centric figure, the 100 million hosts in early 2001 translate to about 300 to 400 million users. And the trend is expected to continue. One study estimates that more than 600 million users will be online by the end of 2002 and more than 1 billion by 2005.

In addition to this rapid increase in the number of users, folks are staying online for longer periods of time. There are several reasons for this, including that there's more to see and do on the Web than there was before. According to AOL, for instance, the average amount of time a user stayed on its system went up about 5 times between 1996 and 2000.

The main reason, however, why people are staying online longer—and certainly the one that's most relevant to security—is that many of today's high-speed connections allow users to remain on 24 hours a day, if they want. Nielsen/NetRatings estimates that the number of users on such high-speed connections in the United States more than doubled in 2000, to more than 11 million. We'll talk more about the many additional security ramifications of permanent high-speed connections later in this chapter, but they're causing the Net to be used a whole lot more by a whole lot more users.

More People Doing More Important Things

Just as more of us are online more often, the Net is becoming a more important part of our day-to-day lives. Many of us rely on e-mail as an essential form of communication. Some of us need the Net to do our jobs, either for an organization or for ourselves. Many businesses, such as Yahoo! and Amazon.com, could not even exist without the Net. So whereas in the 1990s, the Net was a requirement more for hobbyists and specialists, in the 21st century, the Net is essential for the rest of us as well. It's pretty much like water or electricity—we just can't do without it.

With the Internet, we have a utility that we have come to rely on and that is accessible by millions (soon to be billions) of people. The Net is not only accessible but also affectable. And for every million additional people on the Net, you know that so-many-thousand new hackers will try to affect things. Businesses and large organization have to come to recognize these facts, and most are taking protective measures, if somewhat belatedly. But the same realization has not yet trickled down to the rest of us.

We hope that these statistics, along with the rest of this book, will help convince you that all of us need to do whatever we can to make our online experience a safer one—and that in general, doing so is pretty easy.

More and More Attacks

When few of us were on the Net, few hackers were as well. And those hackers who were online didn't have much to hack. They generally went after machines running the Unix operating system, because Unix machines were more prevalent on the Net in the early days and were quite hackable.

To digress for a moment, most of you have probably heard the term "hacker." Although sometimes "hacker" just means "anybody who's good with a computer," it recently has specifically come to refer to someone whose computer skills are used to cause problems for others, usually over the Internet. That's how we're going to use the term in this book.

Even as the Internet began to grow from 1995 to 1998, the rate of hacker attacks remained relatively low. But recently, things have changed dramatically and the number of attacks has increased at a rate even greater than the number of users on the Net. It's not clear exactly what changed. Maybe the number of machines on the Net reached some sort of critical mass that made hacking worthwhile in the eyes of the hackers. Maybe the media glorified hacking to such an extent that it became "fashionable," especially for young people. Regardless, hacking is definitely on the rise. One good measure of this increase is the number of official security incidents reported by the CERT Coordination Center. The CERT (which at one time was short for Computer Emergency Response Team) Coordination Center is the major reporting center for Internet security problems.

As you can see in **Figure 2.2,** sometime around 1998, the incident rate starting increasing significantly, and it's been growing faster than the Internet ever since.

Exactly what an "incident" is and whether it's directly relevant to the rest of us are certainly valid questions. So here's a statistic that we believe will hit much closer to home (so to speak):

In a study performed by Open Door Networks on a typical Macintosh connected through the popular @Home cable network, during a 30-day period in early 2001, an average of eight unique unauthorized access attempts were detected per day.

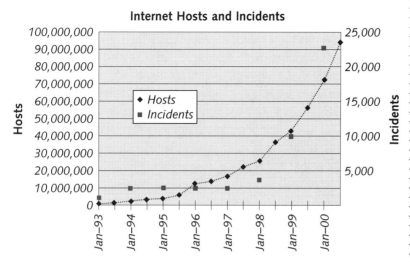

Figure 2.2 The rate of hacking incidents per year.

These access attempts weren't general incidents at some general Internet reporting center; they were specific access attempts made against a specific Macintosh on a widely used cable-modem Internet service. And this study, conducted by the authors, is backed up by many additional reports. At the January 2001 Macworld Expo trade show in San Francisco, during a network managers' forum, an audience member indicated that his newly installed firewall logged so many access attempts that he first thought that the firewall manufacturer was making up those attempts as a marketing ploy! And here's just one of the many reports that Open Door Networks has received on the subject:

"As is probably true with most of your customers, I have been astounded at how many unauthorized attempts to penetrate my computer there are."

Machines that the rest of us use on the Internet are getting attacked, and they are getting attacked at a significant and increasing rate. You do need to worry about online security!

Why Me?

We hope it's pretty clear by now that Internet security is an important issue even for the rest of us. But you still may be wondering why. Why would someone want to attack your machine if it has no secret documents, no Web site to deface, no credit-card numbers to steal (we hope)? What possible benefit could someone gain from accessing or destroying data on your machine?

These are all good questions. And they have two sets of answers. First, you may have more important data on your machine than you think. (We'll look at this issue in the chapter on the physical security of your machine.) But even if you're right about the lack of significant data on your machine (maybe all you do is play games), there is a second set of reasons why your machine is being attacked over the Net.

Here's the key point to realize about most access attempts on your machine:

No one is specifically targeting your machine.

You're right—pretty much no one cares about you in particular. Most hackers out there just want to break into *any* machine. Many are bored high-school or college students looking for a challenge. They want to be able to brag to their friends, "See? Look what I can do to this poor sucker's machine. Am I not cool?"

Being cool used to mean having a powerful car or being on the football team. Now, to a subset of the younger generation, it means being able to wreak havoc at long distance and to leave your mark. Hacking is (sometimes quite literally) the digital version of graffiti.

Another key point to understand is exactly how those access attempts to your machine are being made:

Almost all havoc-wreaking is done through prebuilt applications or scripts.

The havoc-wreaker doesn't need to be some geek who slaves away for nights on end on a specific application to go out and do his dirty work. He (and it usually is a he and a young he at that) simply needs to go to any of a variety of Web sites and download any of a variety of applications or scripts. A simple double-click after that, and the hacker (or "script kiddie," as he's often called) is on his way.

But how does a script kiddie happen to end up hacking your machine? Again, why you? Pretty much because your machine was there, and it was your turn. As you'll see in the chapter on Internet basics, each machine on the Net has an address, just like a phone number. The hacker's script either picks Internet addresses at random or goes through them sequentially. The script uses various techniques to see whether there's a machine at that address and concentrates on address ranges that are more likely to have lots of vulnerable machines (such as the address ranges used by popular Internet providers). When the script finds a machine at a particular address, it moves on to try various built-in attacks against that machine. Those attacks usually are the ones that you'll see if you've added any sort of logging or monitoring features to your machine (see the chapters on analyzing security threats and personal firewalls for ways to do this). If any attack is successful, the script alerts the hacker running it or logs the machine's address to a file for future exploitation; otherwise, it moves on to the next address.

It may seem unlikely that of all the machines on the Net, yours is getting chosen at random eight times a day on average. After all, there are a hundred million machines. But remember that the rate of attacks is increasing faster than the rate of new users. A few years ago, lots of new users were getting on the Net but not lots of new hackers. Now the hackers are catching up. So with all those hackers running all those automated tools (on faster computers and faster connections), they just happen to hit your machine eight times a day! And if trends continue, the situation is just going to get worse.

It Gets Worse

For many reasons, you don't want a script kiddie, or anyone else, to gain access to your machine. These reasons are pretty much the same as the reasons you don't want anyone to gain access to your house. There also are less obvious, but equally important, reasons. The main one is:

You may never know that someone has gained access to your computer let alone what they're doing or have done with the access they've gained.

Some attackers just leave some sort of calling card ("Kilroy was here!") and don't do anything malicious. But other attackers are much more subtle. They may implant an invisible file or application (often called a *Trojan horse*) on your machine that could do all sorts of bad things at some unknown time. For example:

- The hidden application could spy on everything you're doing and then make that information available to the attacker over the Net. It could notice what Web sites you go to, for example, or read your e-mail along with you. Worse yet, it could copy the passwords you type to access Web services or steal the credit-card numbers you enter in supposedly secure Web sites.

- The hidden application could be used to launch an attack on another machine. Attackers often cover their tracks by launching attacks indirectly, through a series of machines, sometimes in different countries. Then, when someone comes looking for the attacker, they find you instead. Although you may not be legally liable for the misuse of your machine in this situation, we don't think any of us wants to have the FBI or other law-enforcement agencies knocking on our door.

- The application could be used in concert with similar applications implanted on other machines for more advanced, distributed attacks. The most popular of these is known as a *distributed denial-of-service attack*. Your machine, and hundreds or thousands like it, could be used in concert to flood a particular Web site with traffic, effectively denying the services of that Web site to legitimate users. In February 2000, such an attack was launched successfully against several major Web sites, including Yahoo! and CNN. And the FBI did go around knocking on a lot of doors.

Broadband Connections Are Especially Vulnerable

Any machine connected to the Internet in any way is susceptible to a random attack at any time. But machines hooked up by increasingly popular broadband connections are more susceptible than most others. *Broadband* in general refers to any high-speed Net connection, but for the rest of us, it usually means a connection through a cable modem or DSL (digital subscriber line). The two key characteristics that make broadband links particularly vulnerable to attack are the same characteristics that make broadband connections so popular in the first place: They're connected 24 hours a day, and they're high-speed.

Unlike traditional dial-up connections, in which you call in, surf the Net, and then disconnect, broadband connections are always active. Because broadband connections are always on, the amount of time a computer is vulnerable to Internet attack is greatly increased compared with dial-up. Any time your computer is on, it's online and vulnerable to attack. Thus, based on raw probability, your computer's going to get attacked much more often on a broadband connection than on dial-up. Beyond this, however, hackers are more likely to go after machines that are connected all the time because they know those machines will be there when they need them, either to activate a Trojan horse they've installed or for some other nefarious purpose. Hackers also may restrict their searches to Internet addresses that they know are used for broadband connections, because they know that machines on those networks will be more useful to them, further increasing the odds of an attack.

Broadband connections are not only always on but also (usually) many times faster than dial-up connections. Speed provides many advantages to a hacker. Hackers look for machines by sending out a query or "probe" to successive addresses until a machine answers and tells the hacker it's there. If a hacker is looking only for machines with fast connections, he can find them quickly because they answer his probe faster. And when a hacker finds a machine, he can carry out attacks against it more quickly.

In the chapter on managing passwords, for example, you'll see that speed is essential to a dictionary attack, in which the hacker tries to figure out your password by trying every word in the dictionary. Such an attack is practical only on a high-speed connection. Additionally, if the hacker wants to use your machine as a launching point for other attacks, speed is critical as well.

Another characteristic of many broadband connections is that your machine is assigned the same Internet address for long periods of time. Even though many such connections claim to give your machine a dynamic address, that address rarely changes. So the hacker can pretty much count on your machine's being available at the same address whenever he wants to get at it—another big advantage to him over a machine on a dial-up connection, because its address changes each time it dials in.

Many of the rest of us still connect through dial-up connections, but broadband connections are increasing at a faster rate than other Net connections. Broadband connections grew from about 4.7 million at the end of 1999 to 11 million at the end of 2000, and the number is expect to grow to 20 to 30 million by 2004. So even if you're not using a broadband connection today, there's a pretty good likelihood that you will soon. You might as well start thinking about safety now.

But I Use a Mac!

Even after everything we've told you about how real the risks are, you might still be thinking, "But I use a Mac! Everyone says the Mac OS is secure and that the Mac is just 10 percent of the machines on the Net. Won't the hackers go after the Windows machines first?"

It's true that the Classic Mac OS (up through the 9.x series) generally is considered to be more secure than either the Windows or Unix operating system. Here are a few reasons:

- The Mac OS was designed for a single user.
- It was not designed to be logged into remotely.
- Its source code is not available publicly.
- It does an excellent job of preventing you from opening security holes accidentally, both through a clear user interface and through warnings when appropriate.
- It just seems to have fewer security holes.

As supporting evidence for the Mac's superior security, in 1999 the U.S. Army chose the Macintosh as the Web server for its main site after its Windows-based server was hacked by a 19-year-old. The World Wide Web Consortium (W3C) also states publicly that "the safest Web site is a bare-bones Macintosh running a bare-bones Web server."

It's true that Windows machines represent 90 percent or so of the machines out there on the Net. In this case, however, the Mac's smaller installed base ends up being a good thing. Remember, most attackers aren't looking for your specific machine; they're looking for any machine. And because the methods of breaking into a Windows machine are different from those for breaking into a Mac (or a Unix machine), most hackers are looking specifically for Windows machines. The popularity of Windows machines also has a snowball effect. Because most hackers are looking for Windows machines, most of the automated scripts that are written target those machines, so most of the script kiddies, who can't do much on their own, end up attacking Windows machines. And when the script kiddies grow up and *really* start to learn things, guess what machines they write new scripts for?

Once again though, specific statistics are a good idea:

In the Open Door study we mentioned earlier in this chapter, fully 40 percent of all the attacks detected specifically targeted Windows machines, with another 2 percent targeting Unix machines. Not a single Mac-specific attack was detected during the month of the study.

So, using a Macintosh does go a long way toward enhancing your overall safety against certain type of attacks. But we could not identify a good 58 percent of attacks as being against a specific type of machine. Also, many other security issues (especially those we list in Chapter 3) apply pretty much equally to all types of computers. In fact, some might even apply to Macs to a greater degree.

Moreover, as many of you are aware, the Mac OS is transitioning to Mac OS X. Mac OS X has, at its core, the Unix operating system. Apple has done a great job of hiding the inherent complexities of Unix underneath the covers of Mac OS X, but those complexities are still there. Many of those complexities are directly related to the myriad security issues that have always been associated with Unix. Unix is the environment of choice for many hackers, who love its command-line complexity and open source code. But until now, there hasn't been much of an installed base for hackers to go after. With the sudden flood of Unix-based machines that Mac OS X is unleashing, you can bet that the Mac is going to become a much bigger target very quickly. As the Mac moves from Mac OS 9 to Mac OS X, and from an '80s OS into the 21st century, it also moves from a secure, little-targeted OS to a less secure, more-targeted OS, with many more unknowns. We'll have a lot more to say about the transition to Mac OS X in later chapters, but it's definitely something to start thinking about now.

See our book's companion website at www.peachpit.com/macsecurity/ *for up-to-date information on Mac OS X security.*

What, Me Worry Too Much?

We hope that you now see the need to worry about security while you're online. Some of you may now even be so scared that you're thinking about pulling the network connection on your Mac right away, especially if that connection's through a cable modem or DSL. But is it possible to be too worried?

Yes.

If you really pulled the plug on your network connection and never connected to the Net again, we would have done you a great disservice. Like most good things in life, the Net is a double-edged sword. But it's 95 percent good edge and 5 percent bad. You don't *not* drive your car because you might get into an automobile accident, and you don't stay home all the time because you're worried that someone might break in. But you do put on your seat belt when you drive, and you do lock your house when you leave for a trip. So there is an appropriate degree of worry for every situation.

How much should you worry? Only you can make that decision. As is true of everything else, the degree to which you worry about online security should be proportionate to the risks involved.

Consider two Mac users. The first connects through a dial-up modem for maybe an hour a day. He uses his Mac mainly for reading e-mail and doesn't keep any important documents or data on the Mac. The second is online through a cable modem and uses both the Net and the Mac quite extensively, sending and receiving e-mail, doing online banking, and keeping track of stock portfolios through the Web. She also keeps financial records and even a book that she's writing on the Mac, plus some work-related items. Clearly, the second Mac user should worry about the security of her machine more than the first. This is not to say that the first user shouldn't worry but that he can afford to worry less, because he has less to lose.

Degrees of worry should translate into degrees of security. As you'll see, you can take many security measures to protect your Macintosh while you're online, just as you can take many security measures to protect your house. You can lock the door; you can lock the windows; you can put in an alarm system;

you can build a security gate. Different degrees of security are appropriate for different situations.

We feel that everyone should at least understand and implement the general security principles outlined in the rest of Part 1 of this book. Beyond that, you'll need to assess things for yourself. As a rough guideline, here are some factors that should increase your "worry index" and, thus, your security measures.

Do you:

- Have a permanent connection to the Net?
- Have a high-speed connection to the Net?
- Leave your Mac on all the time (with a permanent connection to the Net)?
- Depend on your Mac or the Net to do your job?
- Make extensive use of e-mail, especially for exchanging documents?
- Keep important documents or records on your Mac?
- Shop online or use other forms of e-commerce?
- Use Mac OS X, Windows, or Unix?
- Have more than one Mac on the Net?
- Provide any services from your Mac, such as file sharing or a Web site?

You may not understand the reasons behind all of these questions yet, but you certainly should by the end of this book.

Physical Security

The simplest things are often the most important. Have you ever prepared for a long trip by locking all the windows in your house, setting timers on the lights, and maybe activating an alarm system but forgotten to lock the door on your way out? Many of the precautions we describe later in this book are like the security measures you take when you're preparing for a trip. But the measures in this chapter, along with the next few chapters, are like locking the door to your house. They're easy, they're something everyone should do, and they're things people often just plain forget. If you implement only the measures in these chapters, you will have gone most of the way toward a fully secure online experience. On the other hand, if you skip these chapters and implement only the more advanced measures later in the book, you will have gone just a small way toward that secure experience. You will have locked the windows but left the door wide open.

Things that Can Go Wrong

Before the network existed, the computer did. Keeping your computer secure off the Net is half the battle of keeping your computer secure on the Net. If you've been using a computer for a long time, you're probably aware that a long list of bad things can happen to your machine. But the popularity of the Internet has caused many of us to buy a computer for the first time, so we think about Internet security first and general computer security second, which is completely backward. Whether you're new to computers or a 20-year veteran, it's important to review the list of physical things that can go wrong with your machine.

Theft. If you use a notebook computer or live in a big city, you're much more likely to lose the data on your computer (not to mention the computer itself) to theft rather than to someone hacking your computer over the Internet.

Loss. Simply losing a desktop computer is somewhat hard, but if you've ever traveled with a notebook, think about how easy it might be to leave it somewhere by accident.

Hardware or software crash. Computers fail. Sometimes the hardware fails, maybe because of a power surge or hard disk crash. Sometimes a critical section of the hard disk goes bad, and the whole hard disk becomes unreadable. Sometimes a piece of software, even the OS itself, fails catastrophically and corrupts the hard disk. Regardless, the result is the same: Your data's gone or at least inaccessible. Data can sometimes be restored after a crash if you know the right expert, but data restoration is not easy.

Accident. As much as we try to avoid them, accidents happen. Especially in a home environment, many accidents can befall computers. Drinks can get spilled on them; they can fall while we're moving them; they can be "attacked" by pets and small children. An "attack" by your child can be as dangerous as an attack over the Net.

Natural disaster. The effects of a fire, flood, or earthquake can be devastating. We should put our loved ones and ourselves first when taking precautions against such events. But we shouldn't overlook our computers.

Seizure by law enforcement. As computers become part of our daily lives, they also become part of criminals' lives, especially Net criminals. These criminals often work indirectly, through other people's computers on the Net. Even though you're not involved in a crime directly, your computer could be seized and inaccessible for a long period.

Just about any of these events will result in significant, if not total, loss of the data on your computer. Many of them will result in the loss of the computer itself. For these reasons, one of the most important principles you can learn from this book is:

> *Compared with an attack over the Internet, a physical offline loss or failure of your computer is more likely to occur and is almost always more devastating. You should devote at least as much effort to your computer's physical security as you do to its Net security.*

Physical Security First

You can do many relatively simple things to protect your computer physically. Many may seem obvious, but then again, so is locking your door. You may not want to implement all these security measures all the time, but they're worth thinking about.

Protect your computer from theft. Don't position it in the window on a busy street or by a door that's easily accessible. And when you do travel, consider hiding your computer away somewhere, just in case. If your computer has an external monitor, you don't need to hide the monitor—just the main computer and associated external hard disks, if any. Consider using a lock-down cable and even an alarm system if you're in a high-crime area.

Get a power-surge protector. A surprising amount of computer failures (and associated data loss) are due to lightning strikes or power surges during power outages. While you're at it, consider getting an uninterruptible power supply (UPS), which will prevent unexpected shutdown of your computer during a power loss. Unexpected shutdowns often cause disk corruption and data loss.

Don't keep valuable or private information on notebook computers, especially ones you travel with. It's just too likely that something bad is going to happen to that computer, and you risk not only losing the data but also having that data fall into the wrong hands. Almost 90 percent of all computer-related insurance claims filed in the United States in 1999 were for notebook computers.

Encrypt data you consider to be confidential. Depending on how private that data is, if your computer does fall into the wrong hands, you can at least take steps to ensure that no one else can see the data. Mac OS 9 makes encrypting and decrypting files easy.

Protect your computer from family and natural disasters. Consider using it in an office that's off-limits to animals and small children. If you live in an earthquake area, be sure that your computer's on a sturdy desk.

Put your computer off-limits to workers and houseguests. Although most of your friends and coworkers are trustworthy, you don't want to risk giving them access to your data or computer. You should protect your computer the same way that you protect your hard-copy confidential information, such as tax returns.

Back up, back up, back up! This topic is so important that we're devoting the rest of this chapter to it.

Things Will Go Wrong Anyway

No matter how careful you are, and no matter how many preventive measures you take, something's probably going to go wrong with your computer at some time. For most of us, the hard part won't be trying to recover from the physical loss of the computer itself. In fact, the loss may well be the good excuse we've been looking for to get the latest model. But the loss of the data stored on the computer is a whole other matter. That data may be irreplaceable.

Many of us who have used computers for a long time know that backing up our computer's data is essential. But even we long-time users still don't back up as often—or as thoroughly as we should. Those who are relatively new to computers may not even think about backing up at all. Now is the time to review whatever backup procedures you may have in place or to put some in place if you don't have any.

Of all the security measures you can take, both offline and online, backing up the data on your computer probably is the most important, because it protects you both offline and online.

If something goes wrong, due to a physical problem or an online attack, a well-implemented backup strategy will go a long way toward mitigating the problem.

Backup options

Whole books have been written about backing up your computer's data, and those books are worth reading. But just as the Internet introduces new security risks, it introduces new backup options as well.

Many applications can help you back up the data on your machine. These applications can even back up your OS and software, although this software can be recovered in other ways as well. The most popular backup application for the Macintosh is Retrospect from Dantz (**Figure 3.1**). Backup applications such as Retrospect can help you figure out what has changed and what needs to be backed up, can automate the backup process, can back up to the Net, and can even compress and encrypt your data.

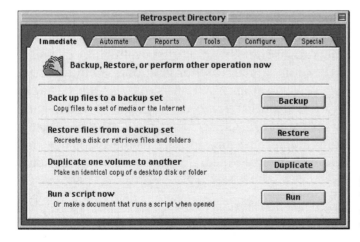

Figure 3.1 Backup applications like Retrospect can automate the backup process, making it more likely that critical backups will always get done.

Getting a backup application is a good idea. But you should make sure that it's what you need. At times, a backup application may be overkill. If you just surf the Web and check e-mail, you may have little to back up. You may need to copy your e-mail folder to an external or network drive occasionally, and that's about it. You can upgrade to a backup application later, as your computer use gets more advanced.

The Internet has had a significant effect on the backup process, and not just because it makes backing up even more critical. One little-noticed side effect of the popularity of the Internet has been the demise of the floppy-disk drive. Today's Macs, including the iMac and iBook, do not have built-in floppy drives. So if you want to back up these machines locally, you may need to get an external backup device, such as a USB or FireWire floppy drive, Zip drive, or writeable CD or DVD drive. On the other hand, you can take advantage of another of the Net's effects on the backup process by using the Net itself as your backup medium.

You have several ways to use the Internet for backup. Many services provide Internet back up, usually for a monthly fee. Two Mac-focused ones are BackJack (*http://www.backjack.com*) and iMacBackup.com. You can also use a backup application such as Retrospect to back up over the Net, if you have a server to back up to. (But don't back up to an FTP server—see the FTP chapter in the Advanced section for the reasons.)

An incredibly simple (and free) backup solution is available for those of us who don't need advanced backup features: iDisk. Apple's iDisk provides 20 megabytes of free Net-based storage that you can use for anything you want. It's accessible from any Mac running Mac OS 9 or later and is built directly into Mac OS X. Being from Apple, iDisk is incredibly easy to use (backup for the rest of us, so to speak). If you have a small amount of stuff to back up, don't need capabilities such as encryption and automation, and are using a machine that doesn't have any external media to back up to, you should look at iDisk.

To use iDisk, sign up for an iTools account through Apple's iTools home page (*http://itools.mac.com/*). As a side benefit of signing up, you get your own mac.com e-mail address. After signing up, to back up files to your iDisk, all you do is mount the disk through the iTools Web site or directly through the iDisk menu item under Mac OS X. Your iDisk shows up on your desktop like a local hard disk. and you use it the same way (**Figure 3.2**). Just drag and drop the files or folders you want to back up into the iDisk folder called Documents. That's it.

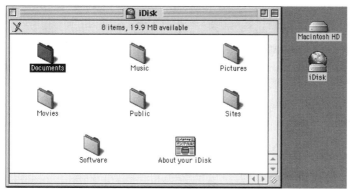

Figure 3.2 iDisk is an incredibly easy to use backup option for the rest of us. Just drag files to the Documents folder, and they're automatically backed up remotely.

You also can do any other operations that you can do on a local hard disk, so if you want to create subfolders for backup or to rename or delete files, you already know how to do it. Restoring files is as simple as dragging them in the other direction. You can even make an alias to the Documents folder and then just drag files to be backed up to that alias. If your iDisk is not already mounted, even that step can be done for you.

You secure your iDisk with the name and password you chose for your iTools account. iDisk uses AppleShare technology, which keeps your password secure over the Net, unlike the popular FTP file-transfer technique, which doesn't (see the Advanced section for more information). The files transferred to and from iDisk, however, are not encrypted. If you're worried that other people might see the contents of the files, you can use Mac OS 9's encryption tools before the transfer.

Even if you use a backup application, keep iDisk in mind: It's especially useful if you're traveling and don't have access to the backup medium you normally use.

Good backup procedures

Whether you use an automated backup application or back up manually, keep several important items in mind:

Back up regularly. Depending on how often you make changes or get new e-mail, you may want to back up daily, weekly, or monthly.

Back up everything you care about. It doesn't take much more time and space to back up everything you don't want to lose.

Make sure that you are backing up the right files. If you are backing up manually, be sure that you back up in the right direction, dragging the newer files over the older ones. Wiping out your recent work with your older backup can be devastating.

Check your backups periodically. You don't want to find out that your backup procedure is not working, or not backing up everything that matters, after you've lost all your data. If you use an automated backup application, try restoring from your backups once in a while. If you back up manually, check the backup medium periodically to make sure that it is readable.

Maintain multiple backups. A file can become corrupted without your noticing it, and you could back up the corrupted file. Keeping some of your older backups around may help you recover from this situation.

Keep both local and remote backups. If the only backups you have are at home with your computer, you may lose the backups along with the computer, for instance due to fire or theft. Every so often, move a backup offsite—to a safe-deposit box or a friend's house, for example. Remote backups are also handy for use as older backups if both a file and its backup become corrupted. If you have a small amount of data to back up, iDisk is an excellent option for your remote backups.

Keep your backups in a secure location. Consider encrypting your backups if you're worried that the data might fall into the wrong hands.

Managing Passwords

Physical security is critical to a safe computing experience, and it makes sense for you to safeguard your Mac whether you surf the Net or not. When you get on the Net, you need to supplement your good physical-security practices with a few simple virtual ones, and you'll be 90 percent of the way toward maximum online safety. One of the simplest and most important online security practices is carefully managing the passwords that are part of your day-to-day Internet experience.

More and More Passwords

You probably first encountered passwords in the online world when you signed up with an Internet service provider (ISP). The ISP may have asked you what you would like to use as an account name and password. When you dial in to your ISP (or even if you use DSL, in some cases), every time you connect, you are asked for that account name and password. Your computer may be set up to provide that information automatically, as shown in **Figure 4.1**(keep reading to see whether doing this is a good idea), but regardless, it's provided every time you connect.

Your ISP needs this information to make sure that you are authorized to connect to the Internet through its system.
It may also use this information for accounting, to make sure that you stay within your total time allowed per month, although almost all ISPs provide unlimited access these days.

Figure 4.1
Using the Mac's built-in Remote Access Control Panel to provide a dial-up ISP with your account name and password before connecting.

Your account name and password are often also used as your e-mail name (the part of your email address before the @ sign) and password. E-mail is the second place most of us encounter passwords on the Net. You don't want just anyone who knows your e-mail address to be able to read your e-mail, so a password ensures that you're the one looking at it. Most e-mail programs can save your password automatically and send it each time you read your mail (again, this may or may not be a good idea). If you have multiple e-mail accounts, you may have multiple passwords, one for each account.

Web-site passwords

Many Web sites require you to log in with an account name and password, using this information to authenticate your identity. Web sites want this information for different reasons, however. Unlike the passwords you use to connect to your ISP or read your mail, some Web-site passwords aren't really for your benefit; they're for the benefit of the Web-site owner. These passwords let the site owner keep track of information about you, such as how often you visit the site, where within the site you go, and which ads you view. In other words, they help the site accumulate marketing data on you, which the owner can use internally or sell to others. An example of such a site is the *New York Times* site (*http://www.nytimes.com*).

Some Web sites, however, use account names and passwords for your protection. If you do any sort of financial management or stock trading online, you wouldn't want anyone who has your account number to be able to conduct transactions. Likewise, if you keep private information online, such as a calendar or stock list, you wouldn't want just anyone to access that information. When you are managing your passwords for Web sites, it is important to distinguish between passwords that are for your benefit and those that are not.

Web-site passwords are implemented in two ways. The first, and increasingly less-common, way is through a dialog box that comes up when you first try to connect to the site. The second way is through a form on the site in which you enter your account name and password. The distinction between these two ways of entering passwords is also important for managing your passwords, as we'll discuss later in this chapter.

Passwords for other services

Account names and passwords are used in other applications as well. If you have multiple users on your Mac, and you have Mac OS 9 or later installed, each user can log in separately. You also have an account name and password for your iDisk and for any FTP (file-transfer protocol) sites that you might log in to.

If you use the Internet much, you're going to accumulate a lot of passwords. Managing these passwords to keep them (and the data behind them) secure is one of the most important areas of online safety. **Table 4.1** summarizes different types of passwords.

Table 4.1

Service	Reason for Password	Notes
Internet login	Making sure you're authorized to connect	Not used for cable and some DSL
E-mail	Making sure that you're the person checking your mail	E-mail application can save password
Web site	Tracking your use	For the Web site's benefit, not yours
Web site	Securing your data or account	For your benefit
Mac login	Seeing which user you are	Applies only if the Mac has multiple users
iDisk	Securing your data	Great for remote backup
FTP	Securing your data	Insecure (see the Advanced section of this book)

Choosing Good Passwords

Most people severely underestimate the importance of picking good passwords and of keeping those passwords secret. Most of us wouldn't set our ATM personal identification number (PIN) to 0000, and none of us would give our PIN to a perfect stranger, right? But not choosing good passwords is like giving your PIN to a stranger and giving that stranger your ATM card as well.

In the online world, your account names and associated passwords are your digital identity. If someone guesses or otherwise finds out a name and password for an account, that person has access to everything in that account. Worse yet, that person can act as you as far as that account is concerned.

A good password has two key properties: It should be hard for someone else to guess, and it should be easy for you to remember. Most people concentrate on the second of these two properties when picking a password, but the first is more important.

Making a password hard to guess

When you're trying to make up a password that's hard to guess, keep several things in mind.

You shouldn't use information about yourself that someone could easily figure out or guess, such as your name or initials; the names of your family members, pets, favorite movie star, or sports figure; or your hobbies or interests. Even information that you might consider to be obscure, such as your place of birth or mother's maiden name, no longer works for passwords, because that information is available to anyone who wants to find it through the Internet.

In fact, you shouldn't use any English word as a password. Computers have become so fast, and have access to so much data, that it's relatively simple for someone to mount a dictionary attack against your password to a particular service.

> *A dictionary attack is an attack in which someone tries every word in the dictionary as your password.*

This method may seem implausible to you, but it's not to someone who has a high-speed Internet connection and a moderately fast computer.

Webster's Third New International Dictionary of the English Language contains around 500,000 entries. Computers can easily perform millions of operations per second, but over networks, those operations are much slower. How easy it is for a computer to guess your password through a dictionary attack depends not just on computer and network speed but also on how fast the service responds to a bad password. (As you'll see, a good service responds to a bad password slowly.) Suppose that a computer can try only 10 passwords per second, which is incredibly slow in the computer world. It would then take the computer 50,000 seconds to try every entry in the dictionary— only about 14 hours. All that a hacker would have to do is start a program in the morning, and he would have tried every word in the dictionary by the time he went to bed.

Computers are also very good at guessing, and they guess the way they try every word in the dictionary: by starting at the beginning and going to the end. So a computer could first guess a, then b, and so on, and then try aa, ab, and so on. A computer could try all possible passwords of up to four letters, whether they're words or not, in about the same amount of time it takes to try every word in the dictionary; there are fewer than 500,000 such combinations. So don't choose a password that contains four letters or fewer.

Computers aren't so good when they have to guess long nonwords, though. Trying every six-letter combination at the same rate would take a computer about a year. You can't be sure what the real rate will be for a particular service, however, and if the computer can try 1,000 passwords per second instead of 10, the time to try six letters drops to three days or so. But throw in numbers as well as letters for your password, and go up to seven characters, and you're back up to a couple of years, even at the faster rate. Eight letters puts computer guessing pretty much out of the question with the current technology. Also, you can use special characters, such as punctuation, to make things even harder.

What makes a password hard to guess? Here's a list:

- It should not be anything that's obviously linked to you, such as your initials, family members' names, or place of birth.

- It should not be an English word or a word in any other common language.

- It should be at least six characters long—and the longer, the better.

- It should use numbers and special characters, if possible. (Don't use all numbers, though; computers are good at guessing them too.)

- If the service considers lowercase and uppercase characters to be different, you should use both.

Table 4.2 lists some examples.

Table 4.2

Easy to Guess	Hard to Guess
david	eiuoiojdue
DLM	e667#4
ventura	**Eee89
puppet	wiopeiur
487637	APEDeokl

Making a password easy to remember

Of course, it's not hard to choose passwords that are difficult for even a fast computer on a fast Net connection to guess. The trick is to also choose passwords that are relatively easy for you to remember. Unlike computers, humans have trouble remembering words as short as three or four letters unless those words have special meaning. Throw in numbers and special characters, plus uppercase and lowercase characters, and it gets difficult to remember one password, let alone the dozen or so that you may accumulate on the Net. Passwords that are hard to guess usually are hard to remember as well.

There are two reasons why passwords should be easy to remember. First, if you forget your password, recovering it is going to be a hassle. Second, if your passwords are too hard to remember, you're going to write them down, severely compromising your online security in the process. We'll say more about both of these issues later in this chapter.

Certain passwords are hard for others to guess but not hard for you to remember. These passwords are the ones you should use. The secret is to figure out a trick that works for you. We all have different ways of thinking about things, so the trick is different for each of us, but here are some examples:

- Pick a phrase that's easy for you to remember; then use the first letter of each word in that phrase. "Four score and seven years ago" (from Lincoln's "Gettysburg Address") would be fsasya or, better yet, Fsasya if uppercase and lowercase are different. Still better would be 4sa7ya.

- If the service allows long passwords, use the whole phrase (Fourscoreandsevenyearsago), as long as it's not linked to you in any obvious way.

- Substitute numbers for letters. Zero can substitute for the letter *o*, the digit 1 for the letter *l*, 5 for an *s*, even 3 for *E* (backward). So password would be pa55w0rd. (Don't use this password, though; it's in a lot of special lists of nonwords that computers should guess first.)

- Use a certain set of keys on the keyboard. The combinations qwerty and asdfg used to be good passwords, because they're easy to type, but now they're too obvious. Something like 3edcvfr4 (down one diagonal and back up another) still makes sense.

Keeping Your Passwords Secret

As we've mentioned, implementing some of the advanced security measures in this book makes little sense unless you first implement some of the more basic ones, such as physical security and good passwords. Likewise, choosing good passwords is pointless if you're not going to keep them secret. The best password in the world is useless if it gets to the bad guys. (Remember the saying, "Three people can keep a secret if two of them are dead.") On the other hand, you may need to tell someone your password in certain rare situations.

How do you tell the difference between someone who really needs to know your password and someone who just wants to know it? It's not easy. When you're establishing an account, you need to give the service your desired account name and password. From that point on, the service may have a specific password policy. With America Online, for example, none of its representatives will ask you for your password. Other services may be different, however.

Always think twice before giving your password to anyone—even your spouse, relatives, or close friends. It's not a question of their trustworthiness (although trustworthiness should be an important part of that thinking twice); it's more a question of risk.

If you don't tell anyone your password, the risk that your password will be disclosed drops significantly.

Just the act of communicating your password to someone incurs risk. If you speak it, who might overhear you? If you write it down (because, if it's a good password, it should be hard to remember), are you sure the person will adequately destroy the paper on which it was written? If you e-mail it, who may be spying on your e-mail? (See Chapter 5 for reasons why you should never send passwords by e-mail.) Your password is much safer if it exists only in your head.

Your password is also at risk of disclosure when you are typing it in the application that needs it. Most applications do not display the password as you're typing it, but even so, you should be sure that no one is looking over your shoulder at what you're typing (a practice so common that it's referred to as shoulder surfing). If you are in such situations often, you may want to consider having the application save the password for you, although this practice also involves risks (see the following section, "Managing Your Passwords").

No matter how careful you are, your password could be compromised, and in most cases, you'll never know. So in addition to telling as few people as possible, you can take a couple steps to minimize the effect of compromised passwords. The most obvious step is not using the same password for more than one service, especially for critically important services. If a hacker does get your password for a particular service, you can bet that he's going to try it in your other services too. If you use the same password for multiple services, you increase your overall exposure.

A second step to minimize the effects of password compromise is changing your passwords periodically. You don't need to change them every week, or maybe not even every month, but you should change them now and then. The longer you use the same password, the more likely it is that someone knows about that password, even if you don't tell anyone. An especially important time to change a password is when you have any reason to believe that it's been compromised. Perhaps there was an unexplained access to one of your services, or perhaps you noticed someone shoulder-surfing. Most services make changing passwords very easy, so if you have any doubt, changing your password is worthwhile.

Managing Your Passwords

What with choosing passwords that are hard to guess, maintaining different passwords for different services, and changing passwords periodically, you probably think you can't keep track of everything without writing all your passwords down somewhere. Although writing passwords on slips of paper is a time-honored tradition, it's one of those traditions that's best eliminated, especially because better alternatives are available.

Using the keychain

Mac OS 9 and Mac OS X have a built-in feature called the keychain that helps you manage your passwords in an easy, secure way. The keychain, which is a control panel under Mac OS 9, is pretty much what it sounds like: a place where you put all your keys (in this case, passwords) for easy access when you need them. When you go to a door that needs a key (a Web site that has a password, for example), you or the application can get the needed key from the keychain and unlock the door (or gain access the site).

To start using the keychain under Mac OS 9, select it in the Control Panels folder. Then name the keychain (you can have more than one, which is useful if the same Mac has multiple users) and create a master password for it (**Figure 4.2**). This password will be used to provide complete access to all the passwords stored by the keychain, so it's even more important than normal that you choose and maintain this password carefully. The keychain even warns you if it detects what it considers to be a poorly chosen password (**Figure 4.3**).

Figure 4.2
Creating a new keychain to manage your passwords.

Figure 4.3 Choosing a good keychain password is critical, since that password can provide access to all the passwords on your keychain. The keychain will warn you if you seem to be choosing a password that is easy to guess.

The keychain is a good idea in principle, but it requires special features from most of the applications that want to use it, and many current applications don't have the needed support. Those that do include the iCab Web browser, AppleShare, Mac OS X's e-mail application and Apple's digital-signature and file-encryption applications. The keychain also has limited built-in support for passwords associated with Web sites, but only certain Web sites work with the keychain. You can use the keychain to store passwords for sites that ask for a password through a dialog box before any part of the site comes up. You cannot use the keychain to store passwords for sites that ask you to enter the password in a form.

Another problem with the keychain is that it can put all your eggs in one basket. Just as you're in big trouble if you put all your keys on a physical key chain and then lose the key chain, if you put all your passwords on the Mac keychain and then "lose" it, you'll be in big trouble too. Losing the keychain could mean forgetting the master password that you use to unlock it or, worse, having that password compromised. In the latter case, someone else would have access to all your passwords if they have physical access to your machine. (Hackers should not be able to access the keychain over the Net, even if they have your master password, but you can never be 100 percent sure.) An additional risk is that while your keychain is unlocked, anyone who has physical access to your machine potentially has access to all the services on your keychain.

Apple has done a good job of mitigating some of the risks involved with the keychain. If someone walks over to your machine, for example, he may be able to access services through your passwords but he can't see what those passwords are without knowing your master keychain password. To prevent unauthorized service access, any time you leave your machine, you can lock the keychain, and the master password must be reentered before any keys are available. You can also set the keychain up to lock automatically after a specified period or any time your machine goes to sleep (**Figure 4.4**). Finally, the keychain can warn you any time an application tries to access any of the passwords it contains, protecting against rogue applications such as Trojan horses. (See Chapter 11 for details about Trojan horses.)

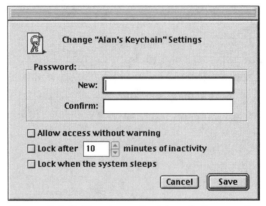

Figure 4.4 Setting important keychain security features.

Other password-management techniques

Another good password-management application is Web Confidential. You can download the Web Confidential shareware application from *http://www.web-confidential.com*. You use it much like the keychain to keep track of your various passwords. Web Confidential can track many passwords in various categories, even passwords for non-Internet items such as your ATM PINs. Like the keychain, Web Confidential has built-in integration with your Web browser, supporting both dialog-box-based and form-based site passwords (**Figure 4.5**).

Web Confidential works with Mac OSes as far back as System 7, so you can use it even if you're not running Mac OS 9 or X. It can invoke and receive information from certain applications automatically. It even integrates well with the keychain, so you can use both applications together if you're on Mac OS 9. Caveats similar to those for the keychain apply, such as the risks associated with an "all your eggs in one basket" approach.

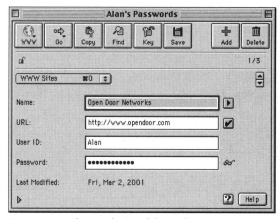

Figure 4.5 The Web Confidential main window for managing passwords.

You can also manage your passwords without a password-management application, even if you have many passwords. Most applications that require passwords allow you to save those passwords within the applications themselves. In many cases, saving passwords within applications makes sense; in other cases, it doesn't.

Saving passwords is especially useful in e-mail applications, for three reasons (**Figures 4.6** and **4.7**):

- You probably check e-mail often, so it saves you from typing the password all the time (as well as risk of disclosure due to shoulder surfing).

- It saves you from having to remember e-mail passwords, especially if you have multiple accounts.

- If someone else gets hold of the e-mail application (and your saved password), the worst he can do is read your e-mail, assuming that you don't use the same password for other services.

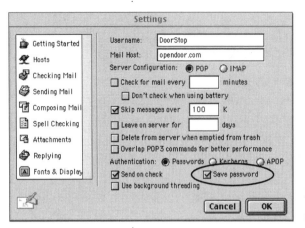

Figure 4.6
The Save password
option in Eudora.

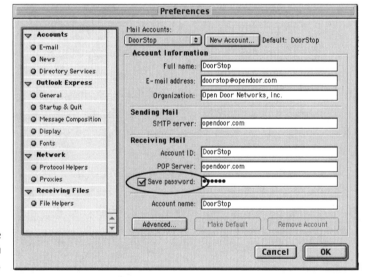

Figure 4.7 The Save
password option in
Outlook Express.

You can also use your Web browser to save your passwords to certain Web sites, and certain Web sites have their own ways of saving your password. Doing so is less advantageous than it is with e-mail, however:

- You probably don't go to specific Web sites as often as you read your mail.
- Different Web sites have different password schemes, so saving your password may not work all the time.
- You may have greater exposure if someone gets access to your Web browser and, hence, to the Web sites for which you've saved passwords.

Other applications that save passwords may have similar risks, so evaluate each application based on its advantages and disadvantages.

One additional general warning: Don't save passwords in applications on notebook computers that you travel with, at least not passwords for any important services. The risk of loss and password compromise is too high.

Another way to manage passwords is a level-of-protection system. As we've said in Chapter 2, you should always consider the risk involved with what you're protecting in terms of how much work (and expense) you should use to protect it. You can take advantage of this principle by grouping your passwords in levels of protection. Here are some examples:

- Some Web sites ask for account names and passwords solely for their benefit, to track you as a user. In these cases, you wouldn't care if someone else were to get your password.

- You can often get away with saving your e-mail passwords within your e-mail application, partly because the risk involved generally is low. If someone got your e-mail password and managed to read your e-mail, you would suffer a loss of privacy but, in general, no significant personal or financial loss.

- If someone got the password to a Web site that you and your family use for online banking, that situation could be very bad.

- You might have passwords that you don't even want anyone in your family to know about—passwords for logging onto a Macintosh that you all share, for example, or passwords that you consider to be critically important, such as your keychain master password or one that enables your Macintosh to be controlled remotely over the Internet (see Chapters 9 and 10).

Because your password-protected services fall into different levels of protection, you can group your passwords and thereby make them easier to remember. You could use the following scheme for the four cases in the preceding list:

- For Web sites that ask for a password solely for their own benefit, use something that's easy to remember and in fact violates most of the rules about good passwords— just your initials, for example. Use that same password for all such Web sites. Why waste brain cells remembering passwords that you don't want to have in the first place?

- For e-mail passwords, whether or not you save them in the application, keep the passwords simple and consider using the same passwords for different accounts if you have them.

- For important family-related Web sites, follow all the password-choosing rules, but keep in mind that in certain rare situations, you may need to share these passwords with a good friend or family member.

- Your most critical passwords should be the hardest for anyone else to guess, and you should never share them with anyone under any conditions. Also, you should type this password only when you're sure no one else is around. If an exceptional condition causes one of these passwords to be shared or potentially compromised, you should change it as soon as possible.

With a level-of-protection scheme, you can ensure that the highest levels of protection are being applied to the most important services and still maintain your passwords in a manageable fashion.

Finally, writing passwords down is generally a bad idea. But that's principally because of what we do after we write our passwords down: We stick the password on the computer monitor. This may work for the Web sites that have passwords solely for their own benefit, but you shouldn't do this for any service that you want to keep secure.

On the other hand, if you write a password down and then lock it in a safe or place it in a safe-deposit box, it's more secure than it would be if it were saved in an application. The written password also serves as a backup in case you forget an important password, and it will be available to your loved ones when you're no longer around. Especially if you seldom need the password, writing that password down and storing it in a secure place may make a lot of sense.

Dealing with forgotten passwords

No matter which password-management system you use, and no matter how much work you do, you're going to forget or lose a password. You may make up a very difficult password and save that password in an application. Then you may upgrade that application and lose your password. (This situation shouldn't happen, but it could.) Or perhaps you don't use a service for a year and don't remember the password when you go back.

You have several options for dealing with forgotten passwords. How you deal with a forgotten password often depends on the level of importance you place on the service involved:

For passwords that you use solely for the benefit of a Web site, simply create a new account and password for yourself. You might want to do this periodically even if you don't forget your password, just to prevent the Web site from obtaining detailed tracking data on you (which is a privacy issue).

For medium-security services such as e-mail, consider contacting your e-mail provider and asking it to change your password to a new one. Your provider probably will require some proof of your identity (it should, anyway), but because the service is not a critical one, providing proof should not be a lot of work. Often, the provider can identify you through caller ID.

Some services ask you to provide a password hint when you first sign up and use that hint to help you remember your password. If you use the hint, be sure that it's something only you can figure out.

For high-security services, you're probably going to have to do a lot of work to recover the password. In many cases, starting from scratch with another account may be better. Doing so may not be practical in many cases, however, such as with a bank account with real money in it. In such cases, you might want to plan ahead, write the password down, and store it in your safe-deposit box, in anticipation of such a problem. Going to your safe-deposit box could be a lot less work than going down to the physical business involved or going to a notary public in an attempt to persuade a particular business that you're really you.

Passwords in the Future

Passwords as we use them today on Internet are, in many ways, an archaic mechanism that needs to be replaced. Several much-improved options are on the horizon.

Digital certificates

The most immediate option, which is available now for certain applications, is a digital certificate (also called a digital ID). Digital certificates are widely used by secure Web servers. When used by a Web server, a digital certificate serves two purposes: to verify to you, the user of the server, that the server is associated with the organization it claims to be with and to encrypt your data for secure transmission to the server. (See Chapter 5 for details on digital certificates as used by Web servers.)

Digital certificates are starting to be available to individual Net users. You can purchase a digital certificate from a company such as Verisign (*http://www.verisign.com*), which verifies that you are who you say you are before issuing you the certificate. The certificate, like everything else digital, is just a bunch of letters and numbers. You can save it in a file for future use or store it on your Mac OS keychain and use it in place of your password in certain applications.

Currently, digital certificates are used mainly for sending secure e-mail. E-mail can be a very insecure application (see Chapter 5 for all the details). Among other purposes, the digital certificate confirms that the mail in fact came from you and was not forged or tampered with in any way. Essentially, you are digitally signing your e-mail with the certificate.

In the future, other applications will use digital certificates, making the ongoing maintenance of passwords less necessary.

Other password options

You probably have seen "Star Trek" episodes in which the captain uses his or her voice to authenticate his or her identity with the computer or a science-fiction movie in which a thumbprint or retinal scan confirms a user's identity. These so-called *biometric* tests are the passwords of the future. Compared with traditional passwords, they identify us more directly, are much more difficult to forge, and can't be forgotten. Mac OS 9 even includes a very basic biometric test as part of the voice-print password login option, and other biometric applications are starting to appear. Right now, however, most biometric tests are generally too expensive or too unreliable for use with personal computers.

Finally, some internal networks used in large businesses are starting to use directory services, which in many cases allow users to log into the system once (currently, through a password or digital certificate) and then give users access to all the services they're authorized to access. See Chapter 17 for details. In the future, such a system could apply to Internet-based services as well.

Safe Surfing

You've secured your computer physically, have a regular system of backups in place, and have chosen good passwords for all your services. But Internet security means more than just setting things up right; you also need to maintain a set of ongoing "safe surfing" practices as you enjoy the online world. Because most of your online activities will have to do with either Web browsing or e-mail, you should concentrate your ongoing efforts on those two applications.

Safe Web Browsing

When you're surfing the Web, and particularly when you're entering information in Web sites, the most important thing to be aware of is whether the Web page you're on is secure. You can also take several other common-sense steps to ensure your security while browsing.

Secure and insecure Web pages

Web pages are secure or insecure. An *insecure* Web page is one that anyone spying on Internet communications can see. The spy can look at the Web page itself or, more important, at any information that you type in the Web page, such as your credit-card number. A *secure* page essentially prevents any type of Internet spying.

Most Web sites are made up of insecure Web pages, which is not necessarily a bad thing, because these Web sites are intended to allow access to anyone who wants it. Search engines, entertainment sites, and most corporate sites are examples of Web sites that exist to provide information or services, not to accept or provide information that must be sent securely. Even most shopping sites need to have only a few secure Web pages, such as those used for entering confidential information such as credit-card numbers. Most of the rest of the pages have no need to be secure.

Determining whether a Web page is secure is straightforward: you should see a security icon in the bottom-left corner of the browser window (**Figure 5.1**). This icon, sometimes in combination with text, indicates the security level of the page being displayed. In Netscape Navigator, you can even click the icon to get additional information.

Netscape secure   *Netscape insecure*

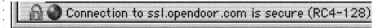

Explorer secure

Explorer insecure

Figure 5.1 Secure and insecure icons for Netscape and Internet Explorer.

Beyond looking at the browser icons, you can set up your browser to warn you about a page's security level each time it displays the page. You usually perform this security setup through the browser's Preferences menu item. You can have your browser notify you whenever you're going to submit data through a page that is not secure, for example. You can also make sure that a Web page is secure by checking that its URL, displayed in the browser's location bar, begins with https:// rather than http://.

Web pages are made secure through a protocol called the Secure Sockets Layer, or SSL. SSL uses digital certificates to provide two forms of security. The first form of security is authentication. Specifically, SSL authenticates the Web site to you, so you know that Web site is legitimate. In the physical world, if you walk into a downtown store and make a purchase, you can be fairly sure that the people to whom you're giving your credit card (or cash) really run the store. But when you type *www.apple.com* in your Web browser, can you really be sure that you're going to a Web site run by Apple Computer? With digital certificates and SSL, you can.

As we mentioned at the end of Chapter 4, a digital certificate definitively identifies its owner. The certificate is issued by an agency that does a lot of work to confirm that the certificate owner is who it says it is. (In the case of Apple Computer, the agency probably checks Apple's certificate of incorporation.) When you go to a secure Web page, SSL checks that page's digital certificate to make sure that the Web page actually is associated with the site name that you typed (or clicked). If you go to the Open Door Networks secure ordering page at *http://www.opendoor.com/order.html*, for example, SSL will check the certificate that page sends back to make sure that the page is being served by the owner of the domain name opendoor.com (Open Door Networks).

If a page's digital certificate does not match the site name you used to get to that page, a dialog box warns you that something may be wrong with the site (**Figure 5.2**). If you see such a dialog box, you should contact the site owner before proceeding further through the site. If you don't see the warning dialog, you can feel secure that the page you're on is the one associated with the name you typed. If you clicked a link rather than typed in a name, you should check the name displayed in the location bar of your Web browser to make sure the link took you to the site you expected, since it's that name that the certificate is going to be checked against.

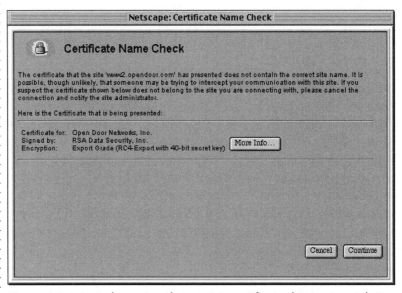

Figure 5.2 A typical warning that a site's certificate does not match its domain name. You should not proceed further into the site until you contact its owner.

The second form of security provided by SSL is data encryption. SSL uses the site's digital certificate to encrypt data transmitted to and from secure Web pages on the site. After the Web site has been authenticated, information in the certificate is used to create an encryption key. That key is then used with an advanced encryption algorithm to scramble the data digitally. Data encrypted in this way is extremely difficult for an intercepting party to read. Only the Web browser and the Web site itself, as parties in the SSL conversation, can read that data. So even if someone is spying on all the network traffic from your machine, or on all the network traffic to a particular site, he won't be able to get any information sent to or from the site (such as credit-card numbers or passwords).

You may have heard of strengths or levels of encryption or of different key sizes. In general, you don't need to worry about the strength of encryption except for the most important transactions. Almost always, even the weakest form of SSL encryption (using 40-bit keys) makes it so difficult to decrypt the data involved that it's just not worth a hacker's effort. A hacker would have to try, on average, half of 2^{40} possibilities, which is about a trillion. Although computers are getting faster all the time, trying a trillion possibilities is still going to take a fast machine several days.

Even though the encryption is still hard to crack, why would any site use a weak form of encryption when stronger forms are available? This question has a couple of answers. First, the stronger the encryption, the more work that's needed on the part of the computer running the site and, hence, the slower the site. Second, for national-security reasons, the U.S. government sometimes prohibits the exporting of stronger forms of encryption. If you're particularly concerned about a specific transaction, most Web browsers will tell you the key size being used. For important transactions, make sure you're using a Web browser that supports strong encryption (any U.S. version should), and look for Web sites that support at least 56 bit keys. Because each bit represents a doubling in security, 56 bits is 2^{16}, or 65,000, times stronger than 40 bits.

Think before you type

Now that you know how to identify a secure Web page, the next thing is to make sure that you look for secure pages when appropriate. In general, the rule should be "Think before you type."

> *If you're typing any information in a Web site, you should always consider the importance of transmitting that information securely.*

Specifically, if you're typing a password or credit-card number, you want to make sure that the page is secure. Beyond that concern, the degree of page security you should look for is more an issue of privacy than of security. To what extent would you be upset if someone other than the intended recipients found out the details of what you're typing? If the information is just what color of T-shirt you want, you probably don't care. If the information is your income level, perhaps you do.

In the early days of the Web and e-commerce, several sites that took credit cards were insecure. The media picked up on this insecurity, making it one of the first issues that most e-commerce sites tackled. These days, most Web sites that request any form of confidential information are secure. An interesting side effect of the early emphasis on credit-card security on the Net is that the relative safety of the physical and virtual worlds has been reversed.

It is now significantly more secure to order most products online than in more traditional ways, such as purchasing them in a store or by telephone.

As long as the Web page you order from is secure, your credit card information is transmitted more securely than if you used it in the physical world. If you go into a store and give a clerk your credit card, he or she will most likely run it through a machine that prints two receipts, each of which includes your credit-card number. One receipt goes into the store's cash register or other such storage area, and one goes to you. In both cases, the likelihood of that receipt's getting lost or stolen is much higher than the likelihood of someone decrypting the information over the Internet. The Internet also removes the risk that someone will go through your or the store's garbage later to retrieve the numbers (a technique known as dumpster diving).

Consider another example. When you're ordering over the phone, you probably don't think twice about using a cordless or cellular phone to place the order. The sale won't involve any printed sales receipt, but someone sitting within a block or two of your house could easily listen in on the conversation on a relatively cheap scanner and write down all the information. That process certainly is much easier than decrypting a 56-bit encrypted SSL conversation.

Security on the Web is always changing. Although most sites now use the password mechanism we've described, some older Web sites still use a kind of password that you enter in a dialog box before you get to the site. In this case, determining whether the password is going to be transmitted securely to the site is difficult. In general, be wary of passwords entered in dialog boxes, and talk directly to the site owner if you're not sure about their site's security.

Who'd Spy on Me?

You may be wondering whether you should be worrying about encryption at all. How many people are really spying on the information being sent on the Internet, anyway? And what are the odds that a spy will see your confidential information? Isn't even unencrypted ordering safer than many pre-Web ordering methods?

The answers to these questions depend, to some extent, on who you believe. The problem is that automated spying tools can look for specific forms of unencrypted data, such as credit-card numbers and passwords, and record that data in a file for future use. So spying may be more widespread than you think. Better safe than sorry, in this case.

Other Web-security issues

You should consider a couple of additional issues when surfing the Web. The first issue is whether a Web site uses Java. Java is a general-purpose programming language. As far as Web surfing goes, you should be concerned with Java's use in applications that are automatically downloaded as part of a Web page. These Java applications, or *applets,* perform functions that Web pages normally can't perform through standard HTML (Hypertext Markup Language) format. Java applets can add cool user interface elements to Web pages, enabling advanced features such as the interactive satellite weather map on the Weather Channel's site (*http://www.weather.com/common/home/maps.html*).

The problem is that the power that lets Java applets do cool things also lets them do uncool things. In theory, a Java applet has full access to your computer and its hard disk. An applet could access your confidential data and send that data back to the Web site or even erase your computer's hard disk. In practice, most Web browsers try to limit this access by preventing or warning you about any operation they consider to be a security risk. On rare occasions, however, vulnerabilities in specific Web browsers allow applets full access. One such vulnerability allowed a Java applet to act as a Web server through the Netscape Web browser, transmitting files on the browser's machine over the Net to anyone who wanted them. Netscape fixed the problem quickly through a new Web browser, but the problem existed for a long time before it was discovered.

Despite rare vulnerabilities, few have reported any real security incidents with Java. Web browsers generally do prevent riskier forms of access by Java applets, and the few security holes that exist usually are discovered by members of the security community, who are always on the lookout for such things. But we may well never hear about some incidents, so in most cases, disabling Java in your Web browser is a good idea. You usually can disable Java and set other security-related options through an Advanced tab in your browser's Preferences dialog box (**Figure 5.3**). If you go to a site that needs Java, you can reenable Java if you feel that doing so is appropriate.

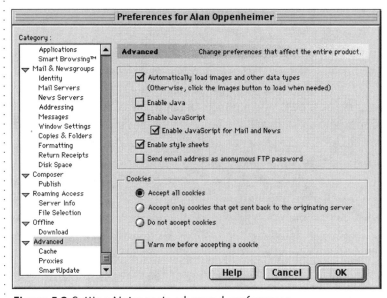

Figure 5.3 Setting Netscape's advanced preferences.

Another set of Web features that provides the same level of vulnerability as Java are Web browser plug-ins. *Plug-ins* are small applications that add functionality to your Web browser by running as part of the browser. The QuickTime plug-in, for example, can display movies within a Web page. Other common plug-ins include RealPlayer and Shockwave. Many popular plug-ins come with your Web browser. Because you usually download plug-ins from the Net, they present another opportunity for a malicious application to get into your machine. In general, you should minimize the number of plug-ins you install with your browser, especially if those plug-ins come from less-well-known developers.

A language related to Java is ActiveX. This language is popular in the Windows world but not used much on Macs, although Microsoft Internet Explorer for Mac supports it. ActiveX has the same risks as Java, and the safest thing to do is to disable it if your Web browser supports it. You can disable it through the "Custom" button in Explorer's "Security Zone" Preference dialog.

Also, don't be confused by a Web language called JavaScript. JavaScript has no real relation to the Java language; it's an extension to the HTML that makes up Web pages. Although somewhat more powerful than standard HTML (enabling features such as changing an icon or text when you move the mouse pointer over it), JavaScript presents less of a security risk than Java itself, because its power is quite limited by comparison. JavaScript also is used more than Java is. Generally, it's safe to leave JavaScript on in your Web browser, although you can disable it if you want (Figure 5.3).

Another Web-security issue to consider is cookies. You've probably heard this silly term before and wondered what it means. *Cookies* are small files that Web sites can store on your computer to keep track of information about you. These files present both security and privacy issues. Cookies can track all sorts of information about where you go on the Web and what you do; they can also track the passwords you use. If you don't type passwords over the Web (using them only in an e-mail application, for example), cookies present only a privacy issue. But if you type a password on a Web site, cookies can present security issues as well. You may want to disable cookies in your Web browser for both security and privacy reasons.

Finally, apply common sense to Web browsing. Order from the larger, more reputable sites wherever possible; the odds are that they'll be better at security issues than the smaller ones (although you have no guarantee). Watch your credit-card statements carefully, looking for unauthorized charges. No matter how careful you are about ordering online or offline, credit-card numbers can get stolen. If you see anything suspicious on your statement, report it to your credit-card company immediately, because doing so usually limits your overall liability to something like $50. (Any larger amount will be covered by the credit-card company.) And just as in the real world, keep away from sites that offer things that are too good to be true because, usually, that's exactly what they are.

Safe E-mail

E-mail probably is the most common Internet service, one that many of us rely on for day-to-day communication. From a security perspective, the e-mail system is a bit more complicated than the Web. When you use the Web, the process involves you and the Web server. But when you send e-mail, intermediaries are involved as well.

When you send an e-mail message, that message is transferred from your machine to a mail server (**Figure 5.4**). That server usually is operated by your ISP or by a Web-mail site, if you use services such as Yahoo! Mail or Hotmail. Your ISP's mail server is responsible for delivering that message to the recipient's mail server, which usually is operated by the recipient's ISP or a Web-mail site. The recipient's mail server holds the mail until the recipient checks his or her mail; at that time, the mail is delivered. Under some conditions, additional intermediate mail servers may be involved.

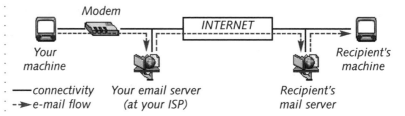

Figure 5.4 Sending e-mail involves several intermediaries, making the system more complex and difficult to secure.

At least four entities usually are involved in sending an e-mail message: you, your ISP's mail server, the recipient's mail server, and the recipient. A message also can have multiple recipients. To simplify matters, however, we're going to consider e-mail security from just two perspectives: what you send and what you receive.

Sending your e-mail password

In Chapter 4, we showed you how to choose, manage, and maintain good passwords. We want to expand on that advice in this section as it applies to the password you use to check your e-mail.

Your e-mail password is sent to your e-mail server when you log in to read your e-mail. The password prevents someone else from pretending to be you and reading your e-mail—and that's about all it does. You may think that your e-mail password prevents someone else from sending mail as you as well, but that usually isn't the case. A hacker has several ways to send e-mail as you if he really wants to. (See "Sending e-mail securely" later in this chapter if you want to be sure that only you can send e-mail as you.)

Your e-mail password does prevent other people from reading your e-mail, which is something you do want. But reading e-mail is as much a privacy issue as it is a security issue. Your online safety may not be compromised if someone reads your e-mail, especially if you follow the practices described later in this chapter. As long as you don't reuse your e-mail password for more critical services and don't save it on a notebook computer that you travel with, you don't need to worry about many other e-mail password-management issues.

As is the case with Web-server passwords and other data, e-mail passwords can be sent securely or insecurely to an e-mail server. An e-mail password is considered to be sent insecurely if anyone spying on Internet communications can look at it. Insecure e-mail passwords generally are less of a security risk than insecure Web-site passwords are, and not simply because someone can do more damage by logging in as you on a Web site than by reading your e-mail. Usually, your e-mail server is provided by your ISP, so logging in to read your e-mail doesn't involve Internetwide communication. The communication is between you and your ISP, so hackers have much less opportunity for spying.

Regardless of the lower risk, making your e-mail password as secure as possible is still good practice. Most e-mail applications and e-mail servers provide a way of sending your password securely through a protocol called APOP (Authenticated Post Office Protocol). APOP encrypts your password to make it difficult to read (although not as difficult as the Web's SSL). You should select this option if it's supported by your e-mail application and server (**Figures 5.5** and **5.6**).

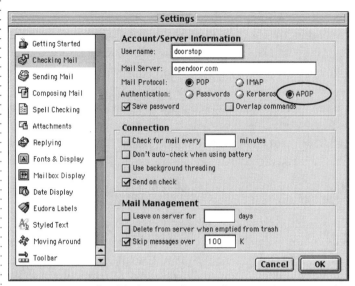

Figure 5.5 You should always select Eudora's APOP option if it's supported by your e-mail server.

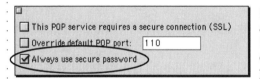

Figure 5.6 You should always select Outlook Express's Secure Password option if it's supported by your e-mail server.

If you use one of the popular Web-mail services, you should take a few extra precautions with your e-mail password. Services such as Yahoo! Mail and Hotmail use Web pages and forms to let you read and send e-mail through your Web browser, rather than through a dedicated e-mail application. Apple's Mac.com e-mail service has Web-based features as well, although you need an e-mail application to send and receive Mac.com mail.

Because some Web-mail services do not support secure passwords, you should check the security of your password by looking at the icon in the bottom-left corner of your browser window.

Many Web-mail systems also use your password for other services, even if you don't want them to, so keep that in mind when you choose and maintain your e-mail password. Your Mac.com password, for example, also is used as the password to your iDisk online storage (see Chapter 3). That service could contain significantly more important data than your e-mail service, because you can use that storage for anything. Unlike some other Web-mail systems, Apple recognizes the potential additional risk of password reuse and transmits passwords securely through the Mac.com site.

Sending e-mail

Your e-mail password is a small but important piece of data that you send through your e-mail application. Most of the rest of what you send through that application (or a Web-mail system) is outgoing e-mail. Protecting outgoing e-mail is both a privacy and a security issue. If people are spying on the e-mail that you send, they might find out things that you don't want them to know but that don't affect your security directly. But they also can find out things that do affect your security directly.

Keep in mind one simple fact about sending (and receiving) e-mail:

Almost all e-mail is insecure.

At least on the Web, most Web pages that need to be secure can be. With e-mail, this option is available in few situations, and sending data in those situations is usually difficult. (See "Sending e-mail securely" later in this chapter for some emerging options, however.) This general lack of security leads to another simple rule for sending e-mail:

Never send credit-card numbers, passwords for other services, or other confidential data by e-mail. You don't know who's going to be watching.

You may think it's highly unlikely that anyone is watching when you send your e-mail. But automated spying applications can pick up things such as credit-card numbers and passwords. If you go to all the trouble of choosing and maintaining a good password for an important service, and then send that password out through e-mail, you may have done a lot of work for nothing.

Sending e-mail securely

With the recent emphasis on Internet security, you would think that e-mail would be more secure. The situation is beginning to change: Secure e-mail options are emerging. One limiting factor with secure e-mail, however, is that it requires the participation of different entities. Not only do the sending and receiving e-mail applications need to support it but the sending and receiving e-mail servers often must support it as well. Therefore, secure e-mail is a complicated subject—one that is too complex for many of us.

Secure e-mail is encrypted in such a way that anyone spying on the message as it's sent can't read it easily. The secure message can also include features beyond basic encryption, such as those enabling authentication and integrity checking of the message. These features assure the recipient that the message really came from you and was not tampered with by an intermediary. The combination of encryption, authentication, and integrity results in a powerful set of features. Just as with secure Web sites and credit cards, secure email actually makes a Net-based service more secure than its physical world equivalent.

Usually, secure e-mail uses a digital certificate of some sort, much like the Web's SSL. In fact, SSL is one of the emerging options for secure e-mail. Like a Web server, your ISP's e-mail server can use a digital certificate to prove to you that it's really your ISP's server and to encrypt your e-mail. Unlike most Web servers, however, your e-mail server then needs to forward your e-mail to another e-mail server, which needs to deliver that e-mail to its intended recipient (Figure 5.4). The odds are that the other e-mail server and the recipient don't support SSL yet, so your message will be only partially protected (between you and your ISP, which probably is the path that least needs protecting). As more applications and providers start to use SSL, this option may make more sense.

Digital certificates are also used in a secure e-mail scheme called S/MIME (Secure/Multipurpose Internet Mail Extensions). With S/MIME, both the sender and receiver of the e-mail message usually obtain personal digital certificates from a company such as Verisign. The sender uses his or her certificate to sign the e-mail digitally before sending it out. The receiver of the e-mail can check the sender's certificate against the message to confirm that the e-mail really came from the sender and that it was not tampered with during transmission (by an intermediate mail server, for example). The receiver's certificate is not used during this authentication process, but it will be used later if the sender wants to encrypt the e-mail as well as sign it.

Without a technique such as S/MIME or some other form of authentication, hackers can easily make e-mail look as though it came from you or anyone else. All they have to do is enter any person's name and e-mail address in an e-mail application, create an e-mail, and send it. Many e-mail servers prevent e-mail from being sent from fake e-mail addresses, but others don't. The hacker needs to find just one server anywhere on the Net to send a forged message—or simply to run one himself.

In addition to sending authenticated e-mail, S/MIME can send encrypted e-mail. That process is tricky, because the sender of the message needs to have the intended recipient's certificate first. If the sender used his or her own certificate to encrypt the message, anyone could decrypt it, just as anyone can verify the sender's signature. In other words, the party that wants to receive encrypted e-mail drives the process, not the party that wants to send it. This setup is the opposite of how authentication through S/MIME works.

The sender uses the recipient's certificate to generate a key and encrypt the e-mail so that only the recipient can read the message. This process is similar to the digital scrambling used in SSL. Messages sent with S/MIME can be both signed and encrypted if the sender has his own certificate and the receiver's certificates available. If you frequently send important messages to a particular party, it's worth the effort to find an e-mail application that supports S/MIME (such as Netscape Communicator) and exchange certificates.

For S/MIME to work, both the sender's and receiver's e-mail applications must support the technology, but the e-mail servers in the middle do not need to support it. S/MIME works within the Internet's standard e-mail protocols, simply encoding the data in the messages that are being sent. By using the standard protocols, S/MIME eliminates the need for any changes in the e-mail servers, which still are passing standard messages.

PGP (Pretty Good Privacy) is another secure e-mail scheme. PGP works much like S/MIME, except that it doesn't use digital certificates; instead, it uses a public-key/private-key pair. When you start using PGP, it generates this pair for you. As the names imply, you keep your private key secret but let anyone know what your public key is. In reality, your public key (like a digital certificate) is a long series of letters and numbers, so you end up storing it in a file somewhere, as you do with your private key. Because your public key is designed to be public, it contains no information that would compromise the secure e-mail process (that is, no secret information). You can send your public key to other people by insecure e-mail or post it on a Web site. Even key servers and other public directories list the public keys of many PGP users (as well as the certificates of S/MIME users, for that matter).

Senders use their private keys to sign e-mail, similar to the way that they would use their certificates with S/MIME. The receiver's e-mail application must support PGP to verify that the e-mail is from the sender and has not been compromised. (PGP sends enough information with the message to allow the receiver to make this verification.) A sender can also use someone's else's public key to send encrypted e-mail, just as they would use someone's certificate in S/MIME. As is the case with S/MIME, both the sender's and receiver's applications must support PGP (a Eudora plug-in provides this support, for example), but the e-mail servers in the middle don't need to do anything special.

Receiving attachments

While sending e-mail, you are at risk of giving away information that you may not want to give away, such as your password or the contents of the e-mail. But the actual risk of access to or destruction of information on your machine, or of misuse of your machine, is low. These risks are much higher when you're receiving e-mail.

For security purposes, understanding the difference between the body of an e-mail message and any attachments to that message is important. The *body* of a message is the text part of the e-mail that's displayed by your e-mail application;

it poses very little security risk (although see the mention in the next section about HTML e-mail). Attachments, however, are a different story. *Attachments* are independent files included with (or attached to) the body of the e-mail. They're like photographs included with a letter. Attachments usually are opened and displayed by an application other than your e-mail reader and can even be applications themselves, which is where much of the security risk associated with them comes in.

When you receive an e-mail with an attachment, your e-mail application will display the body of the e-mail. It will not display the attachment, because it usually doesn't know how. Instead, it will indicate that the e-mail includes an attachment. Different e-mail applications indicate attachments in different ways (see **Figures 5.7, 5.8,** and **5.9**).

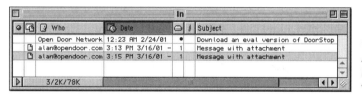

Figure 5.7
A Eudora inbox indicating a message with an attachment.

Figure 5.8
A Eudora message with an attachment.

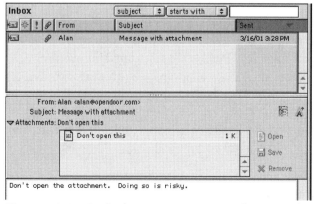

Figure 5.9 An Outlook Express message with an attachment.

Make sure you understand how your e-mail application indicates an attachment, because attachments are how a good percentage of the malicious work on the Internet is performed. When you understand how to spot an attachment, follow one simple rule when you receive one:

> *Do not open e-mail attachments except under rare conditions. In most cases, delete them without opening them.*

If you've sent and received a lot of e-mail, this rule may seem like a rather radical and drastic approach. After all, you probably have sent and received attachments in the past without problems. Attachments have been a useful feature of e-mail for a long time. Unfortunately, the feature has been too useful and has been co-opted by hackers in numerous ways. Attachments provide a convenient and seemingly innocuous way for a hacker to get a specially written application or script running on your machine. And after hackers have their application running on your machine, they own your machine from a functional perspective. They can access all your files; spy on your passwords; and even send e-mail as you, further propagating the mischief. (See Chapter 11 for details on self-propagating e-mail viruses.)

When an attachment first comes in to your e-mail application, it is inert. If you open an attachment (usually, by double-clicking it), that attachment is activated as though you had double-clicked it in the Finder. If the attachment is simply a document that needs another application to be displayed, the associated application launches to display the document. In these cases, because the application is already on your machine, not much additional risk is involved. (But you should look out for certain script- and macro-based viruses; see Chapter 11.) Many times, however, the attachment can be an application, in which case opening it results in that application's being run on your machine. Even if the attachment doesn't look like an application and even if it's named something like picture.jpg or document.txt, it still could be an application. You can't be sure.

The fact that you don't want to run someone else's application on your machine probably is obvious, but it may not be obvious that you've done so. Because a malicious application usually wants to take control of your machine without your knowing about it, that application probably will do something to trick you into thinking that nothing bad happened. It may display a picture or a funny animation. It may return a fake error, saying that something went wrong and the attachment couldn't be opened. But what it really did is something that you won't notice and may not notice for some time, if at all.

How do you know whether it's OK to open an attachment? After all, attachments may be sent legitimately. You should do so only under rare circumstances. You should never open an attachment from someone you don't know, for example, regardless of what the e-mail body says. If you're really interested, you should write the sender back and ask for more details, but continue to be wary of this type of ongoing conversation, keeping in mind how it started (just as you would in the physical world if someone you didn't know came up to you on the street or knocked on your door).

If you know the person who's sending the attachment, opening it is OK, right? Wrong. Remember what we've said about how insecure email is. Someone might easily have forged the e-mail to trick you into opening the attachment. Another not-unlikely scenario is that someone co-opted your friend's machine when he or she opened the attachment, causing you to be sent the e-mail containing that attachment. Many recent viruses, such as the Love Bug virus, have spread this way, with people propagating them because they knew the sender and thought it was OK to open the attachment (see Chapter 11 for details).

If you unexpectedly receive an attachment from someone you know, you probably will want to talk with that person before opening the attachment unless the body of the e-mail makes it clear that the attachment is legitimate. But just because the body says something like "check the attachment," it may not be legitimate. The body should make it clear that the sender meant to send both the e-mail and the attachment. The body should contain something specific that a virus couldn't generate automatically, such as the time of an upcoming meeting or some specific personal information.

Suppose that the attachment came from someone you know and is expected, or that the context of the e-mail makes it clear that the person sending the attachment really meant to send it. Surely it's OK to open the attachment, right? Maybe. Attachments still carry risks of viruses. If the machine that sent the e-mail has a virus, that virus could be passed on through the attachment. Be sure that you have the proper antivirus software installed on your machine before opening the attachment. See Chapter 11 for all the details.

Here's a checklist for what to do if you receive an e-mail with an attachment:

If the e-mail is from someone you don't know, delete the attachment. Follow up with the sender if you want, but be cautious about any conversation that begins this way.

If the e-mail is from someone you know but is unexpected, read the message carefully. Try to make sure that the sender really meant to send you the attachment. If you have any doubt, talk with the sender to be sure. If the sender has any doubt, delete the attachment.

If the e-mail and attachment are expected, be sure that you have up-to-date antivirus software installed on your machine before opening the attachment.

Always delete the attachment if you have any concerns about it, because if you leave it around, you might open it accidentally later. Most e-mail applications do not necessarily delete the attachment if you delete the e-mail message, so check your e-mail application's preferences to be sure. Eudora, for example, does not delete attachments when you delete the associated message, although you can enable this feature as shown in **Figure 5.10**. If your e-mail application does not delete attachments with messages, you'll have to find the attachment and drag it to the Trash separately.

As a corollary to the rules about receiving attachments, think twice before sending attachments, because the person receiving the attachment is going to have to perform the same set of checks as you would (or should have to do so, anyway). Can you convey the same information without an attachment?

Maybe you can include it in the body of the e-mail message. Or maybe you can point the recipient to a Web site that has the information or to a file on an office server somewhere (although risks of viruses still apply if the file is downloaded from a server). If you really feel that you must send an attachment, be sure to include enough context in the body of the e-mail message to make it clear that you intended to send the attachment. Instead of saying something like "Check out this file," be more specific. Say something like "Please review this proposal for the Kingsford project before we meet tomorrow." You would feel a lot better if you had such details, and they should make the recipient feel better as well.

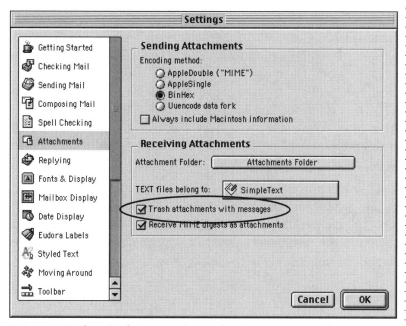

Figure 5.10 The attachments section of Eudora's Settings dialog box.

Other issues with receiving e-mail

Part of the problem with receiving attachments is that you can't be sure that the e-mail is from the person it claims to be from or whether they really intended to send it. This problem applies beyond attachments. You should consider *any* e-mail that you receive as suspect in this regard, even if it includes no attachment. Before acting on the information included in an e-mail, think about what would happen if the e-mail was forged or sent by a virus on the sender's machine. Is the e-mail asking you to disclose any information or take any action that would result in compromised security? An example would be an e-mail message from a trusted friend or colleague, asking for your credit-card number or password. Or perhaps a message asks you to disable your machine's firewall or other form of enhanced security temporarily.

If you have any doubts about the legitimacy of an e-mail, talk with the sender. You would know better than to ask for a password via e-mail, and the sender should, too. (And if senders don't know any better, it's probably time that they did.) Talking with the sender will, at minimum, help increase overall security.

On a related note, be on the lookout for anyone who sends you confidential information through e-mail. If you are ever assigned the password to a service through e-mail, for example, get back to the sender and ask for another password through a more secure channel. (Better yet, tell the sender what password you'd like to receive through a secure channel.) Not everyone will be as well schooled in security issues as you are.

You should also be suspicious of any Web-page links included in any e-mail messages that you receive. Although the risk is small if you've followed the precautions about safe Web surfing earlier in this chapter, you never know exactly what's going to happen if you click a Web link in your e-mail application.

A related issue is the capability to send and receive mail formatted using HTML (Hypertext Markup Language). Generally, HTML provides an advanced way of formatting e-mail text, allowing features such as boldface and font sizes. But advanced HTML can carry some security risks. A link in an HTML e-mail could go to a page on a Web site that downloaded and ran a Java application on your machine. The HTML would obscure the actual details of the link, so you wouldn't know exactly where you were going. Be extremely cautious about clicking links in HTML e-mail.

Another potential security problem with HTML e-mail is JavaScript. If your e-mail application supports JavaScript, you might want to consider disabling its use on all incoming e-mail, probably through a Preferences or Settings menu item. Use of JavaScript in HTML e-mail is quite new, and probably will be subject to security exploits in the future, so better safe than sorry.

Safety with Other Internet Applications

Many people use the Internet only for Web browsing and e-mail. Limiting the number of applications you use is a good idea from a security perspective. Understanding and remembering the issues associated with one or two applications is easier, and these applications being the most popular ones, they're also the best understood. Other interesting Internet applications are available, however.

As a general rule, be cautious when downloading files from the Net through any application. Whether you use your Web browser, FTP, newsgroups, or even a music-sharing service, the files you download could be destructive or contain viruses. Bigger download sites tend to do a good job of scanning for viruses, but be especially wary of files downloaded from less-known sites or from individual users. Some of the recent "peer-to-peer" applications used especially for sharing music are the most worrisome. Although embedding a virus in a legitimate-looking MP3 file would be difficult, peer-to-peer music services are being used more and more to share files of many types. When generic files are used, it becomes relatively simple for someone to embed viruses and other destructive code within the file, making the file as dangerous as an e-mail attachment. Because these sharing services have no central control, anyone who wants to can post a file for downloading.

Instant messaging and chatting services have risks similar to those of e-mail. Because you're communicating in real time, it's easier to get burned, because you don't have time to think about the issues involved. If you receive an instant message from a friend, your tendency is to respond right away without questioning whether your friend really even sent that message. If you're in the middle of a conversation, you might not consider the possibility that one end of that conversation could be hijacked by someone else, who could impersonate you or the person with whom you're talking. Or if someone sends you a file, asking you to open it and tell him what you think, you might open it right away, only later realizing that you could have unleashed a virus on your system.

Many instant-messaging and chatting services are available, and we could write a book just on which security risks apply to which services. Most services, however, should be considered to be insecure from a spying perspective. You should assume that whatever you say is available to anyone who really wants to see it. The most popular services are starting to offer secure communications options, such as PGP security for the ICQ service.

Finally, be wary of any new Internet application. Most application developers concentrate on functionality first and security second (or later). Their goal usually is to get a product to market as quickly as they can, and many developers don't even think about security implications. When an application first ships, security sometimes is not a big concern, because no one knows about the application anyway. As such applications become popular, however, security holes begin to be exposed. If you can, stick to the more established applications until you see that a developer has addressed security in the application. Also, if you wait a while, the Internet security community will have time to evaluate the security ramifications of the new application.

Internet
Basics

Have you ever found that your car won't start in the morning and not had a clue why? Has your car ever developed strange noises that mystified you? If so, you may have wished for a little basic knowledge of how your car works. You don't want a skilled mechanic's knowledge—just enough to help you understand what's happening. Likewise, knowing a few basic concepts about the Internet will help you understand the security risks involved in being connected to the Internet as well as the solutions to those risks. Reading this chapter will prepare you for the chapters that follow.

In this chapter, we'll discuss general concepts pertaining to the infrastructure of the Internet. We'll show you how networking protocols help manage the flow of information on the Internet and how Internet addresses, host and domain names, and port numbers work together to get information to the right service on the right machine. We'll also talk about configuring your Mac's networking capabilities through the TCP/IP Control Panel.

Although the concepts presented in this chapter will be used throughout the book, it is not necessary that you fully understand all concepts before proceeding. Read the chapter, get what you can from it, and then use it as a reference for the rest of the book.

Infrastructure

The Internet consists of many computers all over the world that are networked together. In fact, the Internet is not just a network of computers but a network of computer networks. The word *Internet* comes from *internetwork*, which describes two or more networks that are connected. In this way, users on a local network within Apple can send e-mail to users on a local network within General Motors. This network of networks has no center. The Internet has no main computer, network, or geographical location; it is a *distributed network* (**Figure 6.1**).

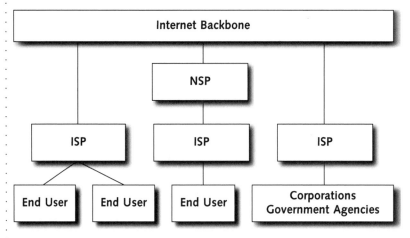

Figure 6.1 A diagram of Internet infrastructure.

You can think of the Internet as having three major components:

- The Internet backbone.

- Internet service providers (ISPs) and large organizations connected directly to the backbone. A special kind of ISP is the NSP (network service provider). NSPs provide Internet services to ISPs, not to end users.

- End users connected to the backbone through an ISP.

The Internet *backbone* is the system of high-speed data lines that make the worldwide connectivity of the Internet possible. Like the Internet as a whole, the backbone is somewhat nebulously defined and always changing. In the early days, the Internet was run by the military, which implemented its own data lines. As the Internet became more popular, the government allowed a few large commercial carriers to provide high-speed lines as part of the backbone. Today, many carriers are commercial providers of data lines for the backbone, with all lines connected through Network Access Points (NAPs).

ISPs and large organizations connect directly to the Internet backbone via expensive high-speed lines known by fancy names such as T3 and OC192 and ranging in speed from 1.5 Mbps (megabits per second) to 10 Gbps (gigabits per second) and beyond.

Common Abbreviations	
K (kilo) = thousand	T (tera) = trillion
M (mega) = million	b = bit
G (giga) = billion	B = byte

These connections make sense for ISPs and users such as government agencies and large corporations, which need high-speed connections to support their many end users. Home users and small businesses connect to ISPs via more affordable connections, using cable, DSL (Digital Subscriber Line), or telephone modems. Cable modems can download data at 3 to 5 Mbps. Telephone modems deliver a maximum 56 Kbps, but the actual speed may be lower.

Internet users in Ashland, Oregon, for example, could choose to have a 100 Mbps line run to their homes via the Ashland Fiber Network (AFN), a municipally owned high-speed fiber-optic network that runs throughout the city (**Figure 6.2**). Such a connection, however, would be prohibitively expensive for a single user. An individual probably would opt for an account with one of AFN's ISPs. For a small fraction of the cost of a 100 Mbps line, a user could have a cable-modem connection to the AFN. Although it runs at only 5 percent of the speed of the faster line, the cable modem would be more than fast enough for almost anything an end user would want to do.

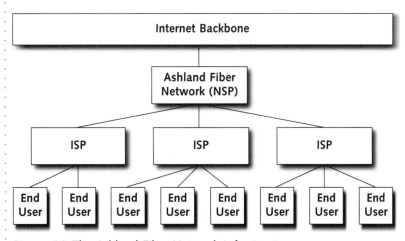

Figure 6.2 The Ashland Fiber Network infrastructure.

Protocols

Because so much data is moved about on the Internet every day, to prevent chaos, the way data is moved must be logical and well defined. A set of rules that defines how to move data on a network is called a *protocol*. The Internet uses a family of protocols known as TCP/IP (Transmission Control Protocol/ Internet Protocol). This protocol dates back to the early days of the Internet, when it was still a military project intended to provide a computer network that would survive nuclear attack.

The TCP/IP protocol fits into an abstract model of networking known as the OSI (Open Systems Interconnect) model. This model describes any network in seven layers, from the physical wires that connect computers on a network all the way up to protocols used by applications, such as Web browsers and mail clients. The complete OSI model is beyond the scope of this book, but **Figure 6.3** shows a simplified model.

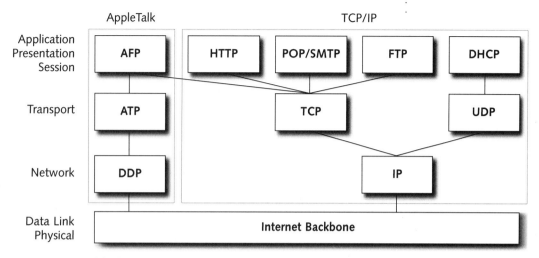

Figure 6.3 Simplified network model.

AppleTalk (on the left side of Figure 6.3) is part of the Macintosh OS and widely known to Macintosh users, but it is not used in relation to the Internet and is shown in the figure only for completeness. The layers of the simplified OSI model are:

Application, Presentation, and Session layers.
The protocols in these layers define how applications obtain information via the network. Mail clients, for example, use POP (Post Office Protocol) to define how the client software contacts a mail server, logs in, determines whether there is new mail, downloads the mail to the user's machine, and logs out. Other common application protocols are HTTP (Hypertext Transfer Protocol), used by Web browsers; SMTP (Simple Mail Transfer Protocol), used for sending e-mail; AFP (AppleTalk Filing Protocol), used for file sharing over both AppleTalk and TCP/IP; FTP (File Transfer Protocol), an older protocol for moving files; and DHCP (Dynamic Host Configuration Protocol), used to obtain dynamic IP addresses (see "IP Addresses and Host Names" later in this chapter).

Transport layer. When data is sent over a network, it is broken into discrete units called *packets*. Large files are sent as a sequence of many packets. Protocols in the Transport layer ensure that all packets sent by one computer are received at the destination computer and that the packets are in the correct sequence. Protocols include TCP (Transmission Control Protocol), which is used by most end-user applications; and UDP (User Datagram Protocol), which is used for more primitive OS services, such as DHCP (see "IP Addresses and Host Names" later in this chapter). TCP and UDP are an important part of firewalls, which we discuss in Chapter 12.

Network layer. The protocol in the Network layer, IP (Internet Protocol), simply determines where information should be sent. It does not attempt to confirm that packets actually reach their destination or that packets reach the destination in the correct order. IP is a lower-level protocol that users never see.

Data Link and Physical layers. These layers are the interface between your machine's networking hardware and the higher layers of the model. An important principle is that any protocol family (such as AppleTalk or TCP/IP) can run over any Data Link layer. Choices for the Data Link layer include Ethernet, PPP (Point to Point Protocol), AirPort (Apple's name for the 802.11b high-speed wireless standard), and the LocalTalk connectivity that Apple built into early Macintoshes. You indicate which Data Link your Mac should use for Internet communications through the TCP/IP Control Panel (see "The TCP/IP Control Panel" later in this chapter).

The most important thing to understand about the OSI model is that layers build on one another. Each layer uses the services provided by the layer below it and provides services to the layer above it. This arrangement is important from a security perspective, because a different form of security can be added at each layer. For example, firewalls (Chapter 12) operate at the Transport layer, potentially blocking TCP (and possibly UDP) packets, whereas most passwords operate at the Application layer.

IP Addresses and Host Names

A computer on the Internet is located by means of its IP address. An *IP address* is a set of numbers that is guaranteed to be unique for each computer on the Internet, much as each combination of area code and telephone number is guaranteed to be unique. An IP address consists of four numbers, each in the range 0 to 255, separated by decimal points, as follows:

192.168.0.2

The numbers in an IP address are hierarchical, with the first number being the most significant. Ranges of IP addresses can be described in this fashion. An intranet might use addresses in the range 192.168.0.0 through 192.168.0.127, meaning that there are 128 addresses, each address starting with 192.168.0 and ending with a number between 0 and 127.

Telephone numbers are guaranteed to be unique because they are centrally administered. People don't just make up the phone number they'd like to use; they get one from the phone company. Similarly, IP addresses are administered by the Internet Assigned Numbers Authority (IANA) and subsidiary agencies. Large users, such as ISPs, large corporations, and government agencies, obtain blocks (sequences) of IP addresses directly from IANA. Users who access the Internet through an ISP don't have to contact an administrative agency; the ISP assigns an IP address to each user's computer.

Static versus dynamic IP addresses

IP addresses can be classified as static or dynamic.

Static means that the machine's IP address is always the same. A static address is required for any machine running Internet services, such as a mail server or Web server, because a server's address must be known for users to contact it. Static addresses require significant configuration by the user through the TCP/IP Control Panel (see "The TCP/IP Control Panel" later in this chapter).

Dynamic means that the machine's IP address is not guaranteed to be the same each time a user connects to their ISP. With dynamic IP addresses, the machine usually contacts a

DHCP server (Dynamic Host Configuration Protocol) to get an address. The DHCP server picks an IP address from a block of addresses allocated to the ISP and temporarily assigns that address to the requesting machine, which can use the address for as long as it's connected to the Internet.

Dynamic IP addresses are common for machines that access the Internet through an ISP. Some ISPs offer more-expensive accounts that come with a static IP address, allowing the account holders to run Internet services (such as a Web server) from their machines. Many businesses are starting to use dynamic IP addresses and DHCP as well, because they require much less configuration on the part of the user.

Public versus private IP addresses

IP addresses can be either public or private. *Public* IP addresses are for use on the Internet. A public address is guaranteed to be unique across all machines connected to the Internet. IANA reserves several blocks of IP addresses for use on private networks, or intranets:

10.0.0.0 – 10.255.255.255

172.16.0.0 – 172.31.255.255

192.168.0.0 – 192.168.255.255

Any intranet can use any IP addresses in these three ranges. For this reason, machines on an intranet using addresses from a private range cannot be connected to the Internet directly, because machines on different intranets might use the same IP address.

Figure 6.4 shows two intranets using the same IP addresses. This system is all right unless the two intranets are connected to the Internet. If they are, machines on the Internet have the same IP address, which is not allowed. If a user on machine A contacts Apple's Web site, for example, the packets from machine A contain a source address of 192.168.0.1. When Apple's Web server sends packets back to the user's machine, it attempts to send them to 192.168.0.1. But in this scenario, that address is not unique, making it impossible to determine whether machine A or B should get the reply packets.

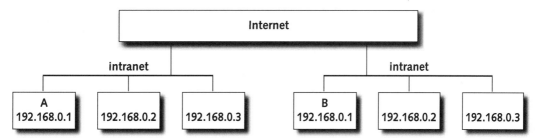

Figure 6.4 Intranets incorrectly connected to the Internet.

Intranets that use private IP addresses but still want to give their users access to the Internet can use a technology known as Network Address Translation (NAT). NAT converts private IP addresses to public ones for use on the Internet. We cover NAT in detail in Chapter 15.

Subnet masks

We've described an IP address as consisting of four numbers separated by dots. You can also think of an IP address as consisting of a network number and a host number. These numbers are analogous to an area code and telephone number, respectively.

As in an area code and phone number, the network number comes first, followed by the host number. In the United States, the area code is always three digits and the phone number seven digits, but network and host numbers can vary in length.

Network and host numbers are derived from the IP address by means of a *subnet mask*. A subnet mask looks like an IP address but is used to break down an IP address into its network number and host number (technically, a bitwise logical AND is done with the subnet mask and the IP address). Suppose, for example, that you have an IP address of 192.168.0.2 and a subnet mask of 255.255.255.0. The first three numbers (192.168.0) are the network number; the last number (2) is the host number on that network. The network number is used to help route packets to the correct network; then the host number is used to route packets to the correct machine on that network (just as area codes get phone calls to the right general area and phone numbers get them to the right telephone).

You probably don't need to worry about the details of how subnet masks, network numbers, and host numbers work. The most you'll probably ever need to do is enter a subnet mask into the TCP/IP Control Panel (covered later in this chapter), but that situation should be rare.

Routers

Normally, machines on a network (that is, machines that have the same network number) can communicate only with other machines on the same network. Routers allow machines on one network to communicate with machines on other networks (**Figure 6.5**).

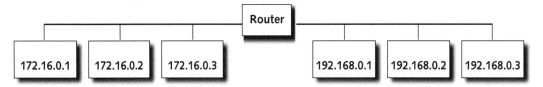

Figure 6.5 A router connecting two networks.

Routers are fundamental to the Internet because they connect the numerous networks around the world that make up the Internet. When you use the Internet, all your traffic goes through one or more routers at your ISP before it gets to the Internet backbone. **Figure 6.6** shows how your ISP may use a router.

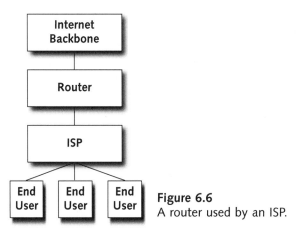

Figure 6.6
A router used by an ISP.

Host names and domain names

Although computers use IP addresses to communicate with one another, people find IP addresses hard to remember. For this reason, many computers that provide Internet services, such as mail servers and Web servers, are given names known as *host names*. To get to Open Door Networks' home page, for example, you can enter the host name *www.opendoor.com* or the IP address 208.1.80.218 in your Web browser. The host name and the IP address both point to Open Door Networks' server, but the host name is much easier to remember.

The host name *www.opendoor.com* is, in turn, based on the domain name opendoor.com. The right to use a domain name is obtained by registering the domain name with a central registry agency, such as Network Solutions Inc. Only the registered owner is allowed to use a particular domain name.

Host names are created with domain names. For example, Open Door Networks is the registered owner of the domain name opendoor.com. Open Door might choose to use the host name *www.opendoor.com* for the machine running its main Web server and the host name *www2.opendoor.com* for the machine running its second Web server. The next logical question is: How does my browser know that *www.opendoor.com* corresponds to the IP address 208.1.80.218? The resolution of a host name to an IP address is done through the Domain Name System.

The Domain Name System

The *Domain Name System* (DNS) is a distributed network of computers known as name servers, which maintain a directory of host names and IP addresses, among other things. When a user types *www.opendoor.com* in a Web browser, the following steps occur:

1. The browser gets the IP address of a name server, as configured with the TCP/IP Control Panel (covered later in this chapter). Usually, your ISP runs the name server.

2. The browser contacts the name server, sending it the host name *www.opendoor.com*.

3. The name server sends back the IP address 208.1.80.218.

4. The browser contacts IP address 208.1.80.218, which is Open Door Networks' main Web server.

Port Numbers

Any computer is capable of running any number of services, from built-in file sharing to mail servers and Web servers. When information comes to a machine on the Internet, how does that machine know what service the information is intended for? Suppose a machine is running both a Web server and a mail server. How does the machine tell a request for a Web page from a request to log into a mail server? It's done with port numbers.

For the purposes of this book, you can think of a port number as representing a particular service. Port 80, for example, is used for Web servers. Packets arriving at a machine that are intended for a specific service contain the port number for that service. The machine's networking software reads the port number and forwards the packet to the correct service for processing. To extend the telephone analogy, the combination of IP address and port number is analogous to the area code, phone number, and extension (**Table 6.1**).

Table 6.1 **Phone-Number Analogy**

	Area Code	Phone Number	Extension
541-555-1212 x49	541	555-1212	49

	Network Number	Host Number	Port Number
IP address 192.168.0.2	192.168.0	2	80
Subnet Mask 255.255.255.0			
Port 80			

Port numbers range from 1 to 65535; most common services use port numbers less than 1024. Common port numbers are administered by IANA, the same agency that manages IP addresses.

Although we said that port 80 is used for Web servers, that isn't quite accurate. Port 80 is the *default* port number for Web servers, but a Web server can also use an *alternate* port number. Suppose that you want to run two Web servers on the same machine. One server could use the default port 80, but the other Web server would have to be configured to use a different port, such as 8080. In this way, the two servers could run on the same machine yet be logically separate. Pages from the first server would have URLs such as *http://www.domainname.com/filename.html*, and pages from the second server would have URLs such as *http://www.domainname.com:8080/filename.html*. The use of alternate port numbers applies to any Internet service that allows its port number to be configured.

Port numbers and IP addresses are fundamental to firewalls, which are important security enhancements (see Chapter 12). **Table 6.2** shows the default port numbers used for common services. For a more complete list, see *http://www.opendoor.com/doorstop/ports.html*.

Table 6.2 **Common Port Numbers**

Service Name	Port Number
Web	80
File sharing	548
Mail (receiving)	110
Mail (sending)	25
FTP	21

The TCP/IP Control Panel

In Mac OS 7.6.1 through Mac OS 9, all the networking data that's required for connection to the Internet is configured in the TCP/IP Control Panel (**Figure 6.7**).

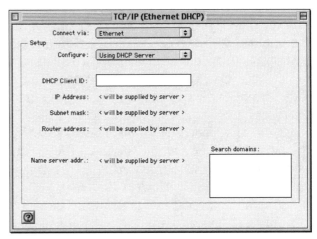

Figure 6.7 The Mac OS 9 TCP/IP Control Panel.

Configuring your Mac for cable-modem access with a dynamic IP address

In most cases, if you're connecting to the Internet through a cable or DSL modem, you'll be using a dynamic IP address. A dynamic IP address eliminates not only the need for you to enter a specific address but also the need to enter various other parameters, such as subnet mask and router address. All these parameters are obtained automatically, along with your machine's IP address.

At the top of the TCP/IP Control Panel is the Connect via pop-up menu (**Figure 6.8**). The choices in this menu correspond to the Data Link and Physical layers of the OSI networking model (refer to "Protocols" earlier in this chapter). Essentially, you choose which networking hardware to use to connect your machine to the Internet.

Figure 6.8 The control panel's Connect via pop-up menu.

You have three choices in the Connect via popup menu:

Ethernet. a high-speed networking interface that sends and receives data at 10, 100, or even 1000 Mbps. Due to its high speed, it is used for most cable and DSL modems as well as most intranet connections.

AirPort. a high-speed wireless connection that theoretically delivers 11 Mbps, although actual speeds are somewhat lower. AirPort is Apple's name for the 802.11b standard (you can see why Apple renamed it). AirPort provides a tremendous degree of freedom to laptop users, at the expense of some additional security risk (see the Advanced section of this book for details).

PPP (Point to Point Protocol). commonly used for dial-up connections. Although they support speeds only as fast as 56 Kbps, phone modems are less expensive than cable modems or wireless hardware. They also are much easier to connect to the Internet while you are on the road. Instead of needing an Ethernet connection or AirPort in your hotel room, you just plug your modem into a telephone line.

To configure a Mac to use a cable modem and a dynamic IP address, you would choose Ethernet from the Connect via pop-up menu. Below the Connect via pop-up menu is the Configure pop-up menu (**Figure 6.9**). The items in the menu vary with the connection method chosen; the figure shows the options for Ethernet.

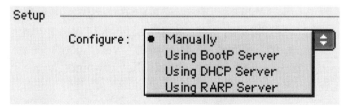

Figure 6.9 The control panel's configure pop-up menu.

If you have been told to use a dynamic IP address, your ISP probably runs a DHCP server. Choose Using DHCP Server from the Configure menu. The Control Panel now appears as shown in Figure 6.7. Notice that there is very little for you to fill in; most data is supplied by the DHCP server. You may have to fill in three items:

- If your ISP supplies IP addresses for name servers, enter those in the appropriate box.

- If your ISP uses DHCP client IDs, enter yours in the appropriate box.

- If your ISP supplies a Search Domains value, enter it in the appropriate box.

That's all there is to do. DHCP is Internet configuration for the rest of us—it's easy.

When your machine obtains an IP address from the DHCP server, that address is displayed in the IP Address field, below the DHCP Client ID (look back at Figure 6.7). The other information supplied by the DHCP server is displayed as well.

If your machine is unable to contact the DHCP server, your machine assigns itself an address from the reserved range 169.254.0.0 – 169.254.255.255, and you will not be able to access the Internet.

Configuring your Mac for cable-modem access with a static IP address

To configure a Mac to use a cable modem and a static IP address, choose Ethernet from the Connect via pop-up menu in the TCP/IP Control Panel. Next, choose Manually from the Configure pop-up menu. At this point, you need to enter the following data, all of which should be supplied by your ISP:

- Your machine's IP address

- Your subnet mask

- A router address (refer to Figure 6.6)

- One or more name-server addresses

- Search Domains value, if your ISP supplies it

Configuring your Mac for dial-up connection

To configure your Mac to use a dial-up connection, you must first configure the TCP/IP Control Panel and then configure the Remote Access Control Panel (**Figure 6.10**). This section describes the process for Mac OS 9.0 and 9.1; the procedure for other OSes is slightly different.

To configure the TCP/IP Control Panel, first choose PPP from the Connect via pop-up menu. Next, choose Using PPP Server from the Configure pop-up menu. You may need to enter one or more name-server addresses, supplied by your ISP; often, you can leave this box blank. If your ISP supplies a Search Domains value, enter it; otherwise, leave the box blank.

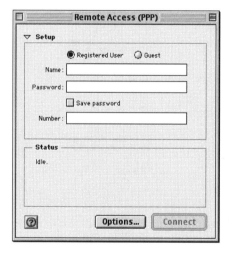

Figure 6.10
The Remote Access
Control Panel.

To configure the Remote Access Control Panel, choose Registered User and enter the requested data. Name is your dial-up account name. Your account name and the telephone number should be supplied by your ISP.

In Mac OS 9.1, the protocol used is always PPP. In earlier versions, you must specify the protocol. Click the Options button; when the Options dialog box appears, click the Protocol tab. From the Use Protocol pop-up menu, choose PPP. You probably should leave the checkboxes set as they are.

TCP/IP configurations

You can use your Mac for different Internet connections at different times—a cable modem at home, an AirPort connection in the local coffee shop, and a dial-up connection on the road, for example. The TCP/IP Control Panel's Configurations dialog box simplifies switching among various types of connections. To use this feature, from the File menu, choose Configurations. The Configurations dialog box opens, displaying a list of available configurations. You can create new configurations by clicking the Duplicate and Rename buttons. When you've selected the configuration you want to use, click the Make Active button.

Mac OS X

You set networking preferences in Mac OS X through its Network Preferences dialog box (**Figure 6.11**).

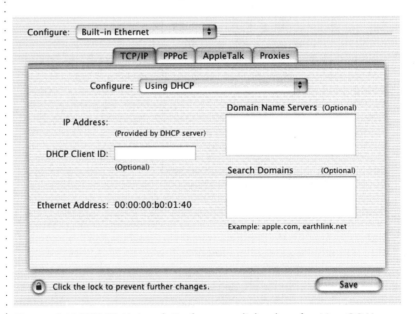

Figure 6.11 TCP/IP Network Preferences dialog box for Mac OS X.

Configuration is similar to Mac OS 9. From the dock, choose System Preferences and then Network. To configure your Mac for use with a cable modem and dynamic IP address, follow these steps:

1. Choose Built-in Ethernet from the Configure pop-up menu at the top of the dialog box.

2. Select the TCP/IP tab.

3. Choose Using DHCP from the bottom Configure pop-up in the TCP/IP tab, and then click the OK button.

That's it. As in Mac OS 9, most data is supplied by the DHCP server. You may have to fill in three items:

- If your ISP supplies you IP addresses for name servers, enter those in the appropriate boxes.

- If your ISP uses DHCP client IDs, enter yours in the appropriate box.

- If your ISP supplies a Search Domains value, enter it in the appropriate box.

Once again, DHCP is Internet configuration for the rest of us—simple and straightforward. For further information on Mac OS X, see Chapter 18.

part ii

Securing
Internet Services

Principles of Securing Internet Services

In this chapter, we present concepts we will use extensively in chapters 8, 9, and 10, which deal with securing Internet services. Although the material in this chapter is not particularly technical, you should read it before going on to the next three chapters. Even if you never intend to provide your own Internet services, these four chapters will give you a good understanding of Internet services that can run on your Mac, the risks they pose, and how to minimize those risks.

Using Versus Providing Internet Services

As an end user, you typically *use* Internet services, not *provide* them. When you get your e-mail or browse the Web, you are using Internet services. When you check or send your e-mail, for example, your e-mail program communicates with a computer at your ISP, which is running mail server software. Your ISP is providing the Internet service called e-mail, and you are using it.

The Mac OS originally did not come with the capability of providing built-in Internet services. If you wanted to run your own Web site, for example, you had to buy special Web-server software and run it on your machine or pay a Web-hosting service to host your Web site. Starting with Mac OS 8, however, the Mac OS came with a Web server, allowing Mac users to provide Web service. Over time, Apple built several Internet services into the Mac OS. We'll describe these services in Chapters 8 and 9.

Providing Internet services creates much more risk than just using them does. Fortunately, most Mac users have no need or desire to provide Internet services, so you may not have this source of vulnerability. And if you do need a Web site, many ISPs provide free personal Web sites with their Internet accounts. The ISP takes on the risks associated with running Web-server software; all you have to do is upload your pages and graphics.

In general, think carefully before enabling a built-in Internet service on your Macintosh. Securitywise, you're better off avoiding it.

Even if you don't want to provide Internet services, you should still read Chapters 8, 9, and 10 so that you know how various services get turned on and will be aware if they do get turned on, either accidentally or maliciously. If you decide that you need to provide an Internet service, Chapters 8, 9, and 10 will help you do so safely.

Levels of Security

You can use four general methods to reduce the risk associated with providing an Internet service. These methods are mutually exclusive; you choose one method for a particular service. From most secure (and most drastic) to least secure, the methods are:

Delete the service from your hard disk. If the software doesn't exist on your disk, it can't pose any risk to you. Deleting a service makes sense if you don't need it now and are sure that you never will.

Disable the service via the Extensions Manager. Many built-in services are implemented through system extensions and control panels, which are like mini-applications that load into memory when the machine is started and stay there. If you use the Extensions Manager (**Figure 7.1**) to disable a service's extensions and control panels, the service won't be loaded into memory the next time your machine starts. If the service isn't in memory, it can't be turned on and can't pose a risk. If you don't need the service now but think you might in the future, this method is the best option. Open the Extensions Manager Control Panel, locate the appropriate control panel or extension, and uncheck the checkbox next to it.

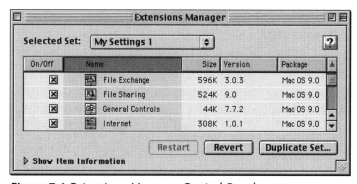

Figure 7.1 Extensions Manager Control Panel.

Turn off the service. If you want to keep a service on standby, disabling it via the Extensions Manager may be awkward, because doing so requires restarting your machine. You can use the service's controls to turn it off, however. Unless the service gets turned on accidentally, it will pose no direct risk.

Turn on the service, and be careful. If you must provide an Internet service, do so carefully, following the guidelines presented in Chapters 8, 9 and 10.

A general principle regarding the security of Internet services will appear again and again in this book:

Take extra security measures, even if they seem to be redundant.

Suppose that a service is running, and you decide to secure it by turning it off. Although turning a service off means that no one can access it, someone who turns it on accidentally or maliciously—usually, with a single mouse click—will make your machine vulnerable again. Most services have several security features. If you use all available security features, many steps will be required to cause significant risk to your machine, making it less likely to happen by accident and more difficult to do maliciously. The more roadblocks you put between yourself and risk, the safer your machine will be.

AppleTalk and TCP/IP

Another general security principle involves AppleTalk and TCP/IP. If a service works over both AppleTalk and TCP/IP, and using the service over AppleTalk is sufficient for your purposes, you should disable its TCP/IP capabilities. Because AppleTalk is not routed over the Internet, using it instead of TCP/IP significantly reduces the risk of unauthorized access to the service.

Note that although AppleTalk normally is not routed over the Internet, on misconfigured cable-modem systems, it can be routed to many users on your local part of the system. As a result, unknown users can access your AppleTalk services, such as File Sharing and Program Linking. You should never assume that AppleTalk poses no risk. Secure each service as though AppleTalk poses the same risks as the Internet.

Users & Groups

Many of the services described in this part of the book have user names and passwords as part of their security features. In particular, many services use the user names and passwords defined in the Users & Groups tab of the File Sharing Control Panel (**Figure 7.2**). Various services enhance security by requiring clients to enter a user name and password before they access the service. File Sharing also uses groups, which define a set of user names. Folders can be shared with a single user or a group.

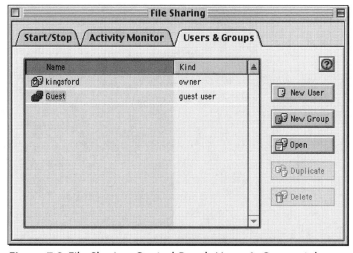

Figure 7.2 File Sharing Control Panel, Users & Groups tab.

You define new users and groups by clicking the appropriate buttons, and you edit them by double-clicking their names in the list. Each user entry has three windows, which you open through the Show pop-up menu in the user entry window (Figure 7.3). **Figures 7.3** and **7.4** show the two windows that are most commonly used.

You use the Identity window to define the user name and password. Although we said in Chapter 4 that longer passwords are better, Mac OS 9 limits you to 8 characters. While not a serious problem, the limit does prevent you from choosing really long passwords. Mac OS X does not have this limitation. You use the Sharing window to allow the user to connect to different types of services (discussed in Chapter 8) as the need arises.

Figure 7.3
The Users & Groups
Identity window.

Figure 7.4
The Users & Groups
Sharing window.

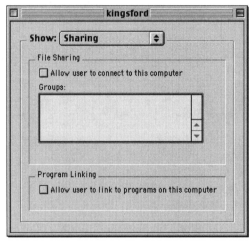

We describe a third window, Remote Access, in Chapter 9. We discuss the use of users and groups in sharing folders in Chapter 8.

Securing Common Mac OS Internet Services

Networking has been part of the Macintosh from the start and has grown steadily in functional power and ease of use. Although networking originally could be used only with Apple's proprietary AppleTalk protocol, Apple has been adding TCP/IP functionality for use with the Internet and intranets. Macintosh networking now offers several services for TCP/IP. Today, users have point-and-click access to built-in networking features that didn't exist even a few years ago, such as File Sharing over the Internet and Web Sharing.

Apple does an excellent job of implementing a basic security rule: default settings should be the most secure. Without exception, you will see that if built-in Internet services are left in their default state, they pose no direct risk to your machine. Creating significant risk requires several steps, making it less likely to happen accidentally.

In this chapter, we look at the most commonly used Internet services built into Mac OS 9 and Mac OS X. We'll describe how each service is used, what risks it poses, and how to mitigate those risks. We mainly describe procedures for Mac OS 9; other OSes may have different dialog boxes and require different steps, but the principles are the same.

File Sharing

When File Sharing is enabled, users anywhere on the Internet can connect to your machine, mount a shared volume (a folder or your whole hard disk) on their desktops, and move files in either direction between their machine and yours by using the standard drag-and-drop interface. You can set up File Sharing so that users have to log in with a user name and password, or you can allow anyone to connect. You can share one or more folders or one or more hard disks. You can allow those who connect to only read files, only write (create, modify, or delete) files, or to read and write files. Users who connect to your machine do so through built-in software such as the Chooser; no special client software is required.

To connect to your machine, a user opens the Chooser, clicks the AppleShare icon, clicks the Server IP Address button, and enters the IP address (or host name, if any) of your machine. Then the user logs in and mounts a shared volume from your machine on his or her desktop. This shared volume looks and behaves like a local disk on the user's machine.

Although File Sharing has been around for a long time, it was accessible only over AppleTalk until Apple's release of AppleShare IP in 1996, which allowed users on TCP/IP-based intranets and the Internet to share files. (Open Door Networks' ShareWay IP application makes it possible to share files over TCP/IP without purchasing the relatively complex AppleShare IP. Apple built ShareWay IP into Mac OS 9.)

In Mac OS 9, you can set up File Sharing over the Internet with a few mouse clicks.

Setting up File Sharing requires three steps:

1. To turn on File Sharing, open the File Sharing Control Panel (**Figure 8.1**). If the center pane of the Start/Stop tab does not say File Sharing On, click the Start button.

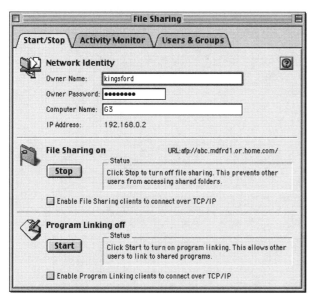

Figure 8.1 The File Sharing Control Panel and its Start/Stop tab.

2. To turn on TCP/IP access, in the Start/Stop tab, confirm that the checkbox labeled Enable File Sharing Clients to Connect over TCP/IP is checked.

3. To share a folder or disk, in the Finder, select the folder or disk to be shared. Then choose File > Get Info > Sharing. The file sharing dialog box appears (**Figure 8.2**); the title of the dialog box contains the name of the selected folder, in this case ShareWay IP Personal. Check the Share This Item and Its Contents checkbox, and assign privileges by choosing a user or group name for Owner and, if desired, for User/Group, and assigning privileges from the pop-up menus labeled Privilege.

Generally, you should make yourself the owner via the Owner pop-up menu. If you want to add privileges for one or more other users, choose that user or group from the User/Group pop-up menu. The user or group you choose will have already been defined in Users & Groups (see the Users & Groups section in Chapter 7). Unless you're sharing the item with the public (read on to see why you shouldn't), assign no privileges to everyone.

Figure 8.2 The File Sharing dialog box.

As you will see, you can take security measures at each of these three steps.

For Mac OS X, the procedures are similar. **Figure 8.3** shows the relevant portion of the Mac OS X Sharing dialog box. To turn File Sharing on, first choose System Preferences from the dock, then choose Sharing and click the Start button. See Chapter 18 for further information on Mac OS X.

Figure 8.3 The Mac OS X Sharing dialog box.

Risk

File Sharing's functionality, along with the ease of configuring it, means exposure to risk. Making a machine accessible to anyone may make sense in a company that has an intranet; the machine might be used only to post companywide information and would be accessible only to users on the local network. Making your personal machine accessible to anyone on the Internet probably is not a good idea. The worst-case scenario is having File Sharing on, TCP/IP access enabled, your whole hard disk shared, guest access enabled, and read/write permissions assigned to everyone. In this scenario, anyone on the Internet can mount your hard disk on his or her desktop and read, alter, or delete most of your files. Even if guest access is off, intruders can try to guess user names and poorly chosen passwords. (See Chapter 4 for information on choosing good passwords.)

A hidden risk in File Sharing is the possibility that your files will be intercepted and read during transmission. This risk probably is not a major one on an intranet, but the Internet always presents the possibility of spies. Someone monitoring Internet traffic can capture, and later read, packets going to or coming from your machine without your ever knowing. This possibility is a problem with File Sharing, because files are not encrypted for transmission.

Another potential risk is that locally misconfigured cable-modem systems may route AppleTalk, resulting in several cable-modem users being on a large AppleTalk network. In this situation, even if you had File Sharing's TCP/IP access turned off, any user on some part of the cable-modem system could open the Chooser, click AppleShare, and see your Macintosh in the list of available machines. Even if you've implemented good security measures, this situation represents a risk. Potential intruders know that you have a shared volume on your machine, and they have only to double-click your machine's entry in the Chooser to try to hack their way in.

A hidden feature of File Sharing—it's in Mac OS 9's built-in File Sharing over IP and all editions of Open Door's ShareWay IP— that increases exposure is ShareWay's registration with SLP (Service Location Protocol). When ShareWay registers with SLP, your machine's File Sharing can be located with an SLP browser, such as that in the Network Browser that is part of the Mac OS. Being registered with SLP may mean that hackers don't have to guess your IP address; they can pick your machine out of a list. This increased exposure means a greater risk of attempted intrusion.

Security measures

So how do you share files but stay secure?

If you will never want to share files, the safest course of action is to delete File Sharing's control panel and extensions from your hard disk. Open the System Folder and then open the Control Panels folder and delete the file named File Sharing. Next, open the Extensions folder and delete the files named File Sharing Extension and File Sharing Library. Be careful you delete the right files. This also eliminates Program Linking (covered at the end of this chapter). Delete these files only if you're sure that you will never want either service. Should you ever decide to run File Sharing, you will need to restore File Sharing from your Mac OS CD.

If you don't need File Sharing now but may in the future, you can do several things:

- Turn off File Sharing. In the Start/Stop tab of the File Sharing Control Panel (Figure 8.1), confirm that the center pane is labeled File Sharing Off. If not, click the Stop button.

- Disable access over TCP/IP. In the center pane of the Start/Stop tab of the File Sharing Control Panel, confirm that the checkbox labeled Enable File Sharing Clients to Connect Over TCP/IP is not checked.

- Don't allow any user to connect. Open the Users & Groups tab of the File Sharing Control Panel. Open each user entry, choose Sharing from the Show pop-up menu, and confirm that the Allow User to Connect to This Computer checkbox is not checked.

- Disable guest access. Guest is a special user name in the Users & Groups tab. When guest access is enabled, anyone can connect to your machine without a user name or password. Open the Users & Groups tab of the File Sharing Control Panel, and confirm that the Allow Guests to Connect to This Computer checkbox is not checked.

- Don't share folders or disks. If you're sure that you've never shared a folder or hard disk and that no one else has either, you can skip this step. Otherwise, you should turn off sharing for each item that has been shared. In the Finder, select the folder or disk; then choose File > Get Info > Sharing. The File Sharing dialog box opens (refer to Figure 8.2). Uncheck the "Share This Item and Its Contents" checkbox.

- Use good passwords for users defined in the Users & Groups window of the File Sharing Control Panel.

- Disable File Sharing through the Extensions Manager. Uncheck the checkboxes for the extensions File Sharing Extension and File Sharing Library and the control panel File Sharing. After the next restart, File Sharing will not be loaded. Note that this step also eliminates Program Linking (covered later in this chapter).

- Use a firewall. A firewall (see Chapter 12) is an easy way to ensure that most potential intruders can't even get to your File Sharing setup via TCP/IP.

By default, most items are configured with the most secure settings. If you have never changed any of these settings on your machine and are sure that no one else has either, you're probably OK.

If you need File Sharing on but not all the time, turn it off when it's not needed. If the service is off, no one can log in. Open the File Sharing Control Panel, click the Start/Stop tab, and then click the Stop button in the File Sharing pane.

When you have File Sharing on, follow these guidelines:

- Unless it's needed, disallow guest access.

- Use good passwords for users defined in the Users & Groups tab of the File Sharing Control Panel.

- Don't share more than you need to share. If possible, confine your shared files to one folder (or at least to a folder hierarchy that does not contain sensitive documents), and share only that folder.

- Determine which users need to connect to your machine, and allow only those users to connect. Open the Users & Groups tab of the File Sharing Control Panel. For each user who needs access to your machine, choose Sharing from the Show pop-up menu, and confirm that the Allow User to Connect to This Computer checkbox is checked. For each user who does not need access to your machine, confirm that the same checkbox is not checked.

- When you share a folder or disk, assign only necessary privileges. If a user or group does not need write privileges, for example, give only read privileges. Unless guest access is required, assign no privileges to Everyone.

- If you're using the built-in File Sharing over TCP/IP that comes with Mac OS 9, you can upgrade to Open Door Networks' ShareWay IP Personal and gain several security advantages, including the capability of limiting TCP/IP access to selected user names, creating a log file, and choosing an alternate port.

- If you want to see who is connected to your File Sharing, open the Activity Monitor tab of the File Sharing Control Panel. You can see who is connected and what folders and disks are available to be shared.

- Encrypt files containing sensitive data before moving them over the Internet. Apple provides an encryption/ decryption tool (see Chapter 9).

- Use a firewall. A firewall is an easy way to limit TCP/IP access to File Sharing, based on the IP address of the client attempting to connect to your machine.

Web Sharing

Web Sharing allows you to run your own Web site from your Macintosh and to share files over the Web. Users can view Web pages on your machine through their browsers just as they can any other Web site. They also can read and download files and possibly upload files.

To start Web Sharing, open the Web Sharing Control Panel (**Figure 8.4**), and click the Start button.

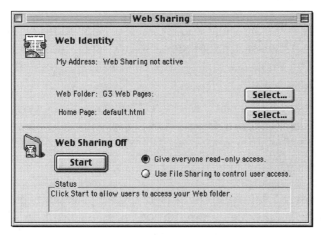

Figure 8.4 The Web Sharing Control Panel.

Among the options you can set are which folder you want to share, the default page, and access permissions.

To specify which folder will be shared, click the Select button to the right of the Web Folder label. The current folder is displayed. As you can with File Sharing, you can choose to share an entire hard disk.

To specify the home page for your Web site, click the Select button to the right of the Home Page label. The selection dialog box that appears displays a list of files, with the current home page highlighted. Select a file; then click OK or None. Clicking None tells Web Sharing to use Personal NetFinder. With Personal NetFinder, a user's browser displays a list of all files and folders in the current folder and allows the user to navigate anywhere in the Web folder. Choosing a file as the home page means that if users enter *http://yourIPaddress/* in their browsers, they will get the file you specified. If users enter *http://yourIPaddress/subfolder/*, however, Web Sharing reverts to Personal NetFinder, displaying a list of all files and folders within the subfolder. Personal NetFinder creates security risks, covered in "Risk" later in the Web Sharing section.

You specify access permissions by using the two radio buttons in the bottom pane. If you click the radio button labeled Give Everyone Read-Only Access, users can connect without a user name and password but can only read files. If you click the radio button labeled Use File Sharing to Control User Access, access is allowed only to users defined in the Users & Groups tab of the File Sharing Control Panel. Depending on the File Sharing permissions assigned, some users may be able to upload files to your disk via Web Sharing if their browsers support uploading.

For Mac OS X, open the Mac OS X Sharing dialog box (Figure 8.3). To enable Web Sharing, click the Start button. See Chapter 18 for further information on Mac OS X.

Risk

In its default configuration, Web Sharing presents little risk. The folder shared is the Web folder supplied with the OS, and unless you've moved documents into this folder, it contains no sensitive data. Although all users can connect, they have read-only access. The default configuration offers little to intruders.

Web Sharing, however, allows you to change several settings, and some changes can increase security risks. The options that affect security are:

> **Web Folder.** This option is the folder to be shared. The default is a folder named Web Pages that comes with the Mac OS. This folder contains only sample files and information on how to use Web Sharing. You can specify that any folder on your hard disk be shared—or the entire hard disk. Specifying folders other than the default may increase risk, because users on the Internet can read any file in the specified folder or any of its subfolders.

Home Page. The default setting for this option is not really a home page. The default is NetFinder, which displays in the user's browser a list of all files and folders in the current folder. Intruders can navigate within the Web folder and any subfolders, looking for interesting file or folder names. If you share your entire hard disk or a folder that contains important data, NetFinder may help trespassers locate sensitive data, such as a file named Stock Portfolio or a folder named Business Records. Specifying a file as a home page means that users get no feedback on what file or folder names are contained in the Web folder—with one exception. If a user who accesses your site guesses a folder name and enters a URL like *http://yourIPaddress/foldername*, Web Sharing will revert to Personal NetFinder and will remain in Personal NetFinder until the user returns to the main Web folder.

Access Permissions. The default setting allows read-only access to all users, the same as most Web sites. You can specify that access be controlled by sharing permissions. This option requires you to turn on File Sharing and then share the Web folder specified in the Web Sharing Control Panel. If for example, you share the Web folder so that user kingsford has read and write permission and user charles has read-only access, only users kingsford and charles can access the Web folder; they will be prompted for their passwords and will have only the specified permissions. User kingsford will be able to upload files to the Web Sharing folder, through a browser or other application that supports uploading.

Access Files Outside Web Folder. Normally, any file or folder outside the Web folder is not accessible. But if you change this setting in Web Sharing's Preferences dialog, users can access files and folders outside the Web folder through aliases in the Web folder. If your stock portfolio file is outside the Web folder, but your Web folder contains an alias to the file (or a folder that contains the file), users could read or download the file.

Allow Guests with Write Permission to Replace Files.
If you check this checkbox in Web Sharing's Preferences dialog, and if you control Web Sharing access by using File Sharing privileges, users with write privileges can upload files (and overwrite your files) if they have a browser or other application with upload capabilities.

Web Sharing supports CGIs. A *CGI* (common gateway interface) is a miniapplication that can be invoked through a Web browser, providing additional functionality to a Web site. A CGI might be used, for example, to accept information in a form and e-mail it to a site owner. CGIs generally pose little security risk, because you choose whether to put them in your Web folder and control what they actually do. Any application that you add to your machine, including a CGI, does increase risks to a small extent, so be sure to evaluate any CGI closely from a security perspective.

Also be aware that controlling access by using sharing privileges opens a potentially serious security hole. If you assign write privileges to a user when you share the Web folder, that user can upload files to the Web folder. That user also can upload CGIs, which they can run from any Web browser—in fact, anyone who knows about the CGI can run it. Presumably, you trust a user with your files before assigning write privileges, but when Web Sharing is configured this way, the user also can run miniapplications on your machine and potentially communicate with other applications on your machine (including the Finder) or other machines on the network. This situation probably is not what you had in mind. Think twice before assigning write privileges to the Web folder.

Security measures

So what should you do to stay safe while using Web Sharing?

If you will never want to enable Web Sharing, you should delete Web Sharing's control panel and extension from your hard disk. Open the System Folder and then open the Control Panels folder and delete the file named Web Sharing. Next, open the Extensions folder and delete the file named Web Sharing Extension. Be sure you delete the right files. Should you ever decide to run Web Sharing, you will need to reinstall it from your Mac OS CD.

If you don't need Web Sharing now but may in the future, you can do several things. Most of these settings are the default settings. Even if you have never opened the Web Sharing Control Panel before, you should do the following:

- Specify a home page. Doing so means that NetFinder will not be used and users will not have a list of your files and folders displayed in their browsers. In the Web Sharing Control Panel, click the Select button to the right of Home Page and specify a document. Using default.html is fine. As noted in "Risk" earlier in this chapter, NetFinder can still be invoked under certain circumstances. Specifying a file as a home page lessens the risk that an intruder will get a list of file and folder names but does not eliminate it.
- Use the default Web Sharing folder. Unless you move documents into this folder, the default folder contains no sensitive data. This folder, named Web Pages, is located either at the root of the hard disk or inside the Documents folder. Click the Select button to the right of Home Page, and locate the Web Pages folder.
- Set read-only access for everyone. Doing so will prevent anyone from uploading pages to your Web folder, possibly overwriting your files. In the bottom pane of the Web Sharing Control Panel, click the radio button labeled Give Everyone Read-Only Access.
- In Web Sharing Preferences, confirm that users are not allowed to access files outside the shared folder via aliases. Choose Edit > Preferences and confirm that the Allow Aliases to Open Files Outside the Web Folder checkbox is not checked.
- In Web Sharing Preferences, confirm that guests with write access are not allowed to replace files in the Web folder.
- Turn off Web Sharing. The bottom pane of the Web Sharing Control Panel tells you whether Web Sharing is on or off. If it's on, click the Stop button.
- Disable Web Sharing via the Extensions Manager. Uncheck the checkboxes for the extension Web Sharing Extension and the control panel Web Sharing. After the next restart, Web Sharing will not be loaded.
- Use a firewall. A firewall is an easy way to ensure that most potential intruders can't even get to your Web Sharing.

If you need Web Sharing on but not all the time, turn it off when it's not needed. If it's off, no one can get in. Open the Web Sharing Control Panel, and click the Stop button.

When you have Web Sharing on, follow these guidelines:

- Unless you have a compelling reason to use NetFinder, specify a home page. If you do need to use NetFinder, confirm that your Web folder does not contain sensitive data. In the Web Sharing Control Panel, click the Select button to the right of Home Page, and specify a document.

- Confirm that the folder you share does not contain sensitive data and does not have subfolders that contain sensitive data. Users may be able to read all the files in your Web folder, and possibly overwrite them, if you use File Sharing for user permissions.

- If you use File Sharing to control user access, confirm that users do not have write access unless they really need it. Choose File > Get Info > Sharing, and in the sharing dialog (Figure 8.2), confirm that Owner and User/Group do not have write privileges unless they need them.

- If you use File Sharing to control user access and you share a folder to a group, confirm that the group contains only users who need access to Web Sharing. Open the File Sharing Control Panel, click the Users & Groups tab, and open the group to see who belongs. If necessary, create a new group.

- If in Web Sharing Preferences, you specify that users are allowed to access files outside the shared folder via aliases, confirm that the aliases point to nonsensitive files or to folders that do not contain sensitive files.

- In Web Sharing Preferences, confirm that users with write access are not allowed to replace files in the Web folder. To do so, choose Edit > Preferences to display the Preferences dialog box, and click the Options tab. Confirm the state of the checkbox labeled Allow Guests with Write Access to Replace Files in the Web Folder.

- Enable logging. Web Sharing's log file is not in the Mac standard WebSTAR-compatible format, making it incompatible with many Mac log-processing applications. A log file might nonetheless be useful for tracking down security violations or attempts. To enable logging, choose Edit > Preferences to open the Preferences dialog box, click the Options tab, and check the Web Sharing Log checkbox. Log files are discussed in Chapter 13.

- Use an alternate port. Alternate ports give you a basic way to hide any Internet service. Using an alternate port for Web Sharing would require users to enter URLs in the format *http://hostname:portnumber/filename.html*. Alternate port numbers typically are greater than 8000. Web Sharing, for example, might use port 8080 as an alternative. To specify an alternate port, choose Edit > Preferences to display the Preferences dialog box, click the Options tab, and type the alternate port number in the Web Sharing Port text box. Host names and ports are discussed in Chapter 6.

- Use a firewall. A firewall is an easy way to limit access to Web Sharing, based on the IP address of the client attempting to connect to your machine.

Program Linking

With Program Linking over TCP/IP, a user can control applications (including the Finder) running on any Macintosh on the Internet that is running Mac OS 9, provided that the target machine has been set up properly.

Program Linking was introduced with System 7 but worked only over AppleTalk until Mac OS 9. When TCP/IP functionality arrived with Mac OS 9, the potential risk involved with Program Linking became much more serious.

To set up your Mac's Program Linking to be accessed from the Internet, follow these steps:

1. Turn on Program Linking. In the Start/Stop tab of the File Sharing Control Panel (Figure 8.1), if the bottom pane is labeled Program Linking Off, click the Start button.

2. Enable TCP/IP access for Program Linking. In the same tab, confirm that the checkbox labeled Enable Program Linking Clients to Connect over TCP/IP is checked.

3. Allow the appropriate users to link to programs. Open the Users & Groups tab of the File Sharing Control Panel. For each user who requires Program Linking access, open the user entry, choose Sharing from the Show pop-up menu, and confirm that the Allow User to Link to Programs on to This Computer checkbox is checked.

When you take these steps, a user on another Macintosh can run an application or an AppleScript that sends commands to, say, your Mac's Finder. The commands can do anything that the target application is capable of doing, although most applications allow only a subset of their actions to be performed through AppleScript. (This subset is defined in the application's AppleScript dictionary.)

Risk

The potential risks related to Program Linking over TCP/IP are high. Although Program Linking cannot be used to launch an application directly on your Macintosh, it can control applications (including the Finder) that are already running on your machine. The Finder generally represents the greatest risk, because it is always running and has many scriptable actions. Intruders can write AppleScripts to tell your Finder to perform actions such as shutting down your machine and moving, renaming, or deleting your files.

Because Program Linking access over TCP/IP is potentially dangerous, guest access is not allowed over TCP/IP. Only registered users can communicate with your machine. Note, however, that allowing guest access over AppleTalk can pose serious risks. Typically, AppleTalk is not routed over the Internet, but in some misconfigured cable-modem systems, AppleTalk may be routed over some portion of the network, exposing your AppleTalk services to access from unwanted users. If you allow guest access to Program Linking on such a system, you expose yourself to serious risk.

Security measures

What steps can you take to keep Program linking safe?

If you will never want to enable Program Linking, remove File Sharing's control panel and extensions from your hard disk. Open the System Folder, open the Control Panels folder inside the System Folder, and delete the file named File Sharing. Next, open the Extensions folder and delete the files named File Sharing Extension and File Sharing Library. Note that this process also eliminates File Sharing (covered earlier in this chapter). Delete File Sharing's files only if you're sure that you will never want either service. Should you ever decide to run Program Linking, you will need to restore File Sharing by reinstalling it from your Mac OS CD.

If you don't need Program Linking now but may in the future, you can do the following things through the File Sharing Control Panel:

- Disable TCP/IP access. In the bottom pane of the Start/Stop tab, confirm that the checkbox labeled Enable Program Linking Clients to Connect over TCP/IP is not checked.

- Disable Program Linking access for all users. In the Users & Groups tab, open each user entry. Choose Sharing from the Show pop-up menu, and confirm that the checkbox labeled Allow User to Link to Programs on This Computer is not checked. Note that this checkbox is not relevant for user Guest. Because Program Linking access over TCP/IP is potentially dangerous, guest access does not apply to Program Linking over TCP/IP. Only registered users can communicate with your machine.

- Turn off Program Linking. Confirm that the bottom pane of the Start/Stop tab is labeled Program Linking Off. If not, click the Stop button.

- Disable Program Linking via the Extensions Manager. Uncheck the checkboxes for the extensions File Sharing Extension and File Sharing Library and the control panel File Sharing. After the next restart, Program Linking will not be loaded. Note that this step also eliminates File Sharing.

- Use a firewall. A firewall is an easy way to ensure that potential intruders can't even get to your Program Linking.

If you need Program Linking on but not all the time, turn it off when it's not needed. If the service is off, no one can access it. Open the File Sharing Control Panel, click the Start/Stop tab, and then click the Stop button in the Program Linking pane.

When you have Program Linking on, follow these guidelines:

- Enable Program Linking access only for users who need it.
- Use a firewall.

Although these precautions are relatively simple, if you follow them, the risks associated with Program Linking can be quite manageable.

Securing Other Mac OS Internet Services

In this chapter, we look at the less commonly used Mac OS Internet services. As in Chapter 8, we'll describe how each service is used, what risks it poses, and how to minimize those risks. We describe procedures for Mac OS 9; other OSes may have different dialog boxes and require different steps, but the principles are the same.

Remote Access

You can use Remote Access in two ways—as a client, to dial up a modem connected to another network or your ISP, or as a server, to allow someone to dial up the modem connected to your machine. (For details on using Remote Access as a client, see Chapter 17.)

In Mac OS 9, you can configure Remote Access as a single-user server, allowing other users to dial in to your machine and get access to your machine and the network it is on (if any). The Remote Access server supports both PPP (Point to Point Protocol) and ARAP (Apple Remote Access Protocol), although with Mac OS 9.1, Apple dropped support for ARAP in favor of the more standard PPP.

Initially, Remote Access was add-on software you installed separately from Mac OS. Starting with Mac OS 8, however, the Remote Access client was installed by default with the system software, although you still had to purchase the server separately until Mac OS 9.

To set up Remote Access as a server, open the Remote Access Control Panel and choose Answering from the Remote Access menu. The Answering dialog box opens (**Figure 9.1**).

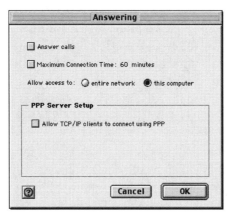

Figure 9.1
The Remote Access answering dialog box.

Check the Answer Calls checkbox. For Mac OS 9 and earlier, the default protocol is ARAP, allowing clients connecting to your machine to access AppleTalk services, including File Sharing via the client's Chooser. If you want to use PPP instead, check the checkbox labeled Allow TCP/IP clients to connect using

PPP. With PPP, both AppleTalk and TCP/IP services will be accessible, and connected users will be able to access the Internet through your machine if it has Internet access.

Unless you've enabled guest access, users dialing up your machine will need a user name and password that match an entry in the Users & Groups tab of the File Sharing Control Panel (see Chapter 7). For each user you want to allow to dial in to your machine, you must edit the user entry in the Users & Groups tab. From the Show pop-up menu in that tab, choose Remote Access. The Remote Access dialog box for the user appears (**Figure 9.2**). Check the Allow user to dial in to this computer checkbox.

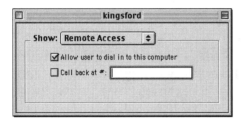

Figure 9.2 Remote Access options for user kingsford defined in the Users & Groups tab of the File Sharing Control Panel.

Risk

If you configure Remote Access as a server, intruders can dial up your machine and attempt to guess a user name and password—unless guest access is enabled through the File Sharing Control Panel, in which case no user name or password is required. After logging in to your Remote Access server, intruders will have two options:

- If intruders connect by using ARAP, they can attempt to access your AppleTalk services. They can open the Chooser, for example, and see your machine and possibly any other machines that are on the same AppleTalk network. By using the list of machines in the Chooser, they can attempt to access File Sharing on each of those machines as well as attempt access to AppleTalk services such as Timbuktu.

- If intruders connect by using PPP, they can attempt to access both AppleTalk and TCP/IP services on your machine, including File Sharing, Personal Web Sharing, and Timbuktu. Each of these services, if enabled, has its own set of security risks, which are covered elsewhere in this chapter and in chapters 8 and 10. Intruders also can access AppleTalk and TCP/IP services on any network to which your machine is connected.

Security measures

What can you do, then?

If you will never need Remote Access as a client or server, delete the service from your hard disk. From your Mac OS CD, run the installer, and uninstall Remote Access. If you don't have access to a CD, open the Control Panels folder and delete the file named Remote Access; then open the Extensions folder and delete the file named OpenTpt RemoteAccess. Be careful to delete the right files. If you ever want to use Remote Access again, you'll have to reinstall it from a system software CD.

If you don't need Remote Access now but will in the future, disable it by using the Extensions Manager Control Panel. Uncheck the Remote Access checkbox in the Control Panels section, and uncheck the OpenTpt RemoteAccess checkbox in the Extensions section. After the next restart, Remote Access will not be loaded.

If you need to use Remote Access as a server, follow these guidelines:

- Allow access only to those users who need it. In the Users & Groups tab of the File Sharing Control Panel, open each user, choose Remote Access from the Show pop-up menu, and confirm that the Allow User to Dial in to This Computer checkbox is checked only for those users who need access.

- If you have other machines networked to yours, allow access to other machines only if necessary. In the Answering dialog box click the Allow Access to This Computer radio button.

- Unless connected users will require access to TCP/IP services, don't choose PPP as the connection protocol. The default protocol used is ARAP, which presents fewer risks. PPP is specified in the Answering dialog box. If the checkbox labeled Allow TCP/IP Clients to Connect Using PPP is not checked, ARAP will be used.

Apple Network Assistant

Network administrators use Apple Network Assistant to manage Macintoshes on a network. The first thing to consider is whether you need to have Network Assistant on your machine.

- If you are using a stand-alone Macintosh (not networked to other machines), you should not have Network Assistant installed on your machine. (If you have a cable modem or dial-up account with an ISP and have no machines connected to your Mac, you have a stand-alone machine.)

  To see whether Network Assistant is installed, look in the Help menu for an item called About Network Assistant. If you find it, open the Extensions folder, drag the file named Network Assistant Startup to the Trash, and restart your machine. Make sure you moved the right file. You also should delete the Network Assistant folder. This folder contains the application Network Assistant Security, which is used to configure the extension. After you complete this step, you can skip the rest of this chapter.

- If you are on an intranet, you should have Network Assistant installed only if your network administrator has asked you to do so. In this case, the rest of this chapter will help you and your system administrator safely use Network Assistant.

Typically, each Mac on a network runs Network Assistant client software, and the network administrator runs the Network Assistant administration application. For each client, the network administrator can observe the client machine's monitor, control their mouse pointer and keyboard, read statistics and other technical information about the state of the machine, and change certain aspects of the machine's configuration.

The Network Assistant client is an optional installation on the Mac OS CD. It is installed as a system extension and an application that is used to configure the extension.

To configure the Network Assistant client, launch the Network Assistant Security application. The default password is xyzzy. The Network Assistant Security dialog box appears (**Figure 9.3**).

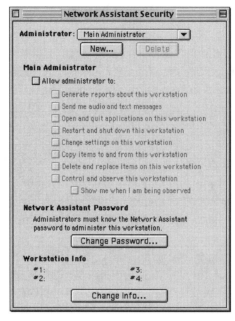

Figure 9.3
The Network Assistant Security dialog box.

You must have at least one administrator defined; typically, you will have only one. Each administrator has a separate set of access privileges. You access administrator definitions via the Administrator pop-up menu at the top of the dialog box. An administrator's privileges are indicated by the checkboxes in the center of the dialog box. The dialog box in Figure 9.3 shows the settings for the default administrator. To define a new administrator, click the New button; when the New Administrator dialog box appears, enter a well-chosen password and a name for the administrator. The new entry will be listed in the Administrator pop-up menu; you can choose it from that menu and change the access privileges by using the checkboxes. Typically, a network administrator will help you configure the client.

Risk

- Anyone on the Internet who has a Network Assistant administration application potentially can gain access to your machine and can read, alter, and delete your files.

The intruder may also be able to run applications. For example, he can turn on your File Sharing and guest access and then share your hard disk, allowing the intruder access to your files in a way that you would not be likely to notice. He may also be able to use your e-mail application, allowing him to read your e-mail and send malicious e-mail under your name.

As with Timbuktu (covered in Chapter 10), the potential for damage is high.

Security measures

So, what can you do?

If you will never need a Network Assistant client, delete the system extension. Open the Extensions folder inside the System Folder, delete the file named Network Assistant Startup, and restart your Mac. Be careful to delete the right file.

If you don't need Network Assistant now but will in the future, don't install it until you need it. If the service is already installed, disable the Network Assistant extension by unchecking the Network Assistant Startup checkbox in the Extensions Manager Control Panel. The next time you start your machine, the Network Assistant client extension will not be loaded.

If you need Network Assistant but not all the time, follow these guidelines:

- Choose a good password for the Network Assistant Security application. You can change the password by clicking the Change Password button in the Network Assistant Security dialog box. When the Change Password dialog box appears, enter the old password and a well-chosen new password. See Chapter 4 for details on choosing good passwords.

- When the service is not needed, you should disable all privileges by unchecking the Allow Administrator To checkbox for each administrator defined.

When you have the Network Assistant client running, follow these guidelines:

- Choose a good password for the Network Assistant Security application. You can change the password by clicking the Change Password button.

- Choose good administrator passwords. You specify a password for an administrator when you create the administrator entry.

- Allow administrators only the necessary privileges. You specify administrator privileges via the checkboxes in the Network Assistant Security dialog box.

- For each administrator, check the Show Me When I Am Being Observed checkbox if you allow remote observation. If this checkbox is checked, a pair of eyeballs will appear in the menu bar when the network administrator is observing your machine.

- Examine Network Assistant's log periodically. From the menu, choose Help > About Network Assistant; when the Network Assistant About box appears, click the Export Log button. The log file contains descriptions of the actions Network Assistant administrators have taken on your machine.

- Use a firewall. A firewall (see Chapter 12) is an easy way to keep unwanted users from trying to access your Network Assistant client.

(For another discussion of controlling machines remotely, see Chapter 10.)

SNMP

Network administrators typically use SNMP (Simple Network Management Protocol) to manage large mixed-platform networks. Machines on the network are managed from a central computer, known as a *console,* that runs SNMP management software. Each machine to be managed runs SNMP agent software. The agent gathers networking statistics and other data from the machine on which it is running, and the console collects data from all agents on the network, making it available to the system administrator. The console also may be able to change the state of certain networking variables on an agent machine.

As with Apple Network Assistant, you should decide whether you need to have an SNMP agent installed on your machine:

- If you are using a stand-alone Macintosh (not networked to other machines, other than through the Internet), you should not have the SNMP agent installed on your machine. (If you have a cable modem or dial-up account with an ISP and have no machines connected to your Mac, you have a stand-alone machine.)

  To see whether SNMP is installed, look in the Extensions folder (inside the System Folder) for files named Open Transport SNMP and OpenTptSNMPLib. If you find those files, drag them to the Trash, and restart your machine. Make sure you removed the right files. You also should delete the SNMP Admin folder. This folder contains the application SNMP Administrator, which is used to configure the extension. After you complete this step, you can skip the rest of this section.

- If you are on an intranet, you should have the SNMP agent installed only if your network administrator has asked you to do so. In this case, the rest of this section will help you and your system administrator use SNMP with minimal risk.

You use the SNMP Administrator application to define sets of permissions, known as *communities,* for an SNMP agent. Communities are similar in concept to user names. One community might allow read and write access to all data; another community might allow read-only access to some data and no access to the rest. The default community is named public. When an SNMP administrator wants to access your machine's SNMP agent, he has to specify your machine's IP address and a community name (**Figure 9.4**).

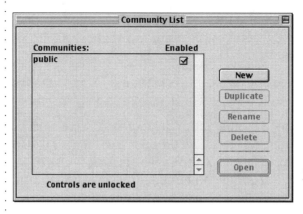

Figure 9.4
The Community
List dialog box.

Starting with Mac OS 8.5, an SNMP agent was available as an optional installation with the system software. As a Macintosh user, you don't need to know how to configure an SNMP agent; your network administrator probably will handle that job. But knowing a few basics that affect the security of your machine is useful.

Risk

Running an SNMP agent on your machine creates the possibility that anyone on your network or the Internet can obtain information about your machine's networking configuration.

Security measures

To safely use an SNMP agent, to disable it, or to completely get rid of it, follow these precautions.

If you will never want to run an SNMP agent, delete the system extensions Open Transport SNMP and OpenTptSNMPLib from your hard disk, and restart your machine. Be careful you delete the right extensions. Should you change your mind in the future, you'll have to reinstall SNMP from your Mac OS installation CD.

If you don't need SNMP now but may in the future, follow these guidelines:

- Don't install SNMP until you need it. If the service is already installed, see the following three items.

- Disable all communities. In the Community List dialog box (which is always open when SNMP Admin is running), uncheck the Enabled checkbox to the right of each community name. When a community is not enabled, it cannot be reached via an SNMP console.

- Lock the controls. When all communities have been disabled, choose Control > Lock Controls; when the Lock Controls dialog box appears, choose a password. After you lock the controls, no one can change the SNMP client without entering the password. See Chapter 4 for guidelines on choosing a good password.

- Disable the SNMP extension by using the Extensions Manager Control Panel. Uncheck the Open Transport SNMP and OpenTptSNMPLib checkboxes. The next time you start your machine, the SNMP extensions will not be loaded.

If you need SNMP, but not all the time, follow these guidelines when you do need it:

- Disable all communities, as described in the preceding list.

- Lock the controls, as described in the preceding list.

When you have SNMP on, follow these guidelines:

- Use hard-to-guess community names or insist that your network administrator provide such names. When an administrator attempts to contact your machine, he must know the IP address of your machine and the name of a community defined in your SNMP agent. Choosing a hard-to-guess community name is a little like choosing a good password; if a potential intruder can't guess it, he can't get in. You should not use the default community named public.

- Lock the controls when you are not using them.

- Don't give more access than necessary. The agent on your machine probably will be configured by a network administrator, who should be careful to allow only access to the necessary data items and write access only where required.

- Use a firewall. A firewall is an easy way to keep unwanted users from trying to access your SNMP agent.

Figure 9.5 A file encrypted with Apple File Security.

Apple File Security

Included with Mac OS 9 is the Apple File Security application, which you can use to encrypt and decrypt files. At the time of encryption, you assign a password to each file. Encrypted files cannot be read until they have been decrypted, which requires knowing the password. Although an encrypted file has the same name as it had before encryption, its icon has a small yellow key in the bottom-left corner (**Figure 9.5**).

The Apple File Security application is located in the Security folder within the Applications folder. Choose a file to be encrypted in one of two ways:

- Locate the file in the Finder and drag it over the Apple File Security application.

- Double-click the application, locate a file through the dialog box that appears, and click the Choose button.

The Apple File Security dialog box appears (**Figure 9.6**). Type a password, specify whether to add the password to the Keychain, and click the Encrypt button. For details on the Keychain, see Chapter 4.

Figure 9.6 Apple File Security dialog box.

File encryption is an additional security measure to protect sensitive data, such as a stock portfolio or business records. An intruder who gains access to your machine can't read an encrypted file unless he knows the file's password.

You also should encrypt files before transmitting sensitive data on the Internet or possibly on an intranet, depending on the intranet's size. Anyone who intercepts an encrypted file during transmission will not be able to read it.

You should consider encryption when you move files that contain sensitive data in any of these situations:

- As e-mail attachments
- Over File Sharing
- To an iDisk folder
- Over FTP

In general, you should use Apple File Security to encrypt sensitive files before transmitting them via any medium that does not encrypt files automatically. You also can use this service to minimize the damage resulting from theft. If someone steals your PowerBook but the most critical data on the disk is in encrypted form, you don't have to worry that the data will be misused.

Securing Third-Party Internet Services

In this chapter, we describe commonly used third-party Internet services. These services let your Macintosh provide Internet capabilities beyond those provided by the Mac OS. As in chapters 8 and 9, we're discussing providing such services from your Mac, not using them through a Web browser, e-mail reader, or other application. If you have not installed third-party Internet services on your machine, you can skip this chapter. If you have installed Internet services but not the ones mentioned here, you can still get ideas about securing those services by reading this chapter.

Timbuktu

Timbuktu from Netopia is similar to Apple Network Assistant (see Chapter 9). Timbuktu allows users to (among other things) access a Mac remotely as though they were present at the remote machine, using that machine's keyboard and mouse. When you connect to someone else's machine by using Timbuktu, a window appears on your monitor that contains an image of the remote computer's monitor; whatever appears on the remote machine's monitor also appears in the Timbuktu window. When you move the mouse pointer in the Timbuktu window on your Mac, the pointer moves on the remote monitor. Using your mouse and keyboard, you can work on the remote machine as though you were actually there (**Figure 10.1**).

This service allows you to do things that you cannot do through File Sharing, such as run applications and configure System software.

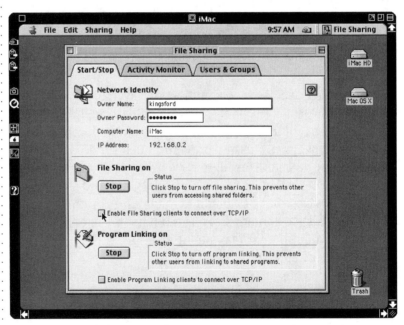

Figure 10.1 Timbuktu controlling a remote Macintosh, named iMac.

The connection can be saved in a connection document on the visitor's machine. In the future, the visitor can establish the connection to the remote machine again by double-clicking the connection document.

Timbuktu is the kind of technology that you may never need, but when you do, little else can take its place. Suppose that you have an order-processing system that requires you to open a database, find new orders, run a database script, run an application to process credit cards, and then run an e-mail script. How do you do these things when you're on the road? You could write an AppleScript and invoke it remotely, but by using Timbuktu, you can look for errors at each step and take any necessary action—a highly desirable setup for order processing.

In addition to allowing control of a remote machine, Timbuktu allows observation of another machine and file transfer and messaging between machines.

Timbuktu must be installed on both machines. To allow someone to connect to your machine, you need to allow public access (read on to see why this practice is strongly discouraged) or create a Trusted Visitor account. Trusted visitors are similar to users defined in the Users & Groups tab of the File Sharing Control Panel, except that Timbuktu maintains its own set of users. Choose Setup > Visitor Privileges to display the Visitor Privileges dialog box. (**Figure 10.2**). Click the New button to create a new visitor entry (**Figure 10.3**). Type a user name and password in the appropriate boxes.

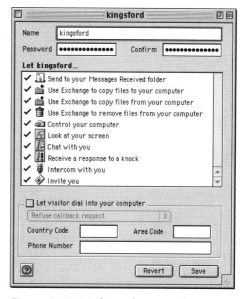

Figure 10.3 Privileges for trusted visitor kingsford.

Figure 10.2 The Visitor Privileges dialog box.

Note that all access privileges are allowed by default, which violates the basic security rule that default settings should be the most secure. Disable privileges that the visitor will not need and then enable incoming access. Choose Setup > Incoming Access to bring up the Incoming Access dialog box (Figure 10.6). To allow others to connect to your machine over the Internet, the TCP/IP checkbox must be checked. Now anyone on the Internet can connect to your machine through Timbuktu, log in with a visitor name and password, and control your machine.

Risk

Timbuktu's ease of setup, along with the power over your machine that it can give intruders, make Timbuktu potentially risky.

Of all the applications that you can install on your machine, Timbuktu probably presents the highest security risk, due in part to its powerful functionality and in part to its popularity. Hackers know about, and are on the lookout for, machines with Timbuktu running. Further, hackers can access your Mac's Timbuktu from either a Mac or a Windows machine, increasing the number of hackers who might try to access your Macintosh.

As long as you stick with the setup described in the preceding section and use good passwords, the chance that intruders will get in is small. But if intruders do get in, they could cause extensive damage.

Intruders could enable guest access for File Sharing and share your entire hard disk, for example. Then they could connect to File Sharing at any time in the future and have complete access to your files, including downloading and deleting them. Because intruders can run applications on your machine, they might run your e-mail application and read your e-mail; send malicious e-mail by using your identity; or download, alter, or delete sensitive data. Intruders could also defeat security measures by disabling or subtly changing your firewall settings or installing a virus. The potential risk is total vulnerability of your data, your system configuration, and your privacy.

Fortunately, Timbuktu has an extensive set of security features.

Security measures

How do you protect yourself whether you are using Timbuktu or not?

If you no longer need Timbuktu, delete it from your hard disk. If the software is not on your hard disk, no one can configure it in such a way as to expose you to risk. In the Extensions folder (inside the System Folder), delete the file named Timbuktu Extension. *Be careful to delete the right file.* Also delete the Timbuktu folder, which contains the Timbuktu application.

If you use Timbuktu rarely, use the Extensions Manager Control Panel to disable the Timbuktu extension when you don't need it. In the Extensions Manager, uncheck the Timbuktu Extension checkbox. Timbuktu will not be available after the next machine restart. To use Timbuktu again, you must enable the Timbuktu extension and restart the machine.

When Timbuktu is running, follow these guidelines:

- Use a master password. When you specify a master password, no one can change Timbuktu's configuration without entering the password. (See Chapter 4 for details on choosing good passwords.) To specify a master password, choose Setup > Preferences to display the Preferences dialog box, and select Master Password in the left pane (**Figure 10.4**). Type a master password in the text box. Then check the appropriate checkboxes to specify that it be required to open the Preferences and Visitor Privileges dialog boxes and to toggle incoming access.

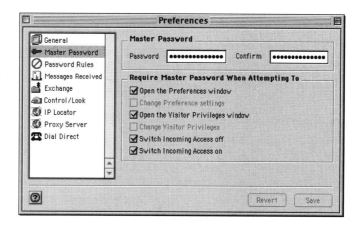

Figure 10.4 Timbuktu's master-password options.

- Assign only the necessary privileges to each visitor.
When you create a Trusted Visitor account, that user is
assigned all privileges by default. You should allow only
those privileges that the visitor actually needs. If in
doubt, err on the side of caution; you can always add
a privilege later.

  The two default accounts, Public Visitor and Ask for
  Permission, should never have any privileges. Public
  Visitor does not require a password to connect to your
  machine and should never be used except under controlled circumstances, such as a private network that has
  no connection to the Internet. Ask for Permission can
  request permission to connect, which requires someone on
  the target machine to acknowledge the request. To edit
  visitor permissions, choose Setup > Visitor Privileges.

- Don't allow common passwords. Select Password Rules
in the left pane of the Preferences dialog box (**Figure
10.5**). Then make the appropriate choices.

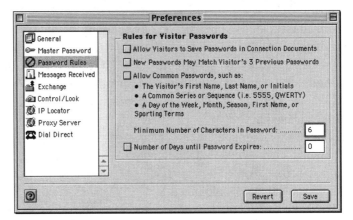

Figure 10.5 Timbuktu's password-rules options.

- Require at least six characters in a password. Select
Password Rules in the Preferences dialog box. In the
Minimum Number of Characters in Password text box,
type the appropriate number.

- Don't allow visitors to save passwords in connection
documents. This setting requires visitors to enter their
passwords every time they connect to your machine,

thereby minimizing the risk that an unwanted user on that person's machine will try to access yours. Select Password Rules in the left pane of the Preferences dialog box, and uncheck the checkbox labeled Allow Visitors to Save Passwords in Connection Documents.

- Specify that new passwords cannot be the same as any of the previous three. This setting prevents visitors from recycling passwords too often. Select Password Rules in the left pane of the Preferences dialog box, and uncheck the checkbox labeled New Passwords May Match Visitor's 3 Previous Passwords.

- Don't allow visitors to dial in to Timbuktu unless doing so is necessary. For each visitor account, confirm that the checkbox labeled Let Visitor Dial into Your Computer is unchecked.

- Don't use IP Locator. This feature allows visitors to locate your machine by using your e-mail address. Normally, a client would need to know the IP address of your computer (or a host name, if any). IP Locator makes your machine much easier to find from anywhere on the Internet, which generally is not a good idea. Select IP Locator in the left pane of the Preferences dialog box, and ensure that no e-mail address has been entered.

- Check Timbuktu's log file periodically for suspicious activity, including frequent access to your machine and long connect times.

- If any critical applications on your machine have the option of requiring passwords, use them, so that Timbuktu intruders can't run them easily.

- Allow access to your machine only if doing so is necessary. To disable incoming access, choose Setup > Incoming Access to display the Incoming Access dialog box, and uncheck all the checkboxes (**Figure 10.6**).

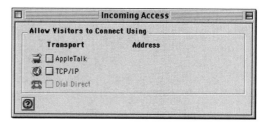

Figure 10.6 Incoming Access dialog box.

- If you allow access to your machine, avoid enabling TCP/IP access, if possible. If AppleTalk access will suffice, allow only AppleTalk.

- Use a firewall. You can use a firewall to block all access to Timbuktu or to allow access only from certain IP addresses.

If you use Timbuktu to control other machines but never want your machine to be controlled, follow these guidelines:

- Allow no incoming access. To do so, choose Setup > Incoming Access to open the Incoming Access dialog box, and uncheck all the checkboxes.

- Disable all services for the default visitor accounts Public Visitor and Ask for Permission. To do so, choose Setup > Visitor Privileges to open the Visitor Privileges dialog box (refer to Figure 10.2). Open each of these two visitor entries, and disable all permissions.

- Delete all visitors other than the two default accounts.

- Don't allow visitors to dial in to Timbuktu. For each visitor account listed in the Visitor Privileges dialog box, confirm that the checkbox labeled Let Visitor Dial into Your Computer is unchecked.

- Use a master password, as we described earlier in this section.

- Check Timbuktu's log file periodically, looking for suspicious activity.

- Use a firewall.

Retrospect

Dantz Retrospect allows you to back up data on your computer from your computer or from another machine on your network. Backing up your files from another machine on your network requires that you have a Retrospect client installed on your computer. The client can be configured for access over AppleTalk or TCP/IP. Network backups usually are done by a network administrator.

Data is stored in units called *backup sets*. The network administrator can put a backup set on a removable medium attached to his machine, in a file on his machine or another machine on the network, or on an FTP site on the local network or the Internet. Even if you use Retrospect on a stand-alone Macintosh, you should read this chapter, because some of the risks pertain to violations of physical security.

Risk

Retrospect presents three main risks:

Unauthorized users could open a backup set. The chance always exists that backup sets can be obtained maliciously. Removable media can be stolen (see Chapter 3), machines containing backup sets can be hacked, and FTP sites can also be hacked. If you don't take proper security precautions, anyone who possesses a backup set can open it with Retrospect and access the files it contains. Even if the intruder doesn't have Retrospect, he can still open the backup set with another application and examine its contents.

Backup data from a machine can be intercepted as it's moved from the machine to the backup set. If you are backing up your machine to a removable medium or to a data file on your machine, this risk doesn't apply. Backing up over your local network or to an FTP site is different, however. Your local network is less likely to have spies than the Internet, although the risk depends on the nature of your network environment. A corporation with 250 Macs on an intranet, for example, is more likely to have mischievous users than a small business with three machines.

Backing up to an FTP site creates much higher risk, due partly to the much greater likelihood of spies. Also, FTP transmits passwords as clear text, making it possible for spies to get your FTP password and access your files on the FTP server (see Chapter 14).

Your data could be backed up by an intruder. This situation might happen in one of two ways. First, if you are on a misconfigured cable-modem system that routes AppleTalk over your local part of the system (see Chapter 7), other users could access Retrospect clients configured for AppleTalk. Therefore, another user on your part of the cable-modem system could back up your files to his machine.

Second, it is possible (though unlikely) for a serious hacker to emulate the Retrospect application across the Internet. After the hacker determines that your machine is running a TCP/IP Retrospect client, he could back up your files to his machine.

Security measures

To safeguard against the unauthorized use of Retrospect to read your backup sets, you can specify a password when you create a backup set. To do so, click the Secure button in the Backup Set Creation dialog box (**Figure 10.7**), which appears whenever you create a new backup set. When you click the Secure button, the Encryption dialog box appears (**Figure 10.8**). If you want a password but no encryption, choose Password Only and click OK. Anyone who attempts to open the backup set will have to supply the password. Note that you must specify the security option you want to use at the time you create the backup set.

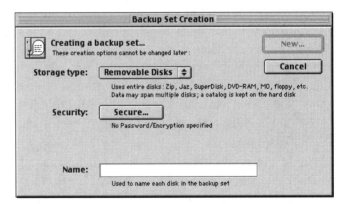

Figure 10.7 Backup Set Creation dialog box.

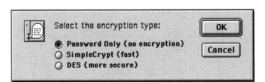

Figure 10.8 Encryption dialog box.

Passwords prevent unauthorized people from using Retrospect to open a backup set. Passwords do not, however, prevent a backup set from being opened with another application or from being intercepted on the network. Going through an entire backup set with, say, a binary editor might be tedious, but someone could do it. Also, a hacker's program could scan backup sets automatically for passwords or credit-card numbers. For this reason, Retrospect allows backup sets to be encrypted.

With encryption, which also requires a password, data that is intercepted on a network or on the Internet cannot be read. Also, backup sets that are obtained maliciously (stolen media or hacked files) cannot be read with other applications. Reading an encrypted backup set requires Retrospect and the set's password. In the Encryption dialog box, choose one of the two encryption schemes (SimpleCrypt is faster, DES provides stronger encryption) and click OK. When you are prompted to do so, choose a password for the set.

A special case of backing up data over a network is backing up to an FTP site, which introduces serious potential risk. Although the possibility of spies on an intranet is small, the possibility of spies on the Internet is so great that you should assume that someone is spying on your activities. Spies can intercept your backup sets en route to the FTP site and read their contents. If you must use FTP backup, be sure to use encryption in conjunction with a well-chosen password.

Also, your FTP password is sent to the FTP site as clear text, meaning that a spy can read it and then use it to access your files on the FTP site. Then the intruder can download and delete the files on the site, including backup sets. For this reason, you should not back up to FTP sites. If you must back up to an FTP site, be sure to use encryption, and don't use your FTP password for any other service.

To prevent the backup of your data from an intruder's machine, you should specify AppleTalk access for the Retrospect client on your machine. Although this method will not eliminate the risk of intrusion, it will reduce that risk considerably. If you must use TCP/IP, install a firewall and configure it to allow access only from the desired backup machine. Firewalls are covered in Chapter 12.

FileMaker Pro

FileMaker's FileMaker Pro is a full-featured relational database that allows access to its files over an intranet or the Internet. If you do not need to share your database files, proceed directly to "Security measures" to see what steps you should take to secure your database.

You can share files in either of two ways:

FileMaker Network Sharing. A FileMaker file on one machine can be opened with a FileMaker application on another machine on the local intranet or the Internet, via AppleTalk or TCP/IP.

Companion Sharing. A FileMaker file on one machine can be made accessible though any Web browser on the local intranet or the Internet. This method of sharing uses FileMaker's Web Companion, which acts as a simple Web server.

This section is based on FileMaker Pro 4; the procedures for other versions will differ slightly. Note that this chapter does not attempt to describe all security risks associated with databases— only those related to Internet access. Consult the FileMaker Pro documentation for full coverage of database security.

Risk

Sharing database files is inherently risky due to the nature of the data these files contain, such as credit-card numbers or financial transactions. Sharing FileMaker files over an intranet is safe to the extent that users on the network can be trusted. One potentially serious security hole exists, however: If a user has export privileges, that user can open a file that is shared on an intranet and then publish it to the Internet.

Sharing FileMaker files over the Internet is much riskier, due to the larger number of hackers and spies. To control the risk of sharing files, FileMaker Pro implements passwords and groups. Passwords limit what users can do (browse, edit, create, and so on); groups limit which layouts and fields are displayed. A group represents one or more passwords. The concept is similar to the Users & Groups tab in Apple's built-in File Sharing (see Chapter 8).

Although well-chosen passwords will keep hackers from accessing your database files directly, spies still can intercept and read files on the Internet.

Security measures

Here's a rundown of what you can do to protect yourself and your database:

If you don't need to share database files, you can follow these guidelines:

- Confirm that all files are single-user and not enabled for sharing via Web Companion. Open each FileMaker file, choose File > Sharing to open the File Sharing dialog box, and confirm that the file is marked as single-user and that the Web Companion checkbox is unchecked (**Figure 10.9**).

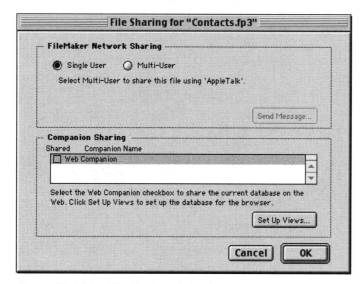

Figure 10.9 The File Sharing dialog box.

- Specify <none> as the networking protocol. Choose Edit > Preferences > Application to display the Application Preferences dialog box. From the Network Protocol pop-up menu, choose <none> (**Figure 10.10**).

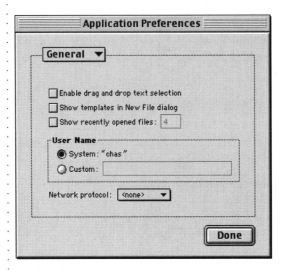

Figure 10.10
The Application
Preferences dialog box.

- When you set up FileMaker's access privileges, think in terms of your database files being shared, even though you aren't going to share them. A little paranoia may save you grief later if someone enables sharing without your knowing about it. Having good passwords and well-assigned privileges will make it that much harder for someone to expose your database to risk. To assign privileges, choose File > Access Privileges > Overview to open the Access Privileges dialog box (**Figure 10.11**).

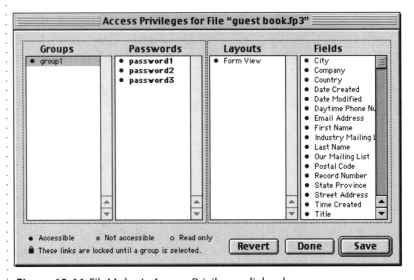

Figure 10.11 FileMaker's Access Privileges dialog box.

Note that the passwords and groups in the figure use example names; you should choose better names.

If you need to share database files, follow these guidelines:

- Don't enable Web Companion unless you need it.
  If FileMaker Network Sharing is sufficient for your purposes, use it instead of Companion Sharing. This choice ensures that your database files will not be accessible to anyone who has a Web browser but not the FileMaker application. Open each database file; then open the File Sharing dialog box (choose File > Sharing) and confirm that the Web Companion checkbox is not checked.

- If your FileMaker machine has AppleTalk connectivity for all potential users, and you don't otherwise need TCP/IP access to your shared database files, specify AppleTalk instead of TCP/IP for the network protocol. To do so, choose Edit > Preferences > Application to display the Application Preferences dialog box. From the Network Protocol pop-up menu, choose AppleTalk.

- Use a good password for each file. You manage passwords from the Define Passwords dialog box, which you open by choosing File > Access Privileges > Define Passwords (**Figure 10.12**).

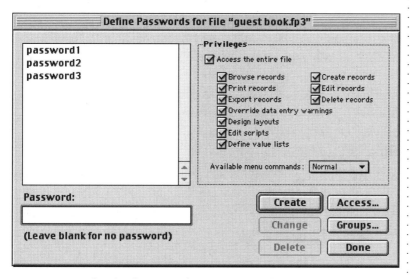

Figure 10.12 The database's Define Passwords dialog box.

- Assign access privileges sparingly. Assign only the necessary privileges to a password or group.

- Use extreme caution in sharing files that contain sensitive data. Database files are not encrypted during transmission, making it possible for spies who intercept them to read them. Share such files on the Internet only if absolutely necessary, and disable access to those files when it is not needed.

- Use a firewall. A firewall can block all access to FileMaker Pro or allow access only from certain IP addresses.

- Use FileMaker's built-in firewall (available only in version 5). When you use this feature, database files shared on the Web can be accessed from only one IP address or one range of IP addresses. While this feature is not as flexible as a full firewall, it provides an added layer of security. To use the built-in firewall, choose Edit > Preferences > Application to open the Application Preferences dialog box. Click the Plug-Ins tab, select Web Companion, and click the Configure button. The Web Companion Configuration dialog box opens. In the Security pane, check the Restrict Access to IP Address checkbox, and enter an IP address. See Chapter 12 for details on firewalls.

- Specify that the shared file is not displayed in the Hosts dialog box (version 5 only). This setting makes shared database files accessible to users who need them, but the files are hidden from view, so users who don't need access won't know that they're shared. To share each file this way, choose File > Sharing to open the File Sharing dialog box; then choose Multi-User (Hidden).

ShareWay IP

ShareWay IP, from Open Door Networks, makes AFP (AppleTalk Filing Protocol) file servers accessible over TCP/IP. Such servers include the Mac's built-in File Sharing, AppleShare servers, and third-party AFP servers such as Windows NT.

ShareWay IP is available in three versions:

Personal Edition. This edition (**Figure 10.13**) is similar to what is built into Mac OS 9. It works with the built-in File Sharing on the machine on which ShareWay is installed, allowing users on a TCP/IP intranet or on the Internet to access the target machine's File Sharing. Even though Mac OS 9 has a limited version of ShareWay built in, the Personal Edition has additional security features.

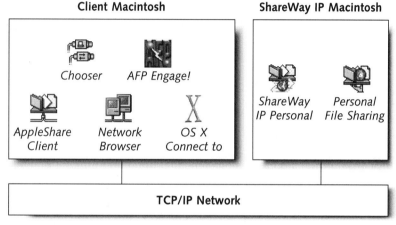

Figure 10.13 ShareWay IP Personal Edition.

Standard Edition. This edition (**Figure 10.14**) can target a file server on the ShareWay machine or another machine connected to the ShareWay machine via AppleTalk. The target file server can be any AFP server.

Pro Edition. This edition (**Figure 10.15**) can target as many as 256 AFP file servers connected to the ShareWay machine via AppleTalk.

Clients on a TCP/IP intranet or on the Internet can use several tools to connect to a ShareWay-targeted file server:

- The Chooser via the AppleShare client, which is built in to every Mac

- The Network Browser, built into Mac OS 9

- Mac OS X's Connect to Server feature

- AFP Engage, add-on client software included with ShareWay IP

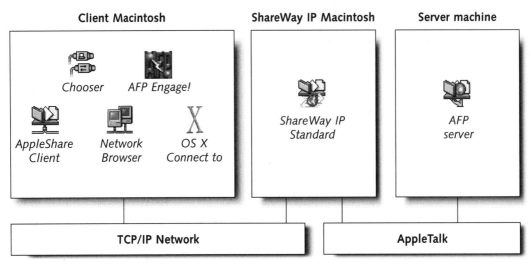

Figure 10.14 ShareWay IP Standard Edition.

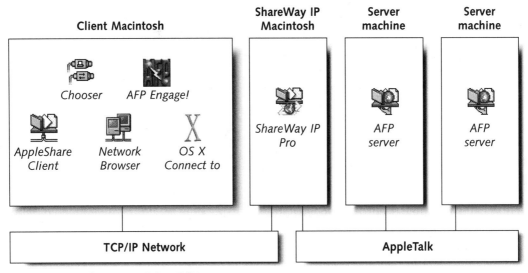

Figure 10.15 ShareWay IP Pro Edition.

Risk

The risk associated with ShareWay IP is essentially that of File Sharing over TCP/IP: Intruders might hack into the file server on the target machine. (We cover security measures for File Sharing in Chapter 8.) The Standard and Pro editions introduce another level of risk. Although users of ShareWay IP Personal Edition know that they have to secure their File Sharing (after all, they just installed ShareWay on their machines), the Standard and Pro editions can target file servers that are not on the ShareWay machine. Users on these other machines have no way of knowing that their file servers are now accessible over TCP/IP, which probably means they're accessible over the Internet. The risk is that these file servers will not be secured properly.

When a machine has been targeted by ShareWay IP, anyone on the Internet can access it through an AFP client (such as the Chooser) simply by entering the IP address assigned to the target machine by ShareWay. Hackers can scan ports and IP addresses for available services, which makes good file-sharing security measures a must.

ShareWay IP presents an additional level of exposure. Like the Mac's built-in File Sharing, all three editions of ShareWay IP register the target servers with SLP (Service Location Protocol). ShareWay's registration with SLP allows users on the same network to use SLP-savvy applications—such as Apple's Network Browser and Mac OS X's Connect to Server feature—to browse for file servers targeted by ShareWay. SLP browser applications present a list of registered file servers in much the same way that the Chooser shows a list of file servers accessible over AppleTalk. The risk is that users on the ShareWay machine's intranet—and possibly users of a particular ISP—don't have to guess IP addresses; they can just select a server from a list. This situation presents a serious risk not only from hackers but also from merely curious users.

Security measures

Each file server targeted by ShareWay IP must be secured (see Chapter 8). If you are using the Standard or Pro Edition, and you target a file server that is not on the ShareWay machine, you must notify the user of the target machine that his or her File Sharing needs to be secured or you must secure it yourself.

The security measures for a target machine are:

- Disallow guest access unless it is needed.

- Use good passwords for users defined in the Users & Groups tab of the File Sharing Control Panel.

- Don't share more than you need to share.

- Determine which users need to connect to your machine, and allow only those users to connect.

- When you share a folder or disk, assign only the necessary privileges.

- Use a firewall on the ShareWay machine. A firewall is an easy way to limit access to File Sharing, based on the IP address of the client attempting to connect to your machine.

The Personal and Standard Editions have security features that are not available in the version that ships with Mac OS 9. To access these features, choose File > Show ShareWay Security to open the ShareWay IP Security dialog box (**Figure 10.16**).

Figure 10.16
ShareWay IP
Security dialog box.

This dialog box allows you to do the following things:

- Disable guest access over TCP/IP. Uncheck the Allow Guests to Connect over IP checkbox. This setting denies guest access over TCP/IP even if the Users & Groups setting allows guest access. This way, you can deny guest access from the Internet but allow it from the intranet via AppleTalk.

- Allow all registered users to connect over IP. When this radio button is selected, any user defined in Users & Groups can access the target server over TCP/IP.

- Allow listed users to connect over IP. This option lets you specify which registered users can access the target server over TCP/IP without affecting access from the intranet via AppleTalk.

- Disallow listed users from connecting over IP. This option blocks TCP/IP access for specific registered users without affecting their access from the intranet via AppleTalk.

ShareWay also allows you to specify an alternate port for File Sharing. Stop ShareWay; then choose File > Set Port Number to bring up the port number dialog box. Type an alternate port number and click OK. Alternate port numbers usually are greater than 8000; 8548 is often used for File Sharing. Using an alternate port is a way to hide File Sharing. Unless the server shows up in an SLP browser, a hacker would have to guess the port number.

Finally, use ShareWay's logging feature to maintain a log file of all connection logins and logouts. To use this feature, choose File > Turn Logging On. The log file is named ShareWay IP Log and is stored in the Preferences folder. You can read and analyze the log file at any time. Log-file-analysis software is discussed in Chapter 13.

Other Applications

You can install many other third-party Internet applications on your Mac. Some of these applications are professional tools, which are covered in Chapter 17. Other backup applications and databases have similar risks to those described in this chapter.

Popular end-user applications include the peer-to-peer services that have sprung up recently, including Napster, Gnutella, and chat services. Although these applications usually are considered to be clients, they also have server aspects that carry some risk. Although many of these applications can share only specific types of files (usually, MP3 music files), others provide more general file-sharing capabilities.

Another category of applications is distributed computing services. The idea behind distributed computing is to break a large, complex computational problem into small pieces and give the pieces to different computers. Each computer solves its small piece and returns the results to the service. An example is SETI@home, which is part of a University of California at Berkeley program engaged in the search for extraterrestrial intelligence. To become involved with SETI@home, you download computational software from the SETI Web site and run it on your machine. A SETI server downloads data to your machine for processing. When your machine is done, it uploads the results to the SETI server.

Risk

Music-sharing services such as Napster and Gnutella, and many chat services, have file sharing capabilities, so you should think of them as carrying all the risks of Apple's built-in File Sharing (see Chapter 8). In addition to the risks of sharing your files with others, a relatively high danger of downloading viruses exists in any peer-to-peer system, because peer-to-peer is more or less anonymous. When you download from a reputable Web site, you can expect that files have been scanned for viruses. But when you download from an essentially anonymous user on the Internet, you have no idea what you're getting.

The risks associated with distributed computing include the following:

- Although SETI@home is run by a distinguished organization, other distributed computing projects may not be, which would raise doubt about the integrity of the software. Is the software virus-free? Does it do only what it claims to do?

- Distributed-computing software is networking software and is always running. How well written is the software? Does the network-communications setup have security holes? Again, in a reputable project, the risk is minimized, but the risk is not zero.

Security measures

When you use any peer-to-peer application, limit what you share, preferably to one folder. Don't share your hard disk. If you download files from other users' machines, use virus-detection software and configure it to scan downloads automatically. See Chapter 11 for more information on viruses.

No specific technical security advice is available for distributing-computing services. Think carefully about engaging in such a project, weighing your contribution to the greater public good against the risks to which you will expose yourself.

If you decide to participate in a distributed-computing project or to use any other third-party Internet software, you should follow the procedures in this book that apply to that software. Using antivirus software is always a good idea.

part iii

Enhancing Overall Security

Viruses

11

In Webster's dictionary, the principal definition of *virus* is "the causative agent of an infectious disease." Although Webster intended this definition to apply in the physical world, the definition is equally valid on the Net. The terms *causative, agent, infectious,* and *disease* all describe very well what a computer virus is, what it does, and why you want to concentrate on avoiding viruses as much in the virtual world as in the physical one.

Like the number of security incidents and hacker attacks, the number of known viruses has been increasing at a rate faster than the number of users on the Internet. Symantec, maker of popular Macintosh antivirus software, reports an increase from 20,500 known viruses at the beginning of 1999 to more than 42,000 going into 2000. No doubt the problem has been getting even worse since then.

What Viruses Are

Webster's alternative definition of *virus,* the one that is relevant to computer security (online or off), is:

a computer program usually hidden within another seemingly innocuous program that produces copies of itself and inserts them into other programs and that usually performs a malicious action (as destroying data).

Let's look at the key phrases in this definition:

Computer program. A virus is a type of computer program, just like a word processor, a Web browser, or an operating system. It does what it's designed to do by running just like any other computer program. Because a virus usually is hidden, however, it almost never looks like a program. Would you run an application called Malicious Virus? As the definition says, a virus usually is embedded within another program, such as an application, a document (many documents are in fact programs that run in the environment of their application), or the OS itself.

Hidden. A virus almost always is hidden so that it can do its dirty work without your realizing it. Viruses can hide in many places, most commonly within an application or part of the OS, but also in documents (see "macro viruses" under "Types of viruses" later in this chapter) or even in places on disks that aren't used for files at all, such as the boot blocks of a disk that you use to start your computer in the first place. Viruses also can hide in invisible files.

Produces copies of itself. Technically, a virus must be self-replicating, which is how it moves from one file and one computer to another. A virus makes copies of itself and inserts those copies where they will be run later. Trojan horses, described later in this chapter, are not always self-replicating but have come to be included with viruses because they meet all the other aspects of the definition.

Malicious. A virus does something bad, even if the bad thing is just use your computer to replicate. Usually, a virus does something worse, either intentionally or unintentionally. See "What Viruses Can Do" later in this chapter for details.

How they work

A virus works through stealth. Because it's a computer program, a virus must be run before it can do anything. But unlike most other computer programs, a virus isn't a program that you run on purpose. The virus has to be stealthy, embedding itself in programs that you do run.

A virus usually embeds itself in, or infects, applications. Some viruses infect specific applications; others infect all applications that they can find. Regardless, when the unaware user runs the infected application, the virus runs as well (or sometimes instead). Viruses also can infect the OS itself— a particularly effective way of making sure that they're run, because the OS is always running. Newer viruses can infect certain types of documents, running when the document is opened by its application.

What can the virus do when it's run? Anything its designer wants it to do within the environment in which it's run. If a virus is run as part of the OS, it can do anything that the OS can do, which is essentially anything the computer can do. If it's run from an application, it can do anything that an application can do (which, up through Mac OS 9, was anything the OS could do but is more limited in Mac OS X). If it's run from a document, it's limited to doing things that documents from that application can do. The fundamental thing that a true virus always does is make copies of itself, which is how it spreads. Then it inserts the copies of itself into other programs, so that it will run again when those programs are run. It also can copy itself to programs on other machines across the Internet or an internal network, in which case it is called a *worm* (see "Types of viruses" later in this chapter).

Beyond copying itself, what a virus does when run may be hidden. A virus hides most of its operations so that you won't notice it and try to wipe it out. Some viruses do only hidden things, such as copy all your passwords as you type them and send them out over the network. The goal of such viruses is to remain hidden, never alerting you to their presence. Other viruses do things that are not hidden, such as display messages or delete files.

Where they come from

Viruses, like other programs, are written by software developers. Most software developers write programs because they can make money by selling them to users or because they think the programs will be useful. The motivation of virus writers is quite different. Most virus writers create viruses for the thrill of being able to affect many computers at a distance. Also, writing viruses is a "cool" thing for a certain subset of people to do. Virus writing has become so popular that virus-writing kits are available, making it easy for just about any software developer to create a virus. Just as script kiddies use premade scripts to launch attacks over the Internet, beginning virus writers use virus kits to create their first viruses.

After virus writers create a virus, they need to unleash it on the world. Viruses usually are buried in legitimate (as *Webster* says, seemingly innocuous) applications that are distributed in the same ways as other applications. Adding insult to injury, you often pay for applications that contain viruses.

Before the Internet became popular, most viruses were distributed through applications on floppy disks. Viruses are one of the many aspects of online security that apply in the offline world as well.

Even if you never connected your computer to the Internet, you would have to worry about viruses, because they could be transmitted to your machine through any application that you install. If you use the Internet, you should worry even more.

The Internet has made viruses a much bigger threat than before. Floppies had to be delivered physically, so a virus might take days or weeks to spread from one machine to another. The Internet, on the other hand, provides many mechanisms for the immediate delivery and spread of viruses:

- You can purchase an application containing a virus and immediately download, install, and run that application.

- You can download and try out an "evaluation" version of an application that contains a virus.

- You can download a virus in an e-mail attachment.

- You can download a virus through any application that copies files from the Internet to your computer (such as those listed in Chapter 5).

The popularity of the Internet has made virus writing much more desirable in certain hacking circles, because viruses can do much more damage much faster. Before the Internet, significantly fewer computers were being used, and those machines were much less accessible. Now machines number in the hundreds of millions, and they can be reached almost instantly. Gratification can be immediate; the virus writer doesn't have to wait weeks for results anymore.

Despite that they originated in the offline world, viruses have evolved into the single biggest security threat in the online world. For that reason, understanding and protecting yourself against viruses is critical to your online safety.

Types of viruses

Viruses come in several types. You need to understand the different types and how they work so that you can take precautions against each type.

Traditional viruses. Traditional viruses infect a piece of software on your computer that is run directly. Usually, that software is an application that you will run as part of your day-to-day activities, but it could also be a piece of operating-system software that is run by the OS itself. On the Mac OS, for example, a virus could infect an extension or control panel, both of which are run at boot time. It could also infect the System file, the Finder, or other pieces of software that need to run for the Mac OS to do its job.

Macro and script viruses. A *macro virus* infects a document, as opposed to an application. A *macro* is a set of instructions in a document that execute together within the scope of the document's application. Macros usually can automate a complex or commonly performed task and can sometimes even do anything you can do manually within an application. A word processing document, for example, might include a macro that changes the font, size, and style of a word at the same time. A spreadsheet might have a macro that duplicates a column of numbers and makes the copies red. Many macros execute automatically when the document in which they reside is opened, guaranteeing that they're invoked whenever that document is opened.

Although a macro virus can execute only instructions that its application allows (as opposed to instructions that the OS allows), many applications have powerful macro capabilities, such as the capability to change and delete documents and to send e-mail. Some of these viruses can move across platforms, because many applications have the same document and macro format on more than one platform (in particular, on Windows and the Macintosh). Macros are powerful but risky from a security perspective.

A *script virus* is essentially the same as a macro virus, being just a complex macro written in a scripting language. Some scripting languages, such as the one used in HyperCard (called HyperTalk), execute in an application. Other scripting languages, such as AppleScript or Visual Basic Script in the Windows world, can execute as applications themselves. Macro and script viruses can be easier to write than traditional viruses, because the macros and scripts are intended more for users of applications than for programmers. When HyperCard first came out, so did many HyperCard viruses. A side effect of HyperTalk's ease of use was that HyperCard viruses were easy to write. VB Script has had a much worse effect on the Windows world in this regard. As many as half of all the Windows viruses reportedly have been written in VB Script. Macro viruses have been growing steadily in popularity. One source estimates that almost half of all viruses are macro viruses.

Worms. A *worm* is a special type of virus that spreads from computer to computer, not just from file to file within a computer. When worms are run, they look for other computers to jump to, not other files on the same computer. They must use the Internet or a local network for this purpose. Worms most commonly find another machine by emailing themselves as attachments. How do they know where to e-mail themselves? Simple—they go through the address book of your e-mail program and e-mail themselves to every address in that list. Because the e-mail appears to come from you, the recipient is more likely to be tricked into opening the attachment (and activating the virus) than if it came from an unknown sender. Worms can spread very quickly in this way.

Trojan horses. A *Trojan horse* (or just Trojan) has all the characteristics of a virus except that it doesn't necessarily go around making copies of itself and infecting other files or machines. But it is a computer program, it is hidden, and it is malicious. Most antivirus software offers protection again Trojans as well as true viruses. Computer Trojan horses are just like the original Trojan horse, which the Greeks presented to the Trojans in the guise of a peace offering. The horse actually harbored warriors who, once inside the otherwise-insurmountable gates of Troy, sneaked out in the dead of night and opened the gates for the invading army. Computer Trojans are not what they appear to be, either; they contain something hidden that has malicious intent. Being applications, they still must be run to carry out their purpose however, just as the Trojan horse had to be brought within the gates of Troy.

What Viruses Can Do

Viruses can do many bad things to your machine and can compromise your online safety significantly, directly or indirectly. We just mentioned some of the things that viruses can do; this section describes some others.

Many viruses are written to do annoying but not intentionally malicious things. A virus might display a message on the fourth day of every month, make annoying sounds at startup, or cause a particular application to behave unusually. But even such viruses end up using memory and disk space and affecting the performance of your machine, if nothing else. Also, if your machine is infected, you can pass the virus on to others, who certainly will not be happy about receiving the virus from you. Thus, no virus is really benign.

Unintentional damage

Some viruses are written to do one thing, innocuous or not, but end up doing other things as well or instead. Most virus writers do not do a good job of testing their viruses, because they don't need to worry about the normal support and upgrade process that traditional developers need to follow and don't need to be concerned if users get a buggy virus. After all, no one will ask for his or her money back if the virus doesn't work right. Because viruses aren't well tested, most of them don't behave as intended under conditions that the virus writer didn't expect.

A misbehaving virus can do two things. Sometimes, the virus becomes inert and does nothing. Because a virus is supposed to do something bad, when it doesn't work, the result is good. But most times when a virus doesn't work right, the results are even worse than intended. Many viruses aren't meant to be malicious, but when they don't work right, they often become malicious.

Viruses need to infect files to propagate, and they need to infect files unobtrusively so as not to be noticed. But infecting files is a difficult operation for a virus writer to perform, especially in a hidden manner, so it's often done incorrectly, at least for certain files under certain conditions. Even though the virus writer may have intended to infect the file without affecting the way the file works, the file may be infected in such a way that it's damaged or destroyed. If the file is an OS file, the OS itself may not work after the infection. A virus written with even the most innocuous intentions can have the worst results.

In addition to infecting files incorrectly, viruses can make at least two other types of errors: they can make errors performing their desired operations, and they can make errors interacting with other programs. Sometimes, a virus incorrectly does what it was intended to do under certain circumstances, such as when it is run in a different version of an application or the OS than expected. In these cases, if you're lucky, little harm will result. But if the error is particularly bad, the virus could crash the application or the machine.

Other times viruses behave poorly when interacting with applications that run on the same machine as they do. Many viruses propagate through residing in memory after they're run, waiting until they encounter the files they want to infect. They also may intercept and change various OS operations. Because viruses take up memory and change the operation of the OS, they change the environment in which other applications run. And because virus writers don't do a good job of testing, viruses often change the environment in ways that other applications don't expect. So applications totally unrelated to the virus also end up behaving strangely or crashing if the virus is active— which is how many otherwise-hidden viruses are discovered.

Intentional damage

As bad as misbehaving viruses can be, behaving viruses can be much worse and are the ones you should be most worried about from a security perspective. Although many viruses are innocuous, some are malicious, and the worst ones may not be the ones that are the most overtly malicious. Overtly malicious viruses may do their damage and move on. But the viruses that are stealthily malicious can have severe and long-ranging effects.

Think about the security measures that this book suggests. Although viruses generally can't affect the physical security of your machine, they certainly can affect your use and management of passwords, your safe-surfing practices, your management of Internet services, and even your installation of advanced security measures. Almost every nonphysical security measure you take can be affected by a virus. Affecting your security measures is often quite difficult for a virus to do, but it's certainly not impossible, and the results can be quite devastating.

Because a virus can take full control of your machine, it could install itself in memory in such a way that it receives notification of everything you do on that machine. It can get a copy of every keystroke and mouse click, and figure out the context in which you type those keystrokes and make those mouse clicks—which application is running and which windows are displayed, for example. So if you type a password—even the best-chosen, best-maintained password—the virus can get a copy of it. Or if you enter a credit-card number in a secure Web site, the virus can get a copy of that number as you type it, before it's encrypted and sent to the Web site via SSL.

When a virus obtains your password or credit-card number, it also can obtain the context in which you type that information. For a password, it can figure out the service in which you typed the password. For a credit-card number, it can obtain any additional information you typed, (such as the expiration date and the name on the card), as well as the address of the Web site for which the information was intended. When the virus has the information it's looking for, it can transfer that information back to its writer in several ways. It can send that information over the Net automatically, for example, or it can wait to be contacted by its writer and pass the information back then.

In addition to spying on everything you type, a virus can defeat other security measures you've taken. If you've disabled unused Internet services, the virus can turn those services back on—which is one reason to consider deleting services that you're sure you're not going to use. If you've set those services up to allow limited access to a limited group of people, the virus can expand those limits. If you've installed additional pieces of security software, such as a personal firewall (see Chapter 12), the virus could turn off the firewall or, worse, configure it to allow certain additional forms of access. After the virus has defeated your security measures, it probably will do things that those security measures were specifically designed to protect against, such as open your machine for direct attack or for use against others in a distributed denial-of-service attack (see Chapter 2). Of all the reasons to be concerned about viruses, this one is the most important:

A virus can defeat just about every security measure you take to protect your online safety.

Be afraid. Be very afraid.

What You Can Do About Them

The main thing you can do about the security risks associated with viruses is not get infected by any. That's easy for us to say, but it's not difficult for you to do either. We describe some virus-prevention techniques in Chapter 5 as part of an overview of safe surfing practices. This section describes virus prevention in more detail.

Going beyond safe surfing

Many safe-surfing techniques are critical to virus prevention. The principal technique for avoiding viruses is not inviting them into your machine by downloading files from the Net. These days, most viruses are transmitted through e-mail attachments, so we'll reiterate the general advice on those attachments from Chapter 5:

Do not open e-mail attachments except under rare conditions. In most cases, delete them without opening them first.

Not opening e-mail attachments, and being sure to remove those attachments from your machine, will go a long way toward preventing viruses. Not downloading files through other techniques will help as well. If you do need to download files, try to get them from the larger sites, which are more likely to have thoroughly checked those files for viruses.

Mac users can usually avoid the other common way in which viruses are transmitted: floppy disks. Apple stopped shipping floppy-disk drives in Macs several years ago. Although Apple didn't eliminate floppy drives to decrease the spread of viruses, it has had that effect. Many older Macs have built-in floppy drives, and you can still add external floppy drives to Macs. But almost no Mac software is distributed on floppy disks these days, so the risks are lower. You should still watch out for macro viruses in documents passed by floppy disks, however, and software distributed on CD-ROM could contain viruses, of course, but manufacturers usually check CD-ROMs carefully.

Mac users also enjoy the same population advantage when it comes to viruses as with many other security issues. Because fewer Macs are being used, fewer hackers learn how to write viruses to attack them. Also, writing viruses for Macs is less desirable, because those viruses probably will spread more slowly and infect fewer machines, so significantly fewer Mac viruses are written than Windows viruses. But at least one class of viruses can affect Macs just as significantly as Windows machines: macro viruses. In this case, the virus could be written for a Windows machine but end up being just as effective on a Mac. Most Microsoft products include cross-platform macro languages, and Microsoft products are favorite targets of virus writers (another example of why being popular is not a good thing in security terms). If you use a Microsoft product on your Mac, you need to be concerned about macro viruses.

Usually most of us have no need for macros. Macros are like the human appendix, which has no real use but can cause great harm when it gets infected. In the case of macros, however, you don't have to wait for an infection to have the problem removed. You can simply turn off macro support in many applications, and from that point on, macros in documents will not be executed. In the unusual situation in which you actually need a macro, you can reenable that feature. Microsoft allows you to configure most of its product to warn you whenever a document with a macro is about to be opened—a feature that is highly recommended (**Figure 11.1**). If you do get such a warning (**Figure 11.2**), you should disable macros in the document unless the document comes from a reputable source and you're sure what the macros are going to do.

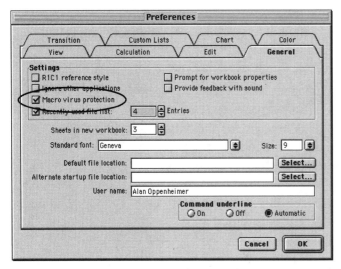

Figure 11.1 You should configure Microsoft products to warn you whenever a document containing macros is opened.

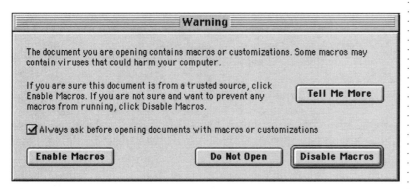

Figure 11.2 A macro-warning dialog box. Usually, you should choose Disable Macros.

Getting an antivirus application

Most of us are going to need to add some files to our computers. No matter how careful we are about opening e-mail attachments, downloading files from the Net, sharing documents, or installing software, at times, we'll run some risk of acquiring a virus. After you've decided to connect to the Internet, viruses are an intrinsic security risk.

The best way to protect your computer against viruses is to get an antivirus application. An antivirus application provides protection through a wide range of automated and manual techniques.

Most antivirus applications include the following features:

Detection of viruses and Trojan horses on your machine. When you first run an antivirus application, such as the popular Norton AntiVirus (**Figure 11.3**), it can scan your whole hard disk for known viruses. It also can scan any file or folder. Most antivirus applications can even detect viruses within archives. An *archive* is a compressed file that contains multiple applications and documents. Because archives frequently are downloaded over the Internet or sent as e-mail attachments, archive scanning is an important feature of any antivirus application. Antivirus applications cannot detect viruses within encrypted files however, because they can't decrypt the files to check for viruses.

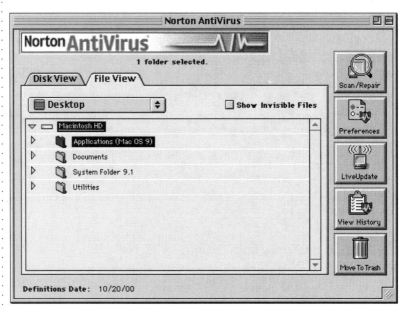

Figure 11.3 Antivirus applications, such as Norton AntiVirus, are critical to online and offline security.

Disinfection. If files on your machine are infected by viruses, the antivirus application may be able to remove the infection and restore those files to their uninfected state. If not, the application can give you advice about what to do. Usually, you'll need to delete the infected files and restore them from backups.

Automated protection. Antivirus applications usually provide several forms of automated protection. Automated protection generally catches viruses before they have a chance to install themselves, and it works even if you forget to tell the app to do anything else. Automated-protection options include scanning whenever an application is run, whenever a document is opened, or whenever a removable medium (such as a floppy disk or CD) is inserted. Automated protection is provided by a system extension on your machine. You can also set up your antivirus application to scan any part of your computer for viruses on a periodic basis.

Antivirus applications can detect both known and unknown viruses automatically. *Known viruses* usually are identified by some type of fingerprint or signature that makes it clear that the file has been infected. The fingerprint may be a subset of the computer instructions that tell the virus how to do its dirty work or some other data unique to the virus. *Unknown viruses* are identified tentatively based on the type of activity they undertake on your computer, although sometimes the antivirus program can interpret normal activity incorrectly as evidence of an unknown virus. See "Using an antivirus application" later in this chapter for information on interpreting data about unknown viruses.

Automated updating. New viruses are written and released every day. Most antivirus applications provide a way to download updates over the Internet to provide protection against the newest viruses. These updates usually are provided by way of virus-definition files, which are read by the application.

E-mail virus protection. In combination with your e-mail program, some antivirus applications can scan incoming attachments for signs of virus infection. Because attachments are one of the primary ways that viruses propagate, this feature is especially desirable. Because this feature is new, however, you should not rely on it to be completely effective.

Installing an antivirus application

Acquiring an antivirus application goes a long way toward protecting your computer against viruses. But you also need to install and use it correctly. Correct installation and use are especially important for security software; otherwise, you may be giving yourself a false sense of security.

You should take one seemingly counterintuitive step before installing your antivirus application.

> *Before installing your antivirus application, you should make sure that your machine doesn't have any viruses on it.*

How do you check for viruses without installing the antivirus application first? And why do you want to check for viruses *before* installing the antivirus app?

We'll answer the second question first. Assuming that you're installing antivirus software for the first time, a decent chance exists that your machine is already infected with a virus. If your machine is infected with a virus, your antivirus application, once installed, would almost always be able to detect and disable that virus. But what if that virus somehow prevented your antivirus application from being installed or from working correctly? Remember that viruses can gain full control of your computer. Viruses are tricky, and a virus could target your antivirus application, which is just another program on your computer. The last thing you want is for your antivirus application to be infected. Such a virus could disable the antivirus application and prevent it from doing its job, so you would think you're protected when you aren't.

Developers of antivirus applications are well aware of this potential for infection, and they take significant steps to try to prevent it. These steps usually are quite sophisticated and almost always are successful. But because the consequences of having your antivirus application infected with a virus are so dire, the safest procedure calls for checking your machine for viruses *before* installing the antivirus application.

How do you scan your machine for viruses before installing your antivirus application? The usual way is to start up your machine off a CD-ROM provided with the antivirus application for this purpose. (You can start up a Mac from a CD by holding down the C key while starting up.) When you start up off a CD, you prevent the launching of any viruses that might have infected your normal system. Your machine is run with the CD's carefully predefined system, which has been fully scanned for viruses. This system probably has a very minimal set of extensions, so you may not be able to do everything you're used to, but all you really want to do is run the antivirus application from the CD and do a full scan of your machine. The first scan may take quite a while, but doing it is worthwhile.

A corollary of the scan-before-installing rule is that to be completely safe, you generally should not download an antivirus application from the Internet, because it could be infected with a virus during download if your machine is already infected. Developers of antivirus applications are aware of this risk and go to great lengths to prevent it, but if you're getting the application for the first time, you should consider acquiring it through some method other than electronic download.

Immediately after scanning your machine for viruses from the CD (and repairing or removing any infected files), you should install and activate your antivirus application to ensure a continuous stream of protection from the first scan onward. You should also make sure that you have the most recent virus-definition file, just in case any new viruses have been discovered since the product was shipped. See the following section for details.

Using an antivirus application

The most important thing to do after installing your antivirus application is use it. This advice may sound obvious, but some people assume that installation is all that's needed. You should make sure that the software's automatic-protection features are enabled (by default, they usually are) to ensure that it is working even if you forget about it. Beyond that, perform manual scans of your machine on a regular basis, just in case a virus sneaked in. Automatic protection may not be able to detect as many types of viruses as a manual scan or may not cover all the ways a virus could get on your machine. Manual scans serve as an important double-check of automatic protection and can be set up to run on a periodic basis.

You also need to keep the application up to date. New viruses are being created on a daily, if not hourly, basis. Developers of antivirus applications make updates available as new viruses are discovered. Because the process is so dynamic, these updates are not made in the application itself, because it would have to change too often. Updates usually are provided in the form of virus-definition files, which are small and easy to download and install. The application learns about the new viruses from the virus-definition file.

You can download virus-definition files manually through your antivirus application or set up automatic downloading on a periodic basis (**Figure 11.4**). Automated periodic updating is a great way to make sure that your antivirus application is always up to date.

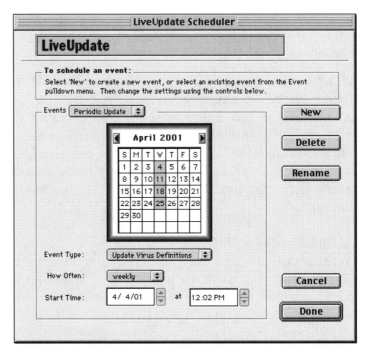

Figure 11.4 Setting up Norton AntiVirus to have it check for updates automatically on a weekly basis.

In "Installing an antivirus application" earlier in this chapter, we recommended that you not download your antivirus application from the Internet, due to the small risk of infection during the download. Can a virus-definition file be infected when you download it? The assumption in downloading a virus-definition file is that your machine has been protected adequately up until that point. If the computer has been protected adequately, it should not be infected with any virus that could infect the virus-definition file. More important, because the virus-definition file is not an application (it's a document) and doesn't use macros, it's particularly hard to infect.

A new undetected virus could theoretically infect your machine before you download a new virus definition file. The unknown-virus-detection feature of your antivirus application comes into play to prevent infection from new viruses. The automatic-protection extension can watch for various types of suspicious activity that may indicate an attempt to infect your machine or the presence of a new virus. A virus needs to copy itself to another file to propagate, for instance, so your antivirus application can watch for this type of copying. If the application detects suspicious activity that may indicate a virus, it can alert you and ask whether you want to allow the activity (**Figure 11.5**).

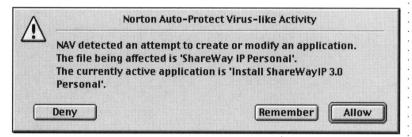

Figure 11.5 Your antivirus application can alert you to viruslike activity.

Not all suspicious activity means that you have an unknown virus. In most cases, you are just doing something that causes suspicious-looking but actually legitimate activity. Installing a new application, for example, looks essentially the same as installing a virus (remember, both are programs). Only you will be able to tell your antivirus application whether to allow the suspicious activity, because only you know whether you're doing something legitimate that looks like a virus. If you have any doubt, disallow the activity and then try to figure out what you're doing to cause the warning. To be sure, you may want to contact the developer of the application that seems to be causing the warning.

> *Whatever you do, don't simply dismiss your antivirus application's warning and allow the activity without thinking about what the warning means first.*

Because an antivirus application does tend to cry wolf sometimes, you'd be amazed by how many people fall into the trap of allowing everything it warns about, thus defeating the purpose of the warning.

By detecting unknown virus activity, your antivirus application adds one more level of protection to the overall system, protecting you against viruses that aren't listed yet in the virus definition file and essentially reducing to zero the odds that a virus will infect the virus-definition file or the antivirus application itself. So downloading virus-definition files over the Net generally is quite safe. You may want to purchase a new copy of your antivirus application every year or two, however, and rescan your system from the new CD that comes with it.

Personal Firewalls

12

In much of this book, we've talked about how to use your Macintosh more securely on the Internet. Chapter 11 talked about adding security to your Macintosh by installing antivirus software. In this chapter, we talk about another way to enhance security on your machine: installing personal firewall software. Antivirus software keeps your machine safe from viruses by telling you when files containing viruses are being downloaded to your machine and disinfecting files that contain viruses. A personal firewall controls access from the Internet to services on your machine, such as File Sharing and Web Sharing. If a firewall blocks access to, say, your File Sharing over IP, no one on the Internet can reach it to try to log in.

In this chapter, we'll discuss what firewalls do; how to choose a firewall; how to configure, test, and troubleshoot a personal firewall; and how a personal firewall can help you identify attacks on your machine. We discuss analyzing and responding to attacks in Chapter 13.

This chapter will occasionally use somewhat technical terms, such as *port* and *packet*. If you have not read Chapter 6, you may want to do so before proceeding or refer to Chapter 6 for terms and concepts you don't understand.

Firewall Basics

For the purposes of this book, a firewall is software that blocks unwanted access from the Internet to services on your machine without interfering with normal Internet client activities. You might configure a firewall to block access to all TCP ports on your machine, for example. No one could reach TCP/IP services running on your machine from the Internet. You would still be able to use Internet services, however: You could read e-mail, browse the Web, and do other Internet client activities. You could also configure a firewall to deny access to all services from anyone on the Internet but allow access to all services from anyone on your local network.

Some firewalls can protect outgoing access, preventing you from using some, or possibly all, Internet services and possibly preventing certain kinds of data from being sent over the Internet.

Although firewalls are most often used to prevent unwanted access to Internet services, they also prevent other types of attacks that use TCP/IP, such as communication with Trojan horses (see Chapter 11) and viruses that have infected your machine. A virus might wait for instructions from the hacker who installed it, for example. Other kinds of attacks can bypass firewalls, such as password dictionary attacks, spying, and breaches of physical security. A firewall is just one of many security tools; a complete security strategy involves all the topics covered in this book.

Firewall types

Firewalls fall into two categories:

Network-global vs. machine-specific. A network-global firewall controls access to all machines on a network, and a machine-specific firewall controls access to the machine on which it's installed. (We talk about network-global firewalls in Chapter 17.)

Personal vs. server. A machine-specific firewall can be a personal firewall, which has a relatively simple interface, or a server firewall, which is somewhat more complex but allows for greater precision in defining the firewall's access rules. Server firewalls are most often employed on machines primarily used as servers, such as Web, e-mail, and FTP servers. These firewalls are more difficult to set up, so their users should be technically competent, but they also allow for more-flexible configurations. Although personal firewalls have a simpler feature set and user interface than server firewalls do, personal firewalls are more than enough for most users. This chapter focuses on personal firewalls.

How firewalls work

The most common use of personal firewalls is to control access to TCP/IP services. When you access a Web site, your browser must open a connection to TCP port 80 on the Web server. Only after the connection is established can you load pages from the site. Your Web browser requests a connection by sending a TCP packet that contains a connection request. The Web server grants the request by sending back an *acknowledgement packet*. If the server denies the request, it sends back a *reset packet*. A similar process applies to any TCP/IP service, including File Sharing and Program Linking.

The basic idea behind firewalls is quite simple. A firewall maintains a set of rules, either created by default or defined by the user. A *rule* specifies whether to allow or deny a connection request, given the IP address that sent the request and the service for which the request is made. As packets containing connection requests arrive at the firewall machine from the Internet, the firewall examines them and, using its rules, passes them on to the appropriate service (allows them) or does not (denies them). For denied connection requests, the firewall sends a reset packet back to the requesting IP address. A reset packet says, in essence, "The computer is online, but the port (service) is not accessible." The Mac OS also sends a reset packet if the firewall allows the connection request but the service is not running.

A firewall may not respond when it denies access to a connection request. Some people describe this lack of response as *stealth* because it effectively hides your machine from hackers. They may think your machine is not online if no response comes back to their connection requests. Stealth mode has problems, however, which we discuss in "Using stealth mode" in this chapter.

A personal firewall can block access to TCP services without affecting outgoing access.

Figure 12.1 shows a firewall configured with one rule: Deny connection requests to all services from all IP addresses. No one on the Internet will be able to access any TCP/IP services on your machine. Two kinds of TCP packets are not affected by the firewall: outgoing TCP packets and incoming TCP packets that are not connection requests.

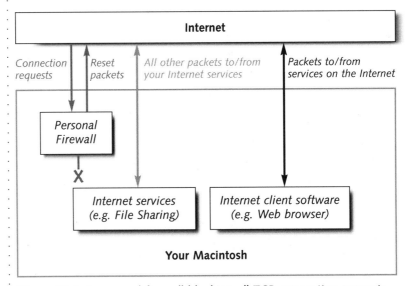

Figure 12.1 A personal firewall blocking all TCP connection requests from the Internet.

Because these two types of packets are not affected, you can still do such things as browse the Web and send and receive e-mail.

In **Figure 12.2,** the personal firewall has been configured with two rules. The first rule allows connection requests to File Sharing (port 548) from IP address 172.16.0.1; the second rule denies all other connection requests.

Note that the first rule does not mean that anyone at address 172.16.0.1 will be able to get into File Sharing. File Sharing over IP must be enabled. If it is not, the Mac OS will send back a reset packet, stating that port 548 is not accessible. If File Sharing over IP is enabled, the user at 172.16.0.1 will be able to log in with a valid user name and password.

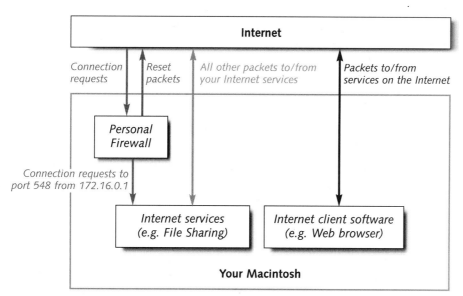

Figure 12.2 A personal firewall allowing connection requests only to File Sharing, only from IP address 172.16.0.1.

This example illustrates the power of the personal firewall as a security tool. You can allow access to File Sharing on your machine from only one machine (at IP address 172.16.0.1), and that machine can access only File Sharing. No other computer on the Internet can access any service on your machine.

The second example also illustrates a firewall's flexibility. You can define rules to allow access to one service from one set of IP addresses and allow access to another service from a different set of IP addresses. You could allow access to all services from anyone on your local network but deny access to all services from anyone on the Internet. Or you could allow access to File Sharing on your home machine from your machine at work but deny access to File Sharing from all other IP addresses and to all other services from all IP addresses. In the second example, only one service on your home machine would be accessible from only one machine on the Internet.

Personal firewalls often work with UDP as well as TCP/IP. UDP is a *connectionless* protocol, meaning that a connection does not have to be opened before a UDP port is used. Because a firewall can't look for just one type of packet to block (the connection request), it must block all UDP packets to a given port.

You may be thinking that a firewall is redundant if you have turned off all Internet services on your machine. In a sense, you're right; under either strategy, no one can access services on your machine. But recall the security principle set forth in Chapter 7: Redundant security measures are best because they make it harder to turn on services accidentally (or maliciously). A firewall is one more thing that you must change to make any service accessible from the Internet. Additionally, firewalls can deter hackers who are trying to access viruses and Trojan horses that may have infected your machine. Finally, firewall logs provide critical data for analyzing and reacting to attacks, as discussed in Chapter 13.

Stateful firewalls

Stateful firewalls represent an emerging technology. These firewalls do more than just allow and deny access to packets based on port number and source IP address; they also remember certain contexts. This technology is useful for accessing services that try to open connections back to your machine. Suppose that you try to contact such a service at address 192.168.0.10, and that server attempts to open a connection back to your machine on a port that the firewall is blocking. A stateful firewall will see that the connection request is from IP address 192.168.0.10, will remember that you just tried to contact a service at that address, and will allow the connection to be opened. This type of firewall makes file downloads that use FTP active mode (see "Downloading files" later in this chapter) much easier.

Stateful firewalls carry their own risks, although those risks are relatively small. The technology is fairly complicated, and with complexity comes additional risk. The principal risk associated with a stateful firewall is that someone could send specially crafted packets that fool the firewall, allowing other unwanted packets to reach applications behind the firewall. Such packets might contain harmful data.

Features

The personal-firewall products on the market offer a wide range of features. Some provide basic functions; others are for advanced users and users on local networks. Our philosophy about security software for the rest of us is that simpler is better. Most users do not need advanced features to secure their Macs on the Internet. Typically, people just want to use the Internet and keep anyone from accessing services on their machines while they do. A simple feature set and user interface mean less likelihood of mistakes in setting up the firewall and greater security for your machine.

A well-designed personal firewall has a basic mode by default. This mode offers only the features that the average user needs (**Figure 12.3**).

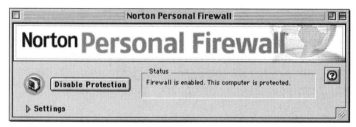

Figure 12.3 Symantec's Norton Personal Firewall in its basic mode.

In Figure 12.3, the firewall is set by default to deny access to all TCP ports from all IP addresses. The firewall is on by default after installation.

A well-designed personal firewall requires no configuration to provide the basic protection that many users need. Also, it should be unobtrusive as it runs; you should not need to interact with it unless you ask to be notified of firewall events (see "Firewall feedback" later in this chapter).

A rule regarding advanced features is:

> *Don't use a personal firewall's advanced feature unless you fully understand what the feature does and are sure that you need to use it.*

Using a feature that you don't understand may cause problems with the basic operation of your machine or even decrease your machine's security. In the example in **Figure 12.4,** you use the Preferences dialog box to switch from basic to advanced mode.

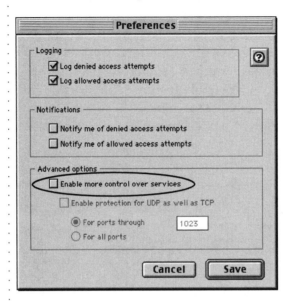

Figure 12.4
The Preferences dialog box with an Advanced options section.

Protocols supported

Networking activity involves many protocols. A personal firewall doesn't have to address all protocols but should work with the most important ones:

TCP/IP is the most commonly protected protocol, because it is used for the most common Internet services, including File Sharing, Web Sharing, Program Linking, Timbuktu and many other services. (For descriptions of built-in and common third-party Internet services, see chapters 8, 9, and 10.)

UDP is a basic Internet protocol used mainly by system-level services such as DHCP (see Chapter 6 and "Protecting UDP services" later in this chapter.)

ICMP is used in network operations, but most important for firewall purposes, it is used to ping machines. A *ping* is a single ICMP packet that causes your machine to reply, letting the sender know that your machine is online. Hackers often look for machines on the Internet by sending a ping to every IP address in a range of addresses. They give machines that respond further scrutiny. (See "Denying access to ICMP" later in this chapter.)

AppleTalk services are not protected by personal firewalls because implementing such a firewall is difficult. Fortunately, with the exception of some cable-modem systems (see Chapter 7), AppleTalk is not routed on the Internet. AppleTalk security on local networks, however, remains an issue; follow the techniques discussed in chapters 8, 9, and 10.

In most firewalls, TCP/IP protection is provided by default, and you can specify other protocols (**Figure 12.5**).

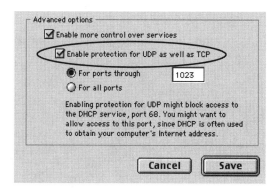

Figure 12.5 Choosing UDP protection.

Firewall feedback

Controlling access to services is a personal firewall's main function. A secondary function is only slightly less important: providing feedback about accesses and attempted accesses to services on your machine. This information allows you to identify possible attacks on your machine and take action if necessary. (We cover analyzing and responding to security threats in Chapter 13.)

A firewall can provide three types of information:

First, a firewall can maintain a log file that records all denied access attempts, all allowed access attempts, or both. You can analyze the log file to help identify possible security problems.

A good log file usually includes the following details for each logged access attempt:

- The date and time of the access attempt
- The result of the access attempt (allowed or denied)
- The port number (service) to which access was attempted
- The IP address and host name (if any) of the machine making the access attempt

Most Mac firewalls create log files in *extended WebSTAR format*. Because applications that analyze log files (see Chapter 13) expect this format, you should look for this log-file format when you consider purchasing a personal firewall. In advanced mode, logging might include such details as the protocol over which access was attempted. Some personal firewalls also allow you to see the most recent lines of a log file in real time (**Figure 12.6**).

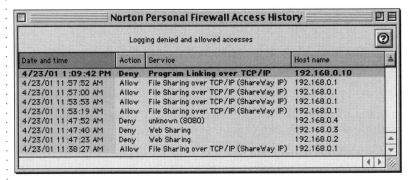

Figure 12.6 A log file's most recent lines, shown in real time.

As a firewall logs accesses, that information appears in a firewall window. Log files can be read and analyzed by log-file-analysis software. (For a full discussion of analyzing log files, see Chapter 13.)

Second, a firewall can notify you via an alert dialog box or a sound whenever it blocks (or allows, or both) an access attempt to a service. Immediate feedback can help you respond to attempted security breaches quickly. Also, because most firewalls normally are unobtrusive, notification is an easy way to get a sense that your firewall is doing something (**Figure 12.7**).

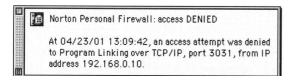

Figure 12.7
Notification of
a denied access
attempt.

Finally, most firewalls have some means of providing additional information about specific access attempts; this information is often displayed on a Web site. Typically, you specify a log line in the log-file monitor window and click a button that takes you to a page on a Web site that describes the access attempt in detail (**Figure 12.8**).

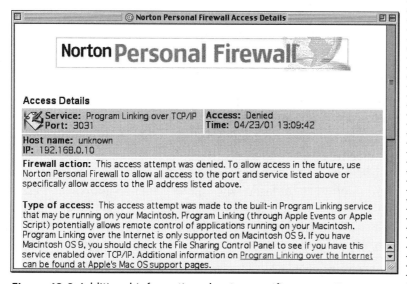

Figure 12.8 Additional information about a specific access attempt.

Other kinds of attacks

Some firewalls detect attacks other than simple attempts to connect to a service. Attacks of this type often involve a sequence of events. The most common are:

Denial of service. By sending many packets of a certain type to a machine, a hacker can overload and possibly crash a machine.

Port scanning. As part of an attack, port scanning usually indicates that a hacker is probing your machine to locate accessible services. The hacker simply tries to open a connection to a large sequence of ports, looking for successful connection attempts.

Ping of death. A hacker can configure an ICMP ping packet in such a way that sending it to your machine will cause your machine to crash. This type of attack affects only Macs OSes before Mac OS 8.

Although attacks such as these can target any computer on the Internet, they are more likely to be directed against machines in large organizations that are running Internet services. These sites have high profiles, and their machines have TCP ports open, tempting hackers to attempt intrusion. If you're a home user with no Internet services running and have a firewall blocking access to all TCP ports, you will be of little interest to most hackers.

Multihoming support

Starting with Mac OS 8.1, you can assign more than one IP address to a Macintosh. One IP address is the *primary address,* which is the address configured in the TCP/IP control panel. Other addresses, known as *secondary addresses*, are entered in a file named IP Secondary Addresses, which is located in the Preferences folder. Assigning multiple IP addresses to one machine is also known as *multihoming.* If you are running only built-in Internet services, or none, you don't need to be concerned about multihoming.

Multihoming is useful when you want to make one server look like many—if you create many virtual Web sites on one machine, for example. With multihoming, owners of virtual sites have their own domain names and also their own IP addresses. This arrangement makes it possible to protect different virtual sites with different rules—if your firewall works with multihoming.

If a firewall supports multihoming, when you define an access rule, you specify not only a service and source IP address but also the IP address on which that service runs. The service IP address for which the filter (rule) is being created may be specified in a pop-up list of IP addresses on the machine (**Figure 12.9**).

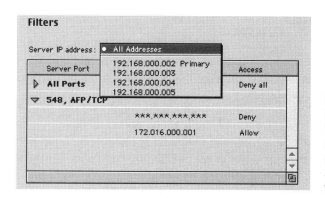

Figure 12.9
DoorStop
Server Edition
allows you to
choose an IP
address for
the service.

You might create an access rule to allow access to one virtual Web site only to users on the local network, another rule to allow access to another virtual site only to users on the administrative staff's network, and so on. You could do this only if each site uses a different IP address.

Another use of multihoming is ShareWay IP Pro, which allows you to provide TCP/IP access to AFP servers on your AppleTalk network. (see Chapter 10). If the ShareWay machine has only one IP address, each machine to which ShareWay provides access must be accessed through that IP address but with nondefault port numbers; the different port numbers distinguish one target server from another. Alternate port numbers are inconvenient, because the user must enter them as part of the URL (see Chapter 7). With multihoming, however, each target server has its own IP address and uses the default port number. If your firewall supports multihoming, you can use it to protect different AFP servers with different firewall rules.

Outgoing-packet protection

Some personal firewalls can protect outgoing packets in either of two ways. First, packets can be blocked if they contain specific data, such as credit-card numbers. This setup prevents your credit-card number from being transmitted in clear text over the Internet (including via e-mail) to an insecure Web site or in a file. Second, outgoing packets can be blocked to or from certain services. This setup can prevent viruses, Trojan horses, and virus-corrupted applications from communicating with the hackers who installed them.

Ease-of-use features

Most personal firewalls have features that simply make them easier to use. In some cases, these features add to your machine's security, by eliminating the possibility of setup errors. Ease-of-use features include:

Export the most recent log lines to a text file.
This feature is a convenient way to look at the most recent accesses to your machine, saving you the trouble of opening the firewall's log file and copying lines into another file.

Look up a host name. Some firewalls allow you to enter a host name and look up the corresponding IP address. This feature can be useful if you want to allow or deny access from a specific host name.

Create configuration sets. If you have a portable machine that you want to use in several environments, you may want to use a different configuration for each environment. At work, you may want to allow access only from certain machines on the local network; at home, you may want to allow no access. Naming and saving these configurations makes it easy to switch settings and eliminates the possibility of misconfiguring your firewall when you switch environments.

Receive notification of upgrades. This feature is purely a convenience. Some firewalls have a menu command that connects to the vendor's Web site and checks for upgrades.

Configuring a Personal Firewall

Most Internet users should follow a simple rule in setting up a personal firewall:

Use the default settings. For most firewalls, these settings will deny access to all TCP/IP services from all IP addresses.

Using the default settings should let you use the Internet without the risk of hackers trying to access TCP/IP services on your machine. After you install the firewall and restart your Macintosh, the firewall should run without further input from you and should deny access to all TCP/IP services from all IP addresses. No one on the Internet will be able to access your File Sharing, Web Sharing, or any of the other TCP/IP services covered in chapters 8, 9, and 10. (Refer to Figure 12.3 earlier in this chapter for an example of a default setup.)

You may wish to change the default settings. For the firewall shown in **Figure 12.10,** you select a service on the left side of the setup dialog box and specify access permissions on the right side. Most personal firewalls use this model for creating rules: specify a service and the IP addresses from which to allow or deny access. By default, the firewall should deny all access.

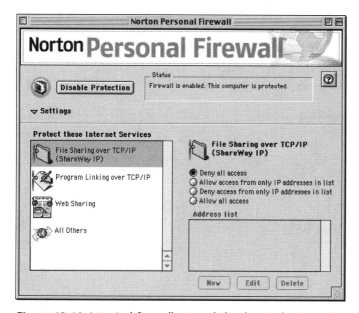

Figure 12.10 A typical firewall setup dialog box in basic mode.

Allowing access to specific TCP/IP services

If you decide to run an Internet service on your Macintosh, you will need to create a firewall rule to allow users to access it.

Allowing access to a service does not mean that anyone can use the service. Users whom the firewall permits to access File Sharing, for example, must still log in with a user name and password. Users who are denied access to File Sharing can't even connect to attempt a login.

To create a rule that allows access to a service, you first specify the service; the procedure depends on the firewall you use. In basic mode, you might choose a service from a list of services. In advanced mode, you might choose a service from a larger list or even define a new service by entering a port number. Tables 12.1 and 12.2 "Services and Port Numbers" later in this chapter list port numbers for common services. To create a rule to allow access to a service, you must also specify the IP addresses from which you want to allow access.

When you create a rule allowing access to a service, allow access to the smallest possible set of IP addresses.

If you decide to host a personal Web page from your machine, you may want to allow access from all IP addresses so that anyone on the Internet can access the page. If you want to share the page with only a few friends, however, you should allow access only from their IP addresses (**Figure 12.11**).

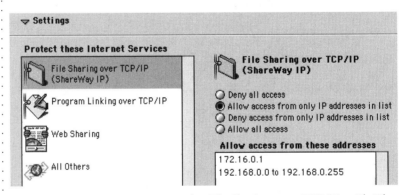

Figure 12.11 Access permissions for File Sharing over TCP/IP, with File Sharing over TCP/IP selected on the left side of the dialog box and access permissions configured on the right side.

The example shown in Figure 12.11 is typical of personal firewalls in that it offers several ways of specifying access to a service. Different firewalls may implement access permissions in a different way. In this example, the options are:

Deny all access. The safest of all settings, this option should be the default for any service. No one will be able to access the service.

Allow access from only IP addresses in list. Access is denied to all IP addresses except those specified.

Deny access from only IP addresses in list. Access is allowed to all IP addresses except those specified.

Allow all access. Anyone on the Internet can access the service.

Most firewalls provide several ways to specify addresses (**Figure 12.12**).

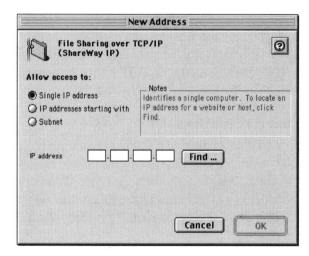

Figure 12.12
You can specify addresses in several ways.

In the example shown in Figure 12.12, you can use the following options to specify addresses:

Single IP address. Because this method specifies only one address, it is the safest option. This method is useful only if the machine to which you want to allow access has a static IP address (see Chapter 6).

IP address starting with. Typically, you specify a range of IP addresses by entering the first one, two, or three fields of an address. If you enter **192.168.0**, for example, you specify the range 192.168.0.0 through 192.168.0.255. IP address ranges are useful for allowing or denying access to whole organizations; they can also be useful for specifying the IP address of a machine with a dynamic address. Although dynamic addresses are different every time, they do fall within a range. Specifying an address range is, in this case, a good compromise between the ideal of a single address (which won't work) and allowing all IP addresses (which creates more risk than necessary).

If you want to specify a range of IP addresses to describe a network, the Subnet option gives you better control of the range.

Subnet. If you want to allow access to a service for everyone on a specific network, you should be able to configure your firewall by choosing this option. You could enter an IP address and subnet mask to specify an address range for the network, for example. Some firewalls have a shortcut feature for your network; the firewall reads the IP address of your machine and the subnet mask, as displayed in the TCP/IP control panel, and computes the address range for your network.

Allowing access to all TCP/IP services

As we stated earlier in this chapter, the general rule for configuring a personal firewall is first to deny access to all services and then allow access to only those services that need it. In some situations, however, it may make sense to reverse this rule and allow access to all services but then deny access only to specific services.

One such situation would be an intranet that is protected by a network-global firewall. Because users on the network would already be protected from the Internet, they might choose to keep their personal firewall configurations simple by allowing access to all services, rather than create individual service entries.

Another situation would be accessing a service that opens multiple ports on your machine, such as the ICQ instant-messaging service. Rather than create an entry for each port, you could turn on access to all ports.

If you allow access to all services, you should make a careful inventory of all services running on your machine and create entries in your firewall for each service, denying access from all but the necessary IP addresses.

Protecting UDP services

For many users, simply protecting TCP/IP services is adequate. At times, however, you will want to protect UDP. Most UDP services that you may want to block use low-numbered ports, and most day-to-day operations use high-numbered ports (above 1023). Many firewalls let you restrict access only to low-numbered ports. The most common reasons to protect UDP services are:

UDP protection can add security to critical services.
UDP services such as SNMP and Apple Network Access (see Chapter 9) create high potential risk. Although these services have built-in security features, the added security of firewall protection is a good idea.

UDP protection can hide certain TCP services. Timbuktu, for example, uses UDP to locate other TCP/IP-accessible Timbuktu machines. Such machines are displayed in a list in the Timbuktu application, much as AFP servers are displayed in the Chooser. By protecting UDP access to the appropriate ports (Timbuktu uses UDP port 1419), such services can be hidden from other users.

Some other services use SLP (Service Location Protocol) on UDP port 427 to make themselves known on a network. File Sharing, for example, registers with SLP, making it possible for the Mac's Network Browser to find such file servers on a local network and display them in a list. By blocking UDP port 427, your File Sharing (or any other services that use SLP) cannot register with SLP. Any hidden services will still be accessible, but potential intruders will not be able to see them in a list.

Denying access to UDP can cause problems in the day-to-day operation of your machine, especially if you deny access to high-numbered UDP ports. If you protect UDP services, you should take the following issues into account:

DHCP. If your machine gets its IP address from a DHCP server, you must allow access to port 68. Ideally, you want to allow access from only the IP address of the DHCP server. To get the DHCP server's IP address, deny access to UDP port 68, restart your machine, and check the log file for a denied access to port 68. The IP address in this log line will be the IP address of your ISP's DHCP server. Configure your firewall to allow access to port 68 from the IP address in the log file. If you don't allow access to port 68, your machine will assign itself an IP address from a private range, and you will not be able to get online.

DNS. If you protect UDP services, you may have problems with DNS (see Chapter 6). When an application contacts a name server to determine the IP address for a host name, the name server sends the IP address back to a random high-numbered port. Unless you allow access to all high-numbered UDP ports, applications will not be able to resolve host names.

Network time servers. If you configured your Date & Time control panel to use a network time server, you must allow access to UDP port 123.

Real-time QuickTime streaming and other real-time services. QuickTime and other audio/video broadcasts are sometimes transmitted via RTP (Real-Time Protocol) and RTSP (Real-Time Streaming Protocol), especially when those broadcasts are live. These protocols use high-numbered UDP ports. See "Configuring a firewall for specific services" later in this chapter for details on how to handle media streaming.

Denying access to ICMP

Some personal firewalls can block ICMP. ICMP is a complex protocol used for various purposes in networking, but from a security perspective, it is significant for its use to ping a machine. A ping is analogous to a sonar ping, which is used to locate objects underwater. A single ICMP packet is sent to a machine. If the machine responds by sending back an ICMP packet, the original sender knows that the target machine is online. Ping is also used to measure network performance by determining round-trip time (the time it takes a packet to reach its destination and return).

Hackers use pings to locate machines on the Internet. A common approach is to ping every IP address in a range of addresses to see which ones respond and examine the machines that do respond. A hacker might use ping to locate a machine on the Internet, do a port scan on the machine to see which TCP/IP services are running, and then try to gain entry to those services. If your machine does not respond to a hacker's ping, the hacker won't know from this simple test that your machine is online. Denying access to ICMP is called *stealth mode* because it makes your machine invisible to this common type of probe (see "Using stealth mode" later in this chapter).

Denying access to ICMP has drawbacks, however. Ping is a low-level protocol that many applications use to determine connectivity and round-trip time, among other things. Blocking ICMP may cause problems with various network services.

Logging

Although your firewall's default configuration should be that full logging is enabled, it is a good idea to confirm that logging is on, because the information that log files provide is useful (see Chapter 13). At the very least, you should log denied accesses. If you are not running Internet services on your machine or are running lightly used services, you should also log allowed accesses. You probably do not want to log allowed accesses if you are running a busy Internet service on your machine, such as a Web site; the log file can become *very* large.

Setting up notification

By default, most firewalls do not notify you of allowed or denied access attempts. Enabling notification is mostly a matter of taste. Some users like to know every time access is attempted; To others, notification is a nuisance. If you're not sure whether notification would be useful, try it; you can always turn it off later.

If you are notified of access attempts via a dialog box (refer to Figure 12.7 earlier in this chapter), the dialog box may interfere with operations on your machine, especially in versions of the Mac OS before Mac OS 9. If you are away from your machine and a notification dialog box appears, it may cause some processes to hang, especially those that involve user interaction.

Using stealth mode

Stealth mode is a relatively new term that different people use to mean different things. Generally, however, stealth mode refers to a machine that does not respond when it normally would. One case is ICMP pings, which hackers commonly use to detect a machine on the Internet. Your machine normally responds to a hacker's ping, letting the hacker know that you're online. By blocking ICMP pings (and, therefore, not responding), you give the appearance of not being online.

Another meaning of stealth mode is not responding to TCP connection requests for specific services (**Figure 12.13**). A firewall that is blocking access to a service normally responds to connection requests for that service by sending back a reset packet, stating the port is not accessible. If you are protecting File Sharing on your machine, and a hacker tries to access it, he will get a response from your machine (the reset packet), saying that port 548 is not accessible. But this packet also tells the hacker that a machine is online at your IP address, so he may try to access other services or launch other kinds of attacks. If however, your firewall does nothing when it receives the connection request, the hacker will be led to believe that no machine is online at your IP address and may move on to another IP address.

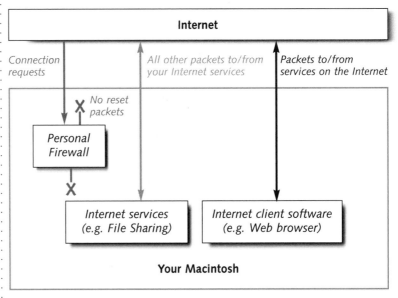

Figure 12.13 Stealth mode applied to all TCP/IP services.

Although stealth mode may sound appealing in terms of increasing security, it introduces problems in normal operations. If you have an alias to an AppleShare server that's accessible through TCP/IP, for example, and that server is behind a firewall that blocks ICMP, that alias will not work unless you run the AppleShare Client Setup utility (available on the Apple Support Web site at *www.apple.com/support/*) to disable the AppleShare client's address verification via pings. Another example is a mail server that uses authentication through the AUTH service. When you send an e-mail, the server attempts to contact your machine on port 113 to confirm your identity. If your firewall denies access to the port, the mail server sees that access is denied, knows that no authentication service is available, and processes your e-mail without authentication. If you use stealth on this port, however, the mail server will wait for a response—anywhere from 30 seconds to a minute or more—before proceeding, making the sending of e-mail unacceptably slow.

Configuring a firewall for specific services

Configuring your personal firewall for use with most services is quite straightforward. You determine the port number that the service uses and allow or deny access to that port from the appropriate IP addresses. Some services, however, require more care.

Timbuktu. Newer versions of Timbuktu are slightly different from older versions. Older versions used port 1417 for control capabilities, and newer versions use port 407 by default but will use port 1417 when communicating with older versions. Follow these tips if you are trying to limit control access:

- To Timbuktu 5.2 or later, from version 5.2 or later, create a firewall rule for port 407.

- To Timbuktu 5.2 or later, from both older and newer versions, create a firewall rule for port 407 and one for port 1417.

- To Timbuktu earlier than version 5.2, create a firewall rule for port 1417.

In general, the easiest process is to create the same rules for both Timbuktu ports. Similar tips apply to limiting observe access to Timbuktu, except that you would use port 1418 instead of 1417.

Downloading files through FTP. If you use FTP for file downloads, you may have problems accessing FTP servers. Many Web sites make files available through FTP, so these problems could be fairly common (see "Downloading files" later in this chapter).

Napster. If you try to download a music file through Napster, that service sometimes opens a connection to TCP port 6699 on your machine to transfer the file to you. You must create a rule to allow access to this port for the machine from which you're downloading the file.

QuickTime and other audio/video streaming. Although many audio/video broadcasts are transmitted via HTTP, they may use RTP (Real-Time Protocol) and RTSP (Real-Time Streaming Protocol), especially when those broadcasts are live. RTP and RTSP don't always open the same port number on your machine, making it difficult to create firewall rules to accommodate them. If your firewall is blocking UDP, you must create rules that allow access to at least UDP port 6970 for QuickTime and probably to several sequentially higher ports as well. You may want to obtain the IP address of the streaming server from the firewall's log file and allow access to all ports from that IP address.

AUTH. AUTH is a general Internet protocol that authenticates clients to servers. When you try to connect to a server (with an e-mail client or Web browser, for example), the server may attempt to contact your machine on TCP port 113 to confirm your identity via AUTH. If your machine does not speak AUTH (Macs generally don't), the server proceeds anyway. Thus, AUTH is not a very useful protocol for Mac users and can create problems in your security monitoring. If your firewall denies access to port 113, you can have many denied accesses in your firewall's log file. To prevent these log entries, allow access to TCP port 113 from the IP addresses of the servers you contact that use AUTH. You can get the IP addresses from your firewall's log file.

Downloading files

You have many ways to download files from the Internet. One of the most common methods is through an old protocol called FTP (File Transfer Protocol). If you follow the basic firewall rule of denying access to all ports and allowing access only to needed services, you may have trouble downloading files due to problems with FTP. You usually get an error message saying that a connection cannot be established. This situation is a problem when you're using an FTP client such as Fetch; it also may be a problem when you're downloading files from the Web. Some sites enable download via HTTP, which is generally safer and easier to use with firewalls, and some sites use FTP. Web browsers can handle either protocol. See Chapter 14 for a discussion of the risks of using FTP.

FTP can operate in one of two modes: active or passive. When you are downloading a file in FTP active mode, your FTP client (or Web browser) opens a connection to port 21 on the FTP server. Then the server tries to open a second connection back to your machine on a high-numbered port. The problem is that you don't know ahead of time which port the server will use, so you can't configure your firewall to allow access to that port (**Figure 12.14**).

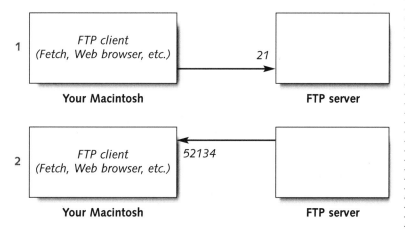

Figure 12.14 FTP active mode.

One way around this problem is to allow access to all ports, but that defeats the purpose of having a firewall. The following solutions are better:

- Configure the Internet Control Panel to specify that FTP transfers use passive mode, in which the FTP server does not try to open a connection back to your machine. Open the Internet Control Panel, click the Advanced tab, and check the Use FTP Passive Mode (PASV) checkbox (**Figure 12.15**). If you are downloading from the Web, configure your browser to use the Internet control panel, if possible.

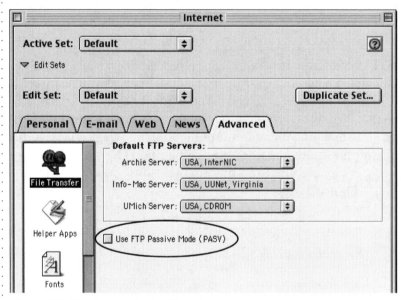

Figure 12.15 Internet Control Panel.

- If your FTP client does not refer to the Internet Control Panel, configure your FTP client to use passive mode. The procedure depends on which FTP client you use, although you typically use the Preferences dialog box.

- If your browser does not use the Internet Control Panel or your FTP client cannot be configured to use passive mode, turn off the firewall, start the download, and turn the firewall back on. Some firewalls allow you to turn them off for a specified number of minutes and then turn themselves back on automatically, eliminating the possibility that you will forget to restart them. A firewall needs to be off only until the download starts (**Figure 12.16**).

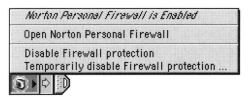

Figure 12.16
Control-strip option for disabling a firewall temporarily.

- Allow access to "all other" services on your machine but from only the IP address of the FTP server. You can get the IP address from your firewall's log file by looking for a denied access to a high-numbered port just after you try to access the FTP site. By creating such a rule for your firewall, you allow the FTP server access to any high-numbered port it chooses. You also allow access to many other ports, but they can be accessed only from the specified IP address. Therefore, a hacker is very unlikely to access your machine through one of those ports.

- Some FTP clients let you specify a set of port numbers for the FTP server to connect back to in active mode. Configure your firewall to allow access only to these port numbers.

- Use a stateful firewall, which allows a connection to be opened by an FTP server to a port that is otherwise protected by the firewall (see "Stateful firewalls" earlier in this chapter).

Testing a Personal Firewall

As you set up your personal firewall, you may want to test it. Testing can confirm two things:

That you configured the firewall as you intended. In particular, if you configured your firewall to allow access to more than one service from more than one IP address, testing can confirm that you specified the correct IP addresses and services.

That the firewall blocks connection requests. Because personal firewalls normally provide no direct feedback, you may gain some peace of mind by testing the firewall and confirming that access attempts are denied when they should be.

You can run two types of tests:

Self-test. Most personal firewalls have a self-test feature that allows you to simulate an access attempt to a service (**Figure 12.17**). Self-testing is quick, easy, and should be sufficient for many users. You choose the service to be tested from a pop-up menu and click the Test button. The firewall simulates an access attempt to the specified service from the firewall machine's IP address and then displays the result—allowed or denied—in the self-test window. A more advanced self-test feature can check non-default configurations. You could specify the IP address to be tested, make a choice from a larger pop-up menu of services, or enter a port number for services that are not listed in the pop-up menu.

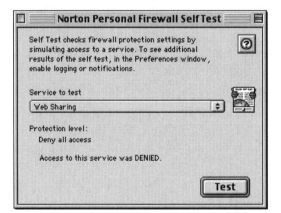

Figure 12.17
A personal firewall's self-test window.

External test. External testing is more difficult than self-testing but provides slightly more credible results. Self-testing is based on the firewall's simulation of receiving a packet designated for a particular service from a particular IP address, but for technical reasons, the test is not quite the same as a packet actually arriving at the firewall from the Internet. Self-testing is adequate for most users, but if your firewall is protecting critical services, you may want to run an external test for peace of mind. Running external tests from a several IP addresses is difficult, however. If you want to test a configuration with many IP addresses, self-test probably would be much easier.

You can perform three types of external tests: ad-hoc, Web-based, and tests that use testing utilities.

In *ad-hoc* testing, a user on another machine tries to access a service behind your personal firewall. This type of test gives you the satisfaction of having a user report that he or she was denied access to a specific service on your machine. Ad-hoc testing is the most "real-world" testing you can do; it also may be the only way to test services that are not covered by Web-based testing.

Web-based tests are performed using the Web sites of companies that test access to your machine for you. In one such service provided by Symantec (*http://security2.norton.com/*), you click a button on a Web page; Symantec sends connection requests to many commonly used ports on your machine and creates a report on the results. Another Web-based testing service is Shields UP (*http://grc.com/default.htm*). Web-based testing has the advantage of testing many ports with little effort on your part. This type of test is not so useful for testing firewall configurations that allow or deny access from specific IP addresses or ranges of IP address, because all Web-based tests are done from the same IP address.

Testing utilities are software programs, such as iNetTools (*http://www.wildpackets.com/*), that do port scans. By doing a port scan on a range of port numbers and inspecting the log file, you can determine the protection provided to each service. Every connection request comes from the same IP address, but with software testing, you have the option of running the same test from several machines, each with a different IP address.

How to test your firewall

How you test your personal firewall depends on the complexity of your firewall configuration and the nature of the services that you are protecting.

 If you want to test a configuration with many services and many IP addresses, self-testing is preferred for its flexibility and ease of use. To confirm that a firewall is working, external testing is slightly more credible.

Most users leave their personal firewalls in the default configuration, denying access from the Internet to all TCP/IP services. If you use this setup and want to convince yourself that the firewall blocks access attempts, you can self-test. Select any service, and click the Test button. If logging and notification are enabled, an entry should appear in your log file, and you should get notification. Because access is denied to all services, you can assume that if one service tests correctly, all the services will. The alternative is to test all 65,535 ports.

If you have a more complex configuration, self-testing will help you determine that the configuration is correct. You can specify the service to be tested and (if your firewall supports it) the IP address from which to simulate the test. Self-test makes short work of testing many services from many IP addresses.

If you are protecting a particularly critical service, such as Timbuktu or Apple Network Assistant, you may want to try an external test. Although self-testing is extremely reliable, it is not the same as packets arriving at the firewall machine from the Internet. You also can run an ad-hoc external test or use a testing utility such as Shields Up or Symantec Security Check.

Testing Mac OS 9 and Multiple Users

If you use the Multiple Users feature of Mac OS 9, you should test your firewall for each defined user to ensure that users are getting the protection you think they are. Norton Personal Firewall, for example, uses the same Preferences file—and, therefore, the same rules—for each user. This firewall also uses a common log file for all users. Other firewalls may differ in their behavior.

Troubleshooting a Firewall

One of the principal goals of a firewall is to be as unobtrusive as possible. Running a personal firewall on your machine may introduce problems with day-to-day Internet operations, however. If you are experiencing problems that you cannot explain, you can try two things:

Check the log file. If you are having problems that you can't explain, check your firewall's log file for denied access attempts that involve the service in question.

Temporarily turn off the firewall. If the problem persists, the firewall is not causing it. If the problem goes away, you may need to create a new rule for the service in question.

TCP problems

Using a firewall to protect TCP services may cause problems with certain operations.

AUTH. If a mail or Web server that you access uses AUTH authentication, the server may try to contact your machine on TCP port 113 every time you send a message. The server is attempting to verify that you are who you say you are. If your firewall denies access to port 113, the server will still process your request, but you will have a denied access entry in your log file for port 113. Over time, you may acquire many such denied entries. To prevent this problem, allow access to TCP port 113 from the IP addresses that use AUTH. You can get these addresses from your log file.

FTP. If you deny access to high-numbered TCP ports, you may have trouble downloading files, even if you don't use an FTP client application. Some downloads from the Web are done via FTP, which Web browsers can handle. For details on the problems you may encounter and how to handle them, see "Downloading files" earlier in this chapter.

Napster. Napster sometimes opens a connection to TCP port 6699 on your machine to transfer a file to you. If you are having trouble downloading files from Napster, try creating a rule to allow access to port 6699 for the IP address from which you're downloading the file.

UDP problems

If you deny access to UDP services, you may introduce problems with the day-to-day operation of your machine, because the Mac OS uses UDP for various behind-the-scenes tasks. Common problems are:

DNS. When an Internet application asks a name server to resolve a host name to an IP address, the name server replies to a high-numbered UDP port on your machine. In Mac OS 9, this port may be 49152, but the port number can vary, making it impossible to create a firewall rule for a single port number that fixes the problem. If you are blocking high-numbered UDP ports, your Internet client applications (such as a Web browser) will complain that host names (*www.apple.com*, for example) are not found. If your firewall allows, you can create a rule that blocks access only to UDP port numbers below 1024. These port numbers are used for the most important services. This rule allows a name server to respond on any high-numbered port.

DHCP. If you are blocking access to UDP ports, your machine may not be able to get a dynamic IP address that's valid for Internet communication; instead, it will assign itself a private IP address in the range 169.254.0.0–169.254.255.255. DHCP, the protocol used to get dynamic IP addresses, uses port 68. If you block UDP, and your machine uses dynamic IP addresses, you must enable access to port 68. Ideally, you should enable access only to the IP address of the DHCP server. To get this address, deny access to port 68 and restart your machine. Examine the log file for a denied access to port 68. The source IP address is the address of the DHCP server. Create a rule that allows access to port 68 from this IP address.

- **Date & Time control panel.** If you specify the use of a network time server in the Date & Time control panel (**Figure 12.18**), you must enable access to UDP port 123.

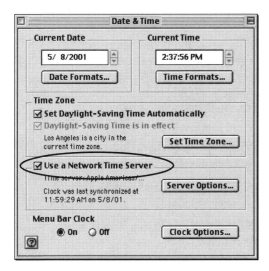

Figure 12.18
Specifying use of a network time server.

ICMP problems

Because ICMP is so widely used in networking operations, denying access to ICMP can have a variety of effects on your machine. See "Stealth mode" earlier in this chapter.

Network Address Translation

Although Network Address Translation, or NAT, (described in Chapter 15) is not intended to be used primarily as a firewall, it does have some of the same functions. Because the machines on a network that use NAT are assigned IP addresses from a private range, no one on the Internet can initiate contact with those machines, although users on those machines can use the Internet. (Chapter 7 discusses private addresses.)

If your network uses NAT, a personal firewall is still a good idea. It is a redundant security measure; it can protect against access attempts from your internal network; and it does logging, which can provide useful information for spotting attempted security breaches.

Services and Port Numbers

Table 12.1 lists port numbers used by common TCP and UDP services, **Table 12.2** lists port numbers used by many other services, and **Table 13.1** lists common attack ports.

Table 12.1 **Built-In and Common Third-Party Services**

Port	Service	Notes	Protocol
68	Dynamic Host Configuration Protocol (DHCP)	Commonly used to obtain a Mac's IP address	UDP
80	Web Sharing		TCP
123	Network Time Protocol		UDP
161	Simple Network Management Protocol (SNMP)		UDP
407	Timbuktu 5.2 or later	Previous versions use other ports	TCP
407	Timbuktu	Handshaking only, before version 5.2	UDP
497	Retrospect		TCP
497	Retrospect	Finding clients on the network	UDP
548	File Sharing over IP		TCP
1417	Timbuktu Control (pre-5.2)	Login is through UDP Port 407	TCP
1418	Timbuktu Observe (pre-5.2)	Login is through UDP Port 407	TCP
1419	Timbuktu Send Files (pre-5.2)	Login is through UDP Port 407	TCP
1420	Timbuktu Exchange (pre-5.2)	Login is through UDP Port 407	TCP
3031	Program Linking over IP		TCP
3283	Apple Network Assistant		UDP
5003	FileMaker Pro	Direct access, not through Web	TCP
5003	FileMaker Pro	For obtaining host list	UDP

Table 12.2 **Other Services**

Port	Service	Notes	Protocol
20	FTP Data	Used only as a source port	TCP
21	FTP Control		TCP
23	Telnet	Common port for attacks	TCP
25	SMTP (e-mail)		TCP
53	DNS	Mainly uses UDP, not TCP	TCP
53	DNS	Sometimes uses TCP	UDP
69	Trivial File Transfer Protocol (TFTP)		UDP
70	Gopher		TCP
79	Finger		TCP
88	Kerberos		TCP
105	PH (directory)		TCP
106	Poppass (change password)		TCP
110	POP3 (e-mail)		TCP
111	Remote Procedure Call (RPC)	Used for many Unix services	TCP
113	AUTH		TCP
119	NNTP (News)		TCP
137	Windows Name Service		UDP
138	Windows Datagram Service		UDP
139	Server Message Block (SMB)	Windows file sharing	TCP
143	IMAP (e-mail)		TCP
311	AppleShare Web Admin		TCP
384	ARNS (tunneling)		TCP
387	AURP (tunneling)		TCP
389	LDAP (directory)		TCP
427	SLP (service location)	Only for large responses	TCP
427	SLP (service location)	Uses TCP for large responses	UDP
443	SSL (HTTPS)		TCP
458	QuickTime TV		UDP
510	FirstClass server		TCP
514	Syslog		UDP
515	LPR (printing)		TCP
554	RTSP (QuickTime server)	Also uses UDP 6970+	TCP

Table continues on next page

Table 12.2 **Other Services** *continued*

Port	Service	Notes	Protocol
554	Real Time Streaming Protocol (QuickTime)		UDP
591	FileMaker Pro Web	Recommended alternative to 80	TCP
626	IMAP Admin	Apple extension	TCP
660	AppleShare Remote Admin		TCP
666	Now Contact Server	Doesn't match actual port assignment	TCP
687	AppleShare User/Group sharing		TCP
1080	WebSTAR Admin	WebSTAR port number plus 1000	TCP
1443	WebSTAR/SSL Admin	WebSTAR port number plus 1000	TCP
2049	Network File System (NFS)		UDP
4000	Now Public Event Server		TCP
4199	Eudora Mail Server Admin		TCP
4347	LANsurveyor Responders	Also uses UDP	TCP
5190	AOL Instant Messenger		TCP
5498	Hotline Tracker	UDP port 5499 for finding servers	TCP
5500	Hotline Server		TCP
5501	Hotline Server		TCP
6346	Gnutella	Music-sharing service	TCP
6699	Napster client	Used when server is in firewall mode	TCP
6970 and up	QuickTime and RealPlayer		UDP
7070	RealPlayer	Also uses UDP ports 6970-7170	TCP
7070	RTSP alternate (RealPlayer)		UDP
7648	CuSeeMe (video)	Client connections; UDP for audio/video	TCP
7649	CuSeeMe (video)	Connection establishment	TCP
19813	4D server	Previously 14566 (6.0 and earlier)	TCP

Analyzing and Responding to Security Threats

13

In this chapter, we talk about how to tell when your machine is being attacked and what to do if it is.

If you have a personal firewall on your Mac, you will probably notice access attempts to various services on your machine from IP addresses you don't recognize as those of friends or colleagues. Some of these access attempts may be attacks; others may not be. How do you tell the difference? And if you do detect an attack on your machine, what can you do about it? This chapter tells you how to generate useful data, how to analyze and interpret the data, and how to investigate and report suspicious activity.

Generating Useful Data

Before you can detect and respond to security threats, you need good data: Who accessed or attempted to access your machine, when those attempts were made, and what services were involved. The log files generated by personal firewalls and various Internet services are an excellent source of information. Creating log files is the first step in detecting and responding to security threats.

Log files

First, use a personal firewall (Chapter 12) and enable its logging features. You should log denied access attempts and usually log allowed access attempts as well. Logging allowed access attempts on a machine with services that have many TCP connection requests (see Chapter 12) can generate a large log file in a short time. A Web server, for example, often gets a connection request for every page and graphic that is downloaded, whereas a file server gets a connection request only when a user logs in. Most of us don't run heavily used Web servers on our machines, so allowed connections should be logged as well.

Useful log-file information includes:

- The date and time of the access attempt;
- The port to which access was attempted;
- The IP address from which access was attempted;
- The result of the attempt (allowed or denied).

Your firewall's log file generally is your first line of defense in spotting security threats. The log provides an overview of all services on your machine and allows real-time monitoring of access made to any service.

Log files generated by Internet services are also useful, providing more detailed information than a firewall log does. A File Sharing log, for example, lists the name of each user who logs in and the date and time of login and logout. If your firewall log file shows an allowed connection to File Sharing from an unknown IP address, you can check the File Sharing log file to see which user logged in at that time and then talk with that user.

Service log files provide more detail on access attempts, helping you fine-tune your investigation. Logging is available for the following services:

- File Sharing over IP (via ShareWay IP Personal Edition)
- Web Sharing
- Timbuktu
- FileMaker Pro
- Retrospect

If you provide any of these services on your Mac, or any other services that generate log files, you should enable logging.

As a log file grows, you may want to start a new one to keep any single log file from becoming unmanageably large. A big log file is slower to work with, and if it gets too big, your analysis software may not be able to open it. You should check log-file sizes periodically. When you get a sense of how quickly a log file grows, you can schedule a time to start a new one.

Compact and store old logs for future use. Because processes such as credit-card billing and law enforcement move slowly, you may not realize that you need the data until months or even years later. As long as you have the disk space, you should never throw away old log files. Open Door Networks once used six-month-old log files to help track down a fraudulent credit-card purchase.

Old data may also be useful for looking at long-term trends. You may want to compare current firewall activity with activity last month, or last year, to see whether access attempts have increased.

Log-file format

Many formats are used for firewall and Internet service log files. For the Macintosh, a standard is the extended WebSTAR format, based on the format used by the popular Macintosh WebSTAR Web server. The extended format makes it possible to use the same general format for applications other than Web servers, such as AFP servers and firewalls.

When you're looking for a firewall or for Internet service software, look for the capability of writing log files in extended WebSTAR format. Such log files are tab-delimited text files, containing lines that indicate the number and meaning of the fields (Figure 13.5).

Real-time information

Although a firewall log file is the single most important source of information, real-time information from your firewall or other services can also be useful. Real-time information can be in the form of notification via a dialog box or a sound or a real-time display of the firewall or service log. Some Internet services, such as File Sharing, also provide real-time monitoring.

Immediate feedback can be useful in two ways:

You become aware of possible security threats while they're happening. If an attack is being made on your machine, you gain an advantage by taking action immediately, even if your machine is fully protected. Contacting the appropriate authorities while an attack is under way may help identify the perpetrator.

You can associate your own actions with firewall events. If your firewall denies access to all ports, and you try to download a file from a Web site that uses FTP (see Chapter 12), you will get an error message from your browser and your firewall will deny an access. Seeing the two pieces of information together will help you identify and remedy the problem and will help you make sense of the log-file entry.

Detecting Suspicious Activity

After you enabled logging for at least your personal firewall, you have the raw data you need to detect security threats on your machine. You can look for suspicious activity in real time or by analyzing a log file.

Establish a baseline

When you install your firewall, you probably will see access attempts to your machine right away. Before you respond to any accesses, take a few days to establish a baseline for your firewall and to learn what kinds of access attempts are normal for your machine. Some access attempts are part of your machine's network operations; some are from your ISP; others are random events. Knowing this will help you spot suspicious accesses.

You may also want to establish a baseline for how many access attempts are made. This information can help you spot days of unusually high activity. Summary reports are easy to generate when you use the appropriate software (see "Log-file analysis tools" later in this chapter). You might decide to run a report of daily totals on the last day of each month, for example.

Store the results for future reference. Such data can help you see long-term trends in overall firewall activity and spot days of abnormally high activity.

What to look for

How do you spot suspicious activity? As you watch real-time events or analyze a log file, look for patterns in the data. Most often, a pattern—not an isolated access attempt—reveals suspicious activity.

Don't be alarmed by every access attempt.

Your firewall's log file will probably reveal many access attempts, but many of them do not involve malicious activity. Possible reasons for access attempts are:

Normal network operations. Many Internet client applications, such as Web browsers and e-mail clients, access a domain name server (DNS) to resolve host names to IP addresses. Depending on how your firewall is configured, you may see name-server responses in your log file. If your machine uses a dynamic IP address, you may see a log entry from the DHCP server right after your machine starts. If you contact a mail or Web server that uses the AUTH authentication mechanism, you may see log entries from the server trying to access the AUTH port on your machine. If you download a file via FTP (see Chapter 12), you may see an access attempt from the download site to a high-numbered port on your machine. If you specified a network time server in your Date & Time control panel, you may see an access to port 123. All these operations happen on an ongoing basis. When you analyze a log file, you may see many entries for one or more of these ports.

ISP activity. Some ISPs contact users' machines, looking for servers that violate their appropriate-use policy. @Home, for example, sends connection requests every few hours to port 119 on subscribers' machines, looking for active news servers. When you analyze a log file, you may see many access attempts to certain services, all from the same IP address, but these attempts may be normal ISP activity. To check, look at the IP address from which the access attempts are coming. If the address is similar to your IP address, there's a good chance that your ISP is making the access attempts. To make sure, call or e-mail your ISP and ask about the specific port number and IP address.

Honest mistakes. Users on the Internet sometimes make mistakes. If a user makes a legitimate attempt to contact a file server over the Internet but specifies the wrong IP address, the connection request goes to the wrong machine (possibly yours). If the user doesn't realize his error, he may try several times before giving up. If you see several access attempts to a service on your machine, you can't necessarily conclude that they're malicious.

To identify suspicious activity, look for several patterns and types of accesses as you monitor your firewall in real time or analyze its log file:

Many denied accesses from one IP address. If the accesses are to different port numbers, that pattern may indicate a port scan (a hacker trying many ports, looking for accessible services). If the accesses are all to the same port, the activity is still suspicious and probably warrants further investigation.

Many denied access attempts to a service during a short period. This pattern may indicate an attempted security attack on your machine, even if the access attempts are from different IP addresses. If one IP address attempts many accesses to the service, this situation is especially suspicious. If many of the accesses are from different IP addresses but occur at around the same time, the activity may be a distributed attack. In either case, you probably want to investigate further.

Any access attempt from an unknown IP address to a service running on your machine. Access attempts to services running on your machine warrant special attention. If you see an occasional attempt, you may want to confirm that your firewall is blocking access from the appropriate IP addresses and to make sure that the service is secured in other ways (see chapters 8, 9, and 10). Many denied accesses from unknown IP addresses may be suspicious so you may want to look into them.

Any access attempt to a high-risk service. You should examine access attempts to high-risk services (see chapters 8, 9 and 10). If any of the accesses are allowed, confirm that they are from IP addresses to which you want to grant access. If not, configure your firewall to deny access to those IP addresses. (If any high-risk services are running on your machine, confirm that they are secured properly, according to the measures we described in chapters 7, 8, 9, and 10.) If you see many access attempts to any high-risk service from one IP address, you may want to investigate further.

Allowed accesses. Unless you are running Internet services on your machine, your firewall should be configured to deny access to all services from all IP addresses. If you see allowed accesses, you should determine whether the services in the allowed log entries are ones to which you intend to allow access and whether the IP addresses from which access is allowed are in the correct range. If not, examine your firewall's rules for each such service, confirming that you specified the correct IP addresses.

As you look for types of accesses and access patterns, you may need to correlate a port number in your firewall's log file with a service name or you may want a description of a particular service. Chapter 12 lists the names and port numbers of many common Macintosh services. And "The Most Common Attacks:

A Case Study," later in this chapter, lists the names and port numbers of common access attempts. If you want a more complete description of a service, your firewall may be capable of querying a Web-based database of service information. Use these resources to make sense of your log file's data.

Real-time monitoring

Real-time monitoring means spotting suspicious activity as it's happening. Rather than analyze a log file that contains information about events that happened in the past, you watch accesses as they happen. You can perform several types of real-time monitoring:

Firewall notification. As mentioned in Chapter 12, firewalls can be configured to notify you of significant firewall events (**Figure 13.1**). An event may be an allowed or denied access or (for some firewalls) an attack.

Norton Personal Firewall: access DENIED

At 04/23/01 13:09:42, an access attempt was denied to Program Linking over TCP/IP, port 3031, from IP address 192.168.0.10.

Figure 13.1 A firewall notification alert.

Firewall monitor window. Most firewalls have a monitor window, which displays (in real time) the most recent lines of the log file (**Figure 13.2**).

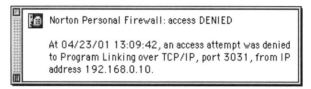

Norton Personal Firewall Access History

Logging denied and allowed accesses

Date and time	Action	Service	Host name
4/23/01 1:09:42 PM	Deny	Program Linking over TCP/IP	192.168.0.10
4/23/01 11:57:52 AM	Allow	File Sharing over TCP/IP (ShareWay IP)	192.168.0.1
4/23/01 11:57:00 AM	Allow	File Sharing over TCP/IP (ShareWay IP)	192.168.0.1
4/23/01 11:53:53 AM	Allow	File Sharing over TCP/IP (ShareWay IP)	192.168.0.1
4/23/01 11:53:19 AM	Allow	File Sharing over TCP/IP (ShareWay IP)	192.168.0.1
4/23/01 11:47:52 AM	Deny	unknown (8080)	192.168.0.4
4/23/01 11:47:40 AM	Deny	Web Sharing	192.168.0.3
4/23/01 11:47:23 AM	Deny	Web Sharing	192.168.0.2
4/23/01 11:38:27 AM	Allow	File Sharing over TCP/IP (ShareWay IP)	192.168.0.1

Figure 13.2 A firewall monitor window.

External monitoring applications. Firewall log analyzers may display log lines in real time, much as a firewall monitor window does. They may also provide summaries of access attempts in the form of graphs or charts. In addition, network-global firewalls may display real-time data.

All these methods allow you to spot suspicious activity as it's happening and then take action. Real-time monitoring is especially good for seeing time-based events, such as port scans and denial-of-service attacks, which generate many log entries in a short period. If you see a large increase in the frequency of access attempts, look closely to see whether they're coming from one or more IP address and whether they involve one or more port numbers (refer to "What to look for" earlier in this chapter).

Although firewalls provide the most comprehensive information about access attempts to your machine, the monitor windows of some Internet services can provide more detailed information. If you have enabled File Sharing over IP, for example, you can use the Activity Monitor tab of the File Sharing Control Panel to see who is currently logged in to File Sharing. If you use the ShareWay IP upgrade to Mac OS 9's File Sharing over IP, you can see the IP address of users who are logged in (**Figures 13.3** and **13.4**).

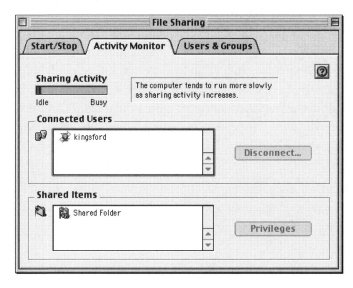

Figure 13.3
Activity Monitor window for built-in File Sharing.

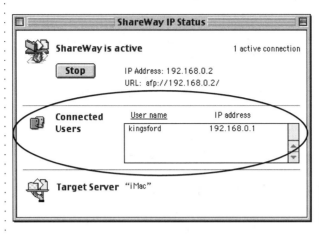

Figure 13.4
Status window
for ShareWay IP.

Because an active service is more vulnerable than one that is turned off or protected from all users by a firewall, you may want to use a service's monitoring capabilities to keep track of who's using it, especially for high-risk services.

Log-file analysis tools

Analyzing log files is the best way to get the big picture on security threats to your machine, because a log file usually covers a larger span of time than any real-time method does. A firewall log file gives you a bigger picture than a service log does, because a firewall reports on activity for all services.

You can analyze a log file in many ways. The most obvious method is to open the log file and read it. The problem with this direct approach is that most log files are much too long and complex to make sense of simply by reading them. Entries are in chronological order, which may not be useful for spotting patterns; also, the file usually contains several types of information, such as date and time, port number, IP address, and result of the access attempt (allowed or denied). A log file that is big enough to be useful is too complex to read. **Figure 13.5** shows typical firewall log lines. Imagine reading a thousand lines of data in this format.

```
!!LOG_FORMAT DATE    TIME       RESULT   HOSTNAME       SERVER_PORT   METHOD
12/18/00             5:38:12    ERR!     208.1.80.221   21            TCP
12/18/00             5:38:13    ERR!     208.1.80.221   21            TCP
12/18/00             16:55:00   ERR!     192.168.0.3    80            TCP
12/18/00             16:57:03   OK       208.1.80.218   548           TCP
12/18/00             14:28:59   ERR!     208.1.80.221   21            TCP
```

Figure 13.5 Typical firewall log lines.

Figure 13.6 shows typical log lines from a File Sharing log. Service-specific logs usually provide more detail than firewall logs do. Notice the information about logins, logouts, and user names.

```
!!LOG_FORMAT DATE    TIME       RESULT   HOSTNAME      URL USER     AFP_METHOD   AFP_STATUS   BYTES_SENT   TIME_TAKEN
1/20/00              10:24:14   OK       192.168.0.2   kingsford    FPLogin      0
1/20/00              10:28:14   ERR!     192.168.0.2   kingsford    FPLogout     -5022        531          0:04:00
1/20/00              10:28:37   OK       192.168.0.2   kingsford    FPLogin      0
1/20/00              10:29:07   OK       192.168.0.2   kingsford    FPLogout     0            452          0:00:30
```

Figure 13.6 Typical File Sharing log lines.

Several kinds of software can help you make sense of a log file:

Spreadsheet. You can read a log file into a spreadsheet and use the spreadsheet's sorting features to group and sort data.

Database. Putting a log file's data in a database is useful. You can group and sort the data, summarize it, and generate reports.

Log file analysis software. These applications are written specifically to analyze and summarize log files. Such applications can display access attempts sorted by various fields (including user name, for log files that contain user names), write summary reports in HTML and plain text, create a log file for each port number, and notify users when certain log-file events take place.

Firewall log-analysis software. These applications are written specifically to analyze firewall logs. Some applications allow users to summarize log files by service or IP address or to display log entries in chronological order. These applications may also be able to locate network administrators for specific IP addresses and generate e-mail to those administrators. Typically easy to use and inexpensive, they often are the best way to go for many users.

Finding patterns in your firewall's log

After you've chosen software to use for log-file analysis, you need to know how to manipulate the log file's data to find patterns. Patterns that you want to look for include:

Many denied accesses from one IP address. In a spreadsheet or database, sort log file entries by IP address, then sort by result (allowed or denied), and then sort by port number. Look for IP addresses that have many entries; then determine whether accesses were made to one port or many ports. If you use a firewall-log analyzer such as Open Door Networks' Who's There? Firewall Advisor, summarize by IP address and sort by number of denied accesses in descending order. For IP addresses with many denied accesses, you can display the services that were accessed by that IP address (**Figure 13.7**).

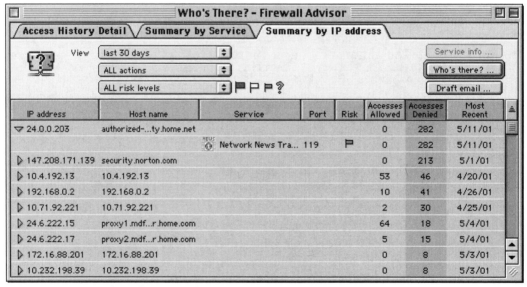

Figure 13.7 Many denied accesses from one IP address.

In this example, the IP address with the most denied accesses is part of @Home's scan of users' machines for network news servers—an otherwise-suspicious pattern that is part of normal ISP activity. Investigation of other IP addresses in this example might reveal suspicious activity, such as access attempts to many ports or to high-risk services such as Timbuktu.

Many denied accesses in a short period. If you use a spreadsheet, sort the log file by date and look for large groupings, which indicate many accesses on one date. By using macros and sorting, you can create a list of daily access totals, making it easier to summarize large log files. In **Figure 13.8,** the COUNT column values were created with macros; those values indicate total number of accesses on the date listed in the DATE column. The spreadsheet is sorted to show the highest COUNT values first. This example shows no unusually active days. If you use a database, create a report of daily access subtotals and look for days with an unusually large number of accesses. If you find a date with many accesses, you can use a firewall log analyzer to analyze log-file data for that date or date range and then summarize the data by service and by IP address, looking for port numbers with many hits, sequences of port numbers, or IP addresses with many hits.

	A	B	C	D	E	F	G
	DATE	TIME	RESULT	IP	PORT	PROTOCOL	COUNT
2	12/21/00	1:50:02	ERR!	208.1.80.221	119	TCP	23
3	12/19/00	1:20:34	ERR!	192.168.0.4	80	TCP	22
4	12/22/00	11:40:57	OK	192.168.0.5	80	TCP	22
5	12/23/00	9:15:21	OK	192.168.0.5	80	TCP	22
6	12/24/00	11:10:52	OK	192.168.0.4	80	TCP	22
7	12/25/00	2:31:32	ERR!	208.1.80.220	119	TCP	22
8	12/26/00	3:20:59	ERR!	208.1.80.221	21	TCP	22
9	12/27/00	6:26:57	ERR!	208.1.80.221	21	TCP	22
10	12/28/00	14:33:01	ERR!	208.1.80.220	21	TCP	22
11	12/29/00	15:23:50	OK	192.168.0.4	80	TCP	22
12	12/30/00	23:14:13	ERR!	208.1.80.221	21	TCP	22
13	12/31/00	6:25:54	ERR!	192.168.0.2	1234	TCP	22
14	1/1/01	22:25:36	ERR!	208.1.80.221	21	TCP	22
15	12/18/00	14:02:55	ERR!	208.1.80.221	21	TCP	21
16	12/20/00	11:19:06	ERR!	208.1.80.218	119	TCP	21
17	1/2/01	6:09:08	ERR!	208.1.80.221	21	TCP	16

Firewall Log

Figure 13.8 Using a spreadsheet to look for days with unusually high numbers of accesses.

Accesses to services running on your machine. With a spreadsheet or database, sort the log file by port number and look for port numbers of services you're running on your machine. With a firewall log analyzer, sort by service and look for the services you're running.

Accesses to high-risk services. With a spreadsheet or database, sort the log file by port number and look for port numbers that correspond to critical services (those covered in chapters 8, 9 and 10). Firewall log-file analyzers often associate a risk with each access. With a firewall log-file analyzer, summarize by service and sort by risk. The highest-risk services should appear at the top of the window (**Figure 13.9**).

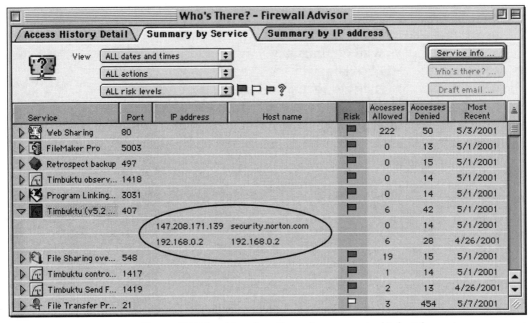

Figure 13.9 Looking for allowed accesses to high-risk services.

This example shows six allowed accesses to Timbuktu, all from a private IP address on the machine's local network. Any allowed accesses from unknown public IP addresses would indicate that the firewall has not been configured properly. The example also shows 14 denied accesses from Symantec's Web-based firewall testing service (see Chapter 12), which had been used to test the firewall.

Is it malicious?

Assessing malicious intent is somewhat subjective. How many access attempts from one unknown IP address do you consider to be suspicious? There's no magic number. The important thing is to be prudent in assessing access attempts to your machine, rather than reactive.

> *Be reasonably sure of malicious intent before you take further action.*

Carefully assess access attempts in the context of potential damage to your machine, the number of attempts from any given IP address, and the frequency of attempts. Access attempts to ports known to be used for attacks (see "Understanding Common Access Attempts" later in this chapter) are suspicious, but because many of those services don't run on the Mac, they may pose no real risk. On the other hand, if many such access attempts are made from one IP address they may warrant investigation, especially if they persist. Be sure that the attempted accesses are not part of your Mac's everyday network operations or from your ISP. The network administrator to whom you may eventually send e-mail probably is busy and won't have time to spend on nonessential issues.

Investigating and Reporting Suspicious Activity

So far, we've talked about using a personal firewall and enabling its logging capability, performing real-time monitoring and log-file analysis, looking for patterns in a firewall log file to find suspicious activity, and using software to find patterns. Now, let's look at what you do if you find suspicious activity.

In many cases, you may not be positive that the intent was malicious, but you should be reasonably sure before you contact a network administrator. Confirm that the accesses are not part of normal network activity, that they're not part of your ISP's operations, and that they are not isolated events.

If you believe that malicious access attempts have been made to services on your machine, contact the network administrator for the IP address from which the accesses initiated.

Finding network administrators

The Internet is made up of many networks that are networked together, and each network has an administrator. Any network may in turn be made up of several smaller networks that are networked together, and each of those smaller networks may have its own administrator. Just as there is a hierarchy of networks, there is a corresponding hierarchy of network administrators. To report suspicious activity, you need to find the network administrator closest to the user at the IP address you're researching.

You can find network administrators by using an Internet technology called *WHOIS*, which is a distributed database maintained by authoritative Internet agencies. The database contains information generated by the registration of domain names and the allocation of IP address blocks by agencies such as IANA (Internet Assigned Numbers Authority).

Most end users do not get IP addresses from an authoritative Internet agency but from their ISPs. Many ISPs do not guarantee that a given user will get the same IP address every time she connects to the Internet. For these reasons, the WHOIS search often will not yield information about the user who attempted access to your firewall machine; information often ends with the user's ISP.

You access WHOIS through the WHOIS protocol. Although some applications use the WHOIS protocol, it is often easier to use one of the Web sites run by the agencies that are part of the WHOIS database. If you want to search the WHOIS database via the Web, use your Web browser to go to one of the following agencies' sites:

> **ARIN** (*http://www.arin.net*) covers addresses registered in North and South America and parts of Africa.
>
> **RIPE** (*http://www.ripe.net*) is for addresses registered in Europe, the Middle East, and parts of Africa.
>
> **APNIC** (*http://www.apnic.net*) covers addresses registered in the Asian-Pacific region.

If you don't know what part of the world an IP address is from, you'll need to try each agency until you find the right one. When you do, the first search may yield information about a network service provider that provides service to an ISP. In this case, you need to do another search based on the results of the first, because the contact at the NSP probably is not the person who can help you. You need to find a contact at the ISP, if possible. **Figure 13.10** shows typical information returned from a WHOIS search.

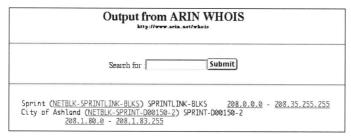

Figure 13.10 A WHOIS search on 208.1.80.220 yielded this information. The data shows no contact information, so you need to use one of the links to make another search.

Each site presents information in a different format. Using WHOIS manually is not a user-friendly process and is probably better left to advanced users.

Fortunately, you can use an easier method. Applications written specifically to analyze firewall log files may have a WHOIS lookup feature that finds the right agency automatically and gets the most detailed information available for a given IP address. Open Door's Who's There? Firewall Advisor includes this function. In addition to summarizing firewall log files, Who's There? can locate a network administrator for an IP address and draft an e-mail to the administrator (**Figure 13.11**).

In this example, the application did a WHOIS search on IP address 24.0.0.203 (an @Home machine that checks users' machines for network news servers). Contact information for the network administrator is displayed at the bottom of the window. WHOIS searches often happen in stages, with each successive search yielding information closer to the ISP. The most pertinent contact information is usually at the bottom of this window.

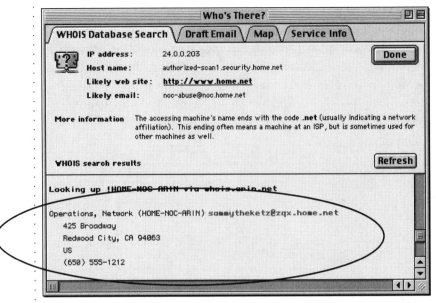

Figure 13.11 Network-administrator contact information for an IP address.

In addition to WHOIS search capability, some firewall log file analyzers can display the location of the registered contact for the IP address, which is useful for attacks that occur from countries you might not know. This feature usually uses an Internet service that returns the latitude and longitude of most IP addresses (**Figure 13.12**).

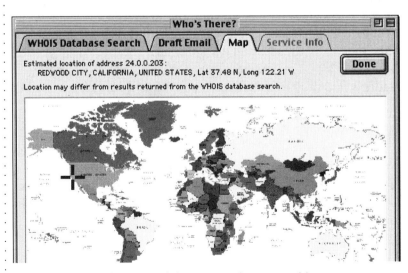

Figure 13.12 The location of the contact for an IP address.

Creating the e-mail

To generate e-mail to the appropriate contact, users of firewall log analyzers may be able to click a button to generate an e-mail draft and another button to send the e-mail though their e-mail client. A sample e-mail draft is shown in **Figure 13.13.** If you do not have a firewall log file analyzer to generate e-mail for you, use the text in Figure 13.13 as a guide to compose your own e-mail.

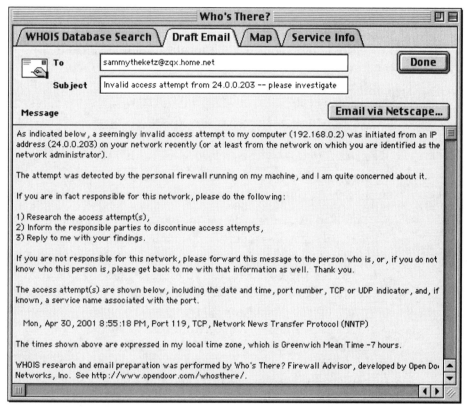

Figure 13.13 The draft of an e-mail to a network administrator.

The application takes the most relevant contact e-mail address (from the final WHOIS search) and uses it in conjunction with an e-mail template stored in the program to generate the e-mail draft.

When you draft an e-mail, remember that network administrators usually want to fight security threats as much as you do. Assume they're on your side. Also realize the suspicious activity you report probably is not coming from the administrator but from a user on his or her network, so be polite and professional in your communications.

Include as much relevant information as you can, including the following:

- The IP address from which access was attempted
- The dates and times of the access attempts
- The port numbers to which access was attempted
- The protocol, if known

Remember that many ISPs allocate dynamic IP addresses to their subscribers, which may make it more difficult to trace an incident to a specific user. An ISP should keep a DHCP log that enables them to correlate a date, time, and IP address to a user, but the task may not be trivial.

If you can't contact the network administrator

If your e-mail to a network administrator is returned with an error, several things may have occurred:

The e-mail address is out of date. The person listed by WHOIS may no longer work for the company responsible for the IP address. You may want to try the phone number listed for the contact. If that attempt fails, try the next contact (the one you found before the current contact in your WHOIS search), explaining that you're trying to report a suspected case of Internet abuse and that the e-mail address listed in WHOIS does not work. Include the same information about the incident. If the contact can't help you, he or she may refer you to someone who can. Most organizations have an "abuse" e-mail address.

The address contains a typo. Take the same measures that you would for an out-of-date address.

The address is fraudulent. In such a case, all the information may be fraudulent. The rest of the information related to that e-mail address probably is fraudulent as well, so you'll need to try the ISP or NSP for that organization.

If you're having trouble reaching the primary contact, and other contacts listed by WHOIS can't help you, you can try one more thing. Do a *trace route*, which lists the IP addresses of all routers (and possibly their host names) between you and the IP address you're researching. Several applications can do trace routes, including WildPackets' iNetTools. When you have a list of router IP addresses, you can use WHOIS to research those addresses, starting with the address closest to the one you're researching (**Figure 13.14**).

Hop	IP address	Host
1	10.72.143.1	*
2	24.6.222.1	bb1-fe1-0.mdfrd1.or.home.net.
3	24.7.75.137	c1-se6-3.ptldor1.home.net.
4	24.7.64.22	c1-pos1-0.snfcca1.home.net.
5	24.7.65.161	c2-pos1-0.snjsca1.home.net.
6	24.7.70.134	*
7	205.171.14.109	svl-core-03.inet.qwest.net.
8	205.171.5.217	bur-core-02.inet.qwest.net.
9	205.171.13.1	bur-core-01.inet.qwest.net.
10	205.171.8.41	lax-core-01.inet.qwest.net.
11	205.171.5.155	sjo-core-03.inet.qwest.net.
12	205.171.22.34	sjo-edge-03.inet.qwest.net.
13	208.46.223.86	*
14	208.1.80.218	

Figure 13.14
A trace route listing.

This example shows a listing from a trace route done on IP address 208.1.80.218. If you could not get valid contact information for this IP address, you could use WHOIS to look up 208.46.223.86—the last router before the IP address you're investigating. If that attempt doesn't yield useful information, you could work your way up the list, using WHOIS to look up each address. You eventually will reach an address that yields valid contact information. Even though the contact you reach in this way may not be the person you ultimately need to talk with, he or she probably could direct you to the right person or tell you how to proceed.

If all else fails, your last resort is law enforcement. This step is fairly drastic, so before you contact a law-enforcement agency, you should do the following things:

- Try all contacts (e-mail, phone, and snail mail) yielded by a WHOIS search on the IP address in question.

- Use a trace route to generate intermediate IP addresses, do WHOIS searches on those address, and try all resulting contacts (e-mail, phone, and snail mail).

- Gather sufficient data in the form of firewall and Internet service log files to support your claim.

- Talk with your own ISP, unless you have some reason to suspect them.

If the suspicious activity persists, using law enforcement may be appropriate, especially if the activity is impairing the use of your machine.

Understanding Common Access Attempts

In this section, we describe the accesses that you are most likely to see as you analyze your firewall's log file. The services are the ones most often reported in a case study done by Open Door Networks, which is described in the following section. The services are listed in descending order of frequency. Many attacks are on services that do not even run on Macintosh computers; hackers usually go after Windows or Unix machines. At the end of this section is a summary table of these services and port numbers. Use this section as a reference for interpreting accesses to your machine. If you don't find a port number in this section, you may find it in Table 12.1 or 12.2, which summarize Macintosh services.

The entries in this section include the service name and port number, a description of the service, and advice on how to respond to access attempts to the service.

Remote Procedure Call (RPC) (111). Access attempts to port 111 are often made by hackers to see whether an application that uses the Remote Procedure Call (RPC) service is running on your machine. RPC is used by several Unix applications that are vulnerable to attack, so a hacker probably is just looking for such a machine.

Few RPC-based applications run on Mac OSes before Mac OS X. You probably do not need to be concerned about these access attempts unless you are running Mac OS X.

Sub7 Trojan Horse (27374). Access attempts to port 27374 are made to a common Windows Trojan horse named Sub7. One of the major advantages of using a Mac is that many, many fewer such viruses exist.

You probably do not need to be concerned about these access attempts.

File Transfer Protocol (FTP) (21). Access attempts to port 21 are made to determine whether an FTP server is running on your machine. This type of access is not the kind of access that occurs when you try to use an FTP client to access an FTP server (see Chapter 12).

You should not have an FTP server running, so you probably don't need to worry about these access attempts. If you are running an FTP server, consider removing it. As described in Chapter 14, FTP servers are insecure, and much better options for sharing files are available.

Domain Name Server (DNS) (53). Access attempts to port 53 are often made to see whether a domain name server is running on your machine. Domain name servers on Unix often contain serious vulnerabilities, so hackers often look for them.

You probably do not have a DNS running unless you've specifically installed one. Your Mac does use DNS services to access Internet services by name but generally should not be running a DNS, so you probably do not need to be concerned about these access attempts.

Web Sharing (HTTP) (80). Access attempts to port 80 are made to try to access a Web server that may be running on your Mac. In Mac OS 8 and 9, the Web Sharing control panel can be used to run a Web server on your Mac.

You should check the Web Sharing control panel to see whether Web Sharing is enabled. If so, follow the steps described in Chapter 8 to make sure that the service is secured properly.

Authentication Server (AUTH) (113). Access attempts to the AUTH service (port 113) probably are made by an e-mail, Web, or FTP server to verify your identity before you access that server. Your Macintosh is probably not running an AUTH server, but your e-mail, Web, or FTP access should work anyway.

These access attempts probably are a normal part of your day-to-day Internet activities. You may want to contact the e-mail, Web, or FTP server's administrator to see whether its AUTH feature can be disabled; otherwise, you probably do not need to be concerned about these accesses.

Wingate/SOCKS/WebSTAR Admin (1080). Access attempts to port 1080 are made to attempt to access applications, including the Wingate Internet Sharing server for Windows, SOCKS proxy servers, and the Admin application for the WebSTAR Web server for Macintosh.

Unless you are running WebSTAR, you probably do not need to be concerned about these access attempts. If you are running WebSTAR, you should configure your firewall to minimize the number of IP addresses that have access to this port.

Gnutella (6346). Access attempts to port 6346 are made as part of the Gnutella file-sharing service. Gnutella is used to download and serve files such as MP3 music files in a distributed manner.

If you are running Gnutella, be sure that you are only sharing the desired files.

Sub7 Trojan Horse (1243). Hackers make access attempts to port 1243 to access the Windows Sub7 Trojan horse. Port 1243 is an alternate port to the more common 27374.

You probably do not need to be concerned about these access attempts.

Netbus (12345). Hackers may have made access attempts to port 12345 to see whether Netbus is running on your machine. Netbus is a Windows application that allows remote control of a Windows machine over the Internet; it does not run on Macs. Alternatively, someone may have used this port number for testing, due to its sequence (1-2-3-4-5).

You probably do not need to be concerned about these access attempts.

Telnet (23). Access attempts to port 23 are made to see whether a Telnet server is running on your machine. Telnet is an application that, on Unix and some Windows machines, allows remote control of the machine through a command-line interface. For this reason, Telnet is a common method of attacking those machines.

Mac OS 8 and 9 do not support a command-line interface and thus do not run Telnet servers. You probably do not need to be concerned about these access attempts unless you are running Mac OS X.

Line Printer Daemon Protocol (LPR) (515). Access attempts to port 515 are made to see whether an LPR (Line Printer) server is running on your machine. The access attempt could be to an actual printer but it is more likely to be to a print server application such as the kind that often runs on Unix machines (and is, like most Unix services, vulnerable to attack).

You probably do not need to be concerned about these access attempts unless you are running Mac OS X.

DNS response (49152). Access attempts to port 49152 are often made, via UDP, as part of your Mac's domain-name resolving process. Whenever you type a host name, your Mac must first convert that name to an IP address before accessing that host.

In most cases, you do not need to be concerned about these accesses. If your firewall is protecting UDP, be sure to allow your domain name server (DNS) access to this port so that domain-name resolving will work.

Napster (6699). Access attempts to port 6699 are made as part of the Napster MP3 sharing service. Napster is used to download and serve MP3 music files.

If you are running a Napster application, you may need to use your firewall to make this service available to any machine from which you are trying to download files. If you are also serving MP3 files, you may need to make this service available to people to whom you want to serve files.

Network News Transfer Protocol (NNTP) (119).
Access attempts to port 119 are made to see whether
your machine is running a network news (NNTP) server.
NNTP servers make available the newsgroups that you
often see on the Net.

The @Home network seems to look for these servers
periodically to make sure that you're not running one.
You may want to contact the ISP. If you don't use
@Home, you probably do not need to be concerned
about these access attempts.

Windows File Sharing (139 and 445). Access attempts
to port 139 are made to see whether your machine is
running a Windows (SMB) file server. Because so many
Windows machines are on the Net, hackers often look
to see whether Windows users accidentally enabled
Windows file sharing in such a way that the hacker
might have access. Port 445 is sometimes used for file
sharing in Windows 2000 and later instead of 139.

You do not need to worry about these access attempts
unless your Mac is running a Windows server such as
DAVE from Thursby Software or Apple's AppleShare IP
(which can act as both a Mac and Windows server).

File Sharing over TCP/IP (AFP) (548). Access attempts
to port 548 are made to the Mac's built-in File Sharing
service. File Sharing is very powerful; it has the potential
to make all the data on your Macintosh available over
the Internet.

If you are running Mac OS 9 or have installed Open
Door Network's ShareWay IP product, check the File
Sharing control panel or ShareWay IP application to see
whether File Sharing is enabled. If so, follow the steps
described in chapters 8 and 10 to make sure that the
service is secured properly.

Alternate Web/Proxy (HTTP) (8080). Port 8080 is often
used as an alternative to the standard Web server port
(80) or for a Web proxy (a type of firewall for intranets).
Certain applications that implement their own HTTP
(Web) server may use this port as well.

Unless you are running a specialized Web-accessible application, you probably do not need to be concerned about these access attempts.

Simple Mail Transfer Protocol (SMTP) (25). Access attempts to port 25 are made to see whether a mail (SMTP) server is running on your machine. Machines running Unix often have mail servers that are vulnerable to attack, so a hacker probably is just looking for such a machine.

Unless your Mac is running a mail server, which is unlikely, you probably do not need to be concerned about these access attempts.

Table 13.1 **Common Access Attempts**

Port Number	Service Name
21	File Transfer Protocol (FTP)
23	Telnet
25	Simple Mail Transfer Protocol (SMTP)
53	Domain Name System (DNS)
80	Web Sharing (HTTP)
111	Remote Procedure Call (RPC)
113	Authentication Server (AUTH)
119	Network News Transfer Protocol (NNTP)
139	Windows File Sharing (SMB)
445	Windows File Sharing (SMB)
515	Line Printer Protocol (LPR)
548	Macintosh File Sharing (AFP)
1080	Wingate/WebSTAR
1243	Sub7 Trojan Horse
6346	Gnutella Music Sharing
6699	Napster Music Sharing
8080	Web Alternate (HTTP)
12345	Netbus
27374	Sub7 Trojan Horse
49152	DNS Response

The Most Common Attacks: A Case Study

This section presents material from a case study done by Open Door Networks that will give you a sense of what the most common attacks are in the real world. This was only one case study, and your experience may differ, but the results should help you interpret access attempts to your machine. If your firewall reports many attempts to access Remote Procedure Call, for example, you should not be surprised, since RPC is the most commonly reported access attempt in the study.

Open Door Networks maintains a Web site called Learn More, where owners of its DoorStop firewall can go for analysis and advice about access attempts detected by DoorStop. The site provides first-level analysis of any access attempt detected by DoorStop (**Figure 13.15**).

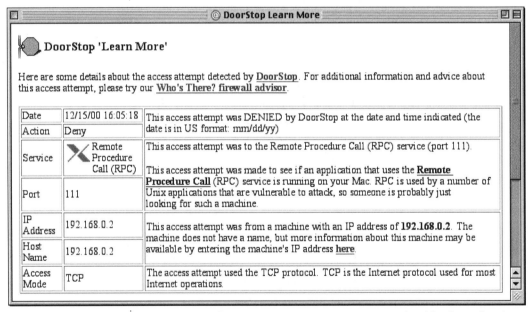

Figure 13.15 The DoorStop Learn More site, used as the basis for the case study.

In the period between January 1, 2001, and March 31, 2001, more than 23,000 access attempts were analyzed by the site. The site thus provides a significant statistical sampling of accesses detected by DoorStop and, by extension, by other Macintosh firewalls as well. To be precise, the sampling is of accesses detected by DoorStop *and* analyzed by DoorStop users through the Learn More Web site (users may choose not to analyze access attempts that they feel they understand).

By comparing your firewall's log against this study, you can see if access attempts to your machine match the profile. If so, you are probably experiencing the same level of attack as most Macintosh users on the Net. If not, you may wish to look more extensively at the differences. You should focus on general trends rather than specific details, since the exact details of the Internet are always changing.

The study also graphically illustrates that most access attempts are to systems other than Macs. The large Unix component emphasizes the additional risk Mac users will be assuming as they move to Mac OS X (see chapter 18).

The following table and charts list the access attempts most commonly analyzed through the "Learn More" Web site. The attempts fall into four categories:

Unix. The most frequent access attempts appear to be searching for Unix services, such as RPC (Remote Procedure Call) and DNS (Domain Name Server). RPC is used as the basis for many Unix services that have been shown to be vulnerable to attack, and many Unix DNS implementations are also known to be flawed from a security perspective. FTP is classified as a Unix service for purposes of this study, since the large majority of all FTP servers run on Unix.

Windows. As expected, a large number of access attempts were Windows-specific, in particular attempts to contact the Sub7 Trojan Horse.

Day-to-day. Many reported "attacks" were actually due to normal day-to-day Internet usage of the Macintosh reporting the "attack," including AUTH authentication and music sharing service usage. Note that day-to-day usage of FTP clients for downloading files is not included in the FTP entry in this study, which only represents attempts to access FTP servers (FTP client usage results in access attempts to random high-numbers ports, as indicated in chapter 12, not to the FTP server port).

Service. Some of the access attempts represent either attacks or legitimate access attempts to services that could be running on the Mac, such as Web or file sharing. There is no way to tell from the bulk data whether each of these access attempts was an attack or not.

Table 13.2 **Most Commonly Reported Services**

Service	Port	Category	Count
Other	other		5257
Remote Procedure Call (RPC)	111	Unix	3689
Sub7 Trojan Horse	27374	Windows	3296
File Transfer Protocol (FTP)	21	Unix	2074
Domain Name Server (DNS)	53	Unix	1303
Web Sharing (HTTP)	80	Service	1217
Authentication Server (AUTH)	113	Day-to-day	934
Wingate/WebSTAR*	1080	Windows	894
Gnutella Music Sharing	6346	Day-to-day	854
Sub7 Trojan Horse	1243	Windows	729
Netbus	12345	Windows	602
Telnet	23	Unix	557
Line Printer Protocol (LPR)	515	Unix	366
DNS response	49152	Day-to-day	292
Napster Music Sharing	6699	Day-to-day	289
Network News Transfer Protocol (NNTP)	119	Day-to-day	272
Windows File Sharing (SMB)	139	Windows	225
Macintosh File Sharing (AFP)	548	Service	221
Web alternate (HTTP)	8080	Service	203
Simple Mail Transfer Protocol (SMTP)	25	Unix	187

*Port 1080, listed in the Windows category, is also used for remotely administering the WebSTAR Web server, so some of its accesses may belong in the Service category.

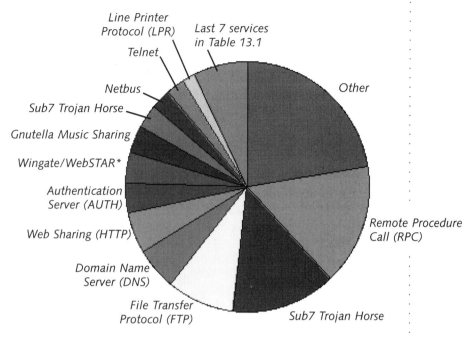

Figure 13.16 Most commonly reported access attempts by service.

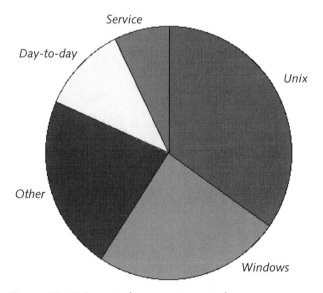

Figure 13.17 Reported access attempts by category.

part iv

Advanced Topics

Just Say No to FTP

You may have noticed that the acronym *FTP* appears throughout this book. Usually, the acronym is in close proximity to words such as *don't, insecure,* and *avoid*. The reason: FTP (File Transfer Protocol) represents one of the least secure protocols on the Internet. Despite this, FTP is also one of the most common protocols on the Internet, even though significantly more-secure, easier-to-use alternatives are available.

What Is FTP?

FTP, as its name implies, is a common protocol for transferring files from one machine on the Internet to another. It was developed in the early days of the Internet, when security was not a significant concern. Like most Internet protocols, FTP is client–server: As an end user, you usually run an FTP client application on your machine, and it speaks to an FTP server somewhere else on the Net. The client can copy files to or from the server and perform other file-related tasks, such as listing directories and deleting files.

The most common use of FTP is through anonymous FTP. Anonymous FTP does not use passwords in any way and does not even purport to provide security. Servers usually use anonymous FTP to make files available to anyone who wants those files. If you download a shareware application, a software upgrade, or a long public document from a Web site, for example, those files may be transferred to your machine through anonymous FTP. (At other times, the server makes files available directly through HTTP, the protocol used by Web servers themselves.) Your Web browser, which can act as an FTP client, may shield the details of the protocol from you, but if you look at the download link carefully, you'll see that it begins with ftp:// instead of http://.

Anonymous FTP does not impose much in the way of security risks, although all forms of FTP can create some problems when used with firewalls (see Chapter 12). Also, all forms of FTP send all their data unencrypted, so transferred files are subject to spying. As long as you never have to enter a password, however, you do not need to be significantly concerned about FTP security.

FTP becomes a security problem when you *do* have to enter a password. This situation may seem to be backward, because passwords are supposed to increase security, but with FTP, they often have the opposite effect. An FTP password is a simplistic attempt to provide some form of security for file transfers that need it. A principal use of password-based FTP is to transfer (upload) files from a local copy of a Web site to a Web server. If you maintain your own Web site but have it hosted on a server somewhere else, you may upload that site to that server via FTP. To make the transfer, you enter your account name and password in your FTP client application, which then connects to the server and lets you upload the files (assuming that the server validates you). Even Webmasters at large organizations often use FTP for this purpose.

Servers also use password-based FTP to make files available to a limited set of users. Users have to enter their account names and passwords in their FTP client applications before they connect to the FTP server. The server validates names and passwords before letting clients connect and access the files.

Why Is FTP So Bad?

FTP was developed in the late 1960s, when the Internet was little more than an experimental project connecting a few universities. The goals of that project did not include the creation of a secure system. After all, access to the network was limited, and the data being exchanged wasn't all that important; the ability to exchange data was what mattered. The network was largely designed by academics for academics. Little thought was given to business or consumer use; hence, little thought was given to security.

The Internet is now the opposite of the way it was in the 1960s. It no longer provides limited access to 10 or 20 U.S. universities; hundreds of millions of people can access it. Instead of being used almost solely for the exchange of academic data, the Internet is used for the exchange of almost any type of data you can imagine, much of it confidential. And instead of being used mainly by the people who were involved in its development, the Internet is used by just about everyone. Most people use it for good, but some do not.

Negative security

As we explain in Chapter 12, FTP was designed well before the concept of a firewall existed, and it works very poorly with all types of firewalls. FTP is also difficult to use, requiring users to run special-purpose client applications to transfer files and often storing those files in formats that make them hard to read. The worst thing about FTP, however, is that the design of password-based FTP often results in *negative* security. In many cases, anonymous FTP, which was designed to have no security, is more secure than password-based FTP. If anonymous FTP has no security, password-based FTP must have negative security. Why is password-based FTP security so bad?

First, the use of names and passwords in FTP gives users and server administrators a false sense of security. If you type a name and password to access a service, you expect that the service is adequately protected. Or if you configure a server to require a name and password, you expect that the name and password will protect something on the server. Even though an FTP server does verify that a user's name and password are valid for the server, a fundamental defect in the protocol makes that verification of limited value and the protection inadequate relative to expectations. A false sense of security is worse than no security.

There is an even bigger concern however:

> *Beyond the false sense of security, the principal reason why FTP passwords provide negative security is that their use can compromise the security of other services by making your user name and password available to any hacker who wants them.*

Although you may question how and why FTP makes your user name and password available (see the following section), you should be able to see that this availability can result in negative security and that you will often be able to increase your overall Internet security by not using FTP passwords in the first place.

How FTP decreases security

Password-based FTP can decrease Internet security through a fundamental defect in the protocol. Many security flaws are complex and difficult to explain, but the security flaw in FTP is simple:

> *FTP transmits both your user name and your password to the server in clear text. Neither user name nor password is encrypted in any way. Anyone who is spying anywhere on the Internet between you and the FTP server can easily obtain your user name and password.*

To make matters even worse, the clear-text user name is pre-ceded by *USER* and the clear-text password is preceded by *PASS* (**Figure 14.1**). You may not understand the other pieces of the FTP packets in this figure, but you can pick out the user name and password easily.

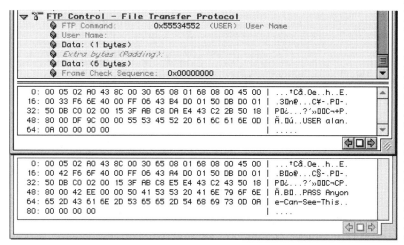

Figure 14.1 FTP makes your user name and password obvious to anyone who can see the traffic between your FTP client and the FTP server.

Figure 14.1 was not created for this book; it was obtained from one of the many so-called sniffer applications—in this case, the Macintosh EtherPeek application. Sniffer applications, which are useful for diagnosing network problems and devel-oping network software, can display data from any packets on the network to which their machines are connected. These applications are essential to the ongoing development of the Internet, but like most useful tools, they can be misused.

You may question how many hackers have access to a place on the Internet between you and the FTP server to which you're talking. You may also question how many hackers would have the time and desire to monitor sniffer traces for FTP names and passwords, even if those names and passwords are obvious. You'd probably be surprised by the answers.

To spy on your FTP conversations, hackers do not have to obtain physical access to a place on the Internet between you and your FTP server. Usually, they hack into a machine that's already on the Net (most often running Unix, which hackers know best and can hack most easily). Once they've hacked in, they take over that machine to run sniffer software (**Figure 14.2**). Because sniffer software is unobtrusive and doesn't affect the machine or network on which it's running, that software can run undetected indefinitely. All the hacker needs to do is check on the software periodically to see what it's found. If that software happens to be on a machine that's on a network between you and your FTP server, or on your server's network (at your ISP, for example), the software will be able to pass your FTP user name and password on to the hacker.

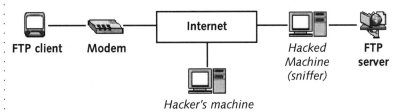

Hacker's machine

Figure 14.2 A hacker doesn't need physical access to a network to monitor the conversation between you and your FTP server.

The hacker doesn't even need to monitor the sniffer software at all. Because FTP user names and passwords are obvious, the software can look for and track that information itself, accumulating a list and giving that list back to the hacker when he checks in. A sniffer application can even use the Internet to send any FTP user names and passwords it sees to the hacker the instant it sees them. Within seconds of your typing your user name and password, that information could be in the hands of hackers throughout the world.

A real-world scenario: hacking a Web site through FTP

You've probably read about Web sites being hacked and defaced with sayings such as "Kilroy was here." One way that hackers intrude on Web sites is by exploiting the negative security of FTP. This section explains how this process works.

If the hacker has physical access to a network that's part of the Internet infrastructure—at an ISP, for example—he may sneak a machine running sniffer software onto that network. If not, he has to find a machine somewhere on the Net that he can hack and use to run the sniffer software. In some cases, the hacker is trying to deface a particular Web site, in which case he needs to run the software on a machine on a network through which traffic passes to get to the Web server that hosts that site. If the hacker is looking to hack just any Web site, he can be less specific about which machine he hacks. Regardless, the hacker can try many machines and eventually will find one that he can access.

Despite FTP's glaring lack of security, it remains a popular upload method, and some ISPs and Web-hosting companies still don't offer any alternative. If a Web-site owner wants to make changes on his or her site and uses FTP to log on and upload the changes, the sniffer can get all the information the hacker needs. When the sniffer sees what it's looking for, it records the user's name and password, as well as the IP address of the FTP server to which the user was connecting. That address conveniently appears in the FTP packets along with the user name and password. The sniffer software can also record other things, such as the IP address of the user's machine, for future nefarious purposes. (A person who uses FTP passwords may implement lax security in other ways.)

The sniffer software accumulates a list of FTP names, passwords, and server addresses and transmits that list over the Internet to the hacker. The hacker then assumes the identity of the Web-site owner by logging into the same FTP server that the site owner used, entering the site owner's name and password. After logging in, the hacker can get a list of all the site owner's files and add, change, and delete them. The changes made through FTP apply directly to the Web site just as they would if the site owner had made those changes. The site is defaced by the changes immediately.

Things can get a lot worse

Using FTP to maintain a Web site risks the security of that site. If you maintain a Web site at an ISP or Web-hosting service, you don't want to use FTP. But as bad as having your Web site defaced is, FTP's negative security can result in much more significant problems for you, the Web-server owner, and the Internet as a whole.

From your perspective, having any of your passwords compromised decreases your overall Internet security. If hackers know a name and password that you use for one service, they have at least a clue as to what you might use for other services. If you follow the password-management rules in Chapter 4 and choose good passwords, that hint shouldn't help a hacker figure out your other passwords. But many people have related passwords, and they may use the same password for multiple services. If you feel that you need to ignore the advice in Chapter 4 about reusing passwords, please at least do the following:

> *Do not, under any circumstances, use an FTP password for any other service. You need to assume that your FTP password is public information, and using it for any other service will compromise that service to almost the same extent that FTP is compromised.*

Remember how easy it is for sniffer software to gather lists of FTP user names and passwords? It's a simple step from gathering such a list to disseminating the information. FTP names and passwords can become known throughout hacker circles in a matter of days, if not hours. You need to prevent those lists from compromising the security of your other Internet services.

FTP can be the crack a hacker needs to break into and take over the machine on which a Web server is running. Web-server owners should limit what their site owners can access through FTP, so if someone's FTP password is compromised (or if someone who has a Web site on the server wants to hack the server), little damage can be done to other Web sites on that server. But if FTP is set up incorrectly, the compromise of one Web-site owner's password can open much of the server machine to compromise. Worse, bugs in the FTP implementation itself (especially on Unix servers) can help hackers gain control of the server. Finally, in some systems, anyone who has FTP access can upload applications such as CGIs (common gateway interface modules, described in Chapter 17) and execute those applications on the server. Essentially, a hacker can implant a virus on the server when he gains access to any site owner's FTP account.

You might wonder why an ISP or Web-hosting service would run an FTP server that requires users to log in with a name and password, thereby compromising both users and the server.

Part of the reason is historical—FTP has been the protocol of choice for transferring files on the Internet for decades—and part has to do with education. Many server owners just aren't aware of the security risks associated with FTP. Further, good alternatives, such as those described in the following section, became available only recently.

You might feel that if your Web-hosting service runs an FTP server, it's OK for you to use that server; any problems are the host service's responsibility. To some extent, that assumption is accurate. But do you really want to contribute to the ongoing Net security problem? A hacker can use your compromised FTP account to compromise the whole machine on which the FTP server is running (**Figure 14.3**). Then he can use the compromised server to compromise other machines on the same network, such as by running sniffer software and finding out what's happening on the network. With those details, he can take over additional machines. The more machines a hacker can take over, the more he can affect the overall security of the Internet, such as by launching a distributed denial-of-service attack. Your use of FTP to maintain a single Web site probably doesn't have much overall affect on the security of the whole Internet, but the widespread use of FTP does.

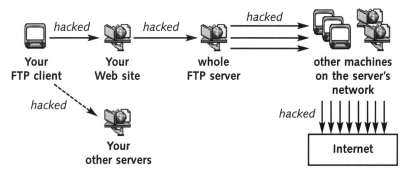

Figure 14.3 Use of FTP can have a cascade effect, resulting in degraded security for the entire Internet.

What Can You Use in Place of FTP?

FTP has served a much-needed role on the Internet, enabling the downloading of files and the uploading of Web sites. When few options were available, the security costs associated with FTP were worth paying. But much more secure alternatives are available now, offering many other advantages as well. Whether you transfer files over the Internet occasionally or run a server that facilitates file transfer for other users, you should consider these alternatives.

The Macintosh alternative

If you want to transfer files between Macs, the alternative to FTP is clear. Apple Filing Protocol (AFP) is significantly more secure than FTP and is integrated directly into the Mac OS, making it significantly easier to use as well. AFP was designed in the 1980s for use with the AppleShare File Server. Apple-Share was designed for the networks that Apple's business and educational customers used, so security was an important aspect of its design. Apple learned from the mistakes of FTP and other file-transfer protocols of the time and made sure that user names and passwords would not be sent in clear text. AFP does even better than that; in many cases, it never sends the password over the network.

When an AppleShare client logs in to most AFP servers, the server generates a random number and sends that number to the client (**Figure 14.4**). The client uses the password as an encryption key, encrypts the random number, and sends the encrypted random number back to the server. The server can verify that the correct password was used by encrypting the number itself and comparing the two encrypted values, which will match if the client has the correct password. AFP also authenticates not only the client to the server but also the server to the client. This two-way authentication prevents a hacker on the network from setting up a machine that masquerades as the server.

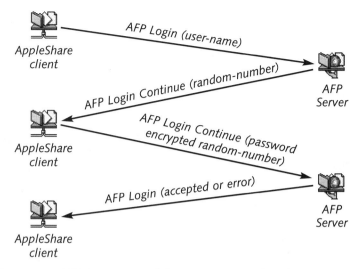

Figure 14.4 AFP does not send the user's password in clear text. Usually, AFP doesn't send that password at all, making it much more secure than FTP.

Until 1997 or so, AFP and AppleShare worked only over AppleTalk. Now AFP also works over TCP/IP, enabling it to be used for file transfer over intranets and the Internet. An AppleShare client that supports AFP over TCP/IP has been built into the Mac since Mac OS 7.5, and a server in the form of File Sharing has been built in since Mac OS 9.0 (**Figure 14.5a** and **b**). Before Mac OS 9, you could also obtain an AFP over TCP/IP server through Apple's AppleShare IP and Open Door Networks' ShareWay IP products. AFP's integration into the Mac OS makes it much easier to use than FTP—an additional security advantage, because the easier something is to use, the more likely you are to use it correctly. See Chapter 8 for details on sharing files with AFP.

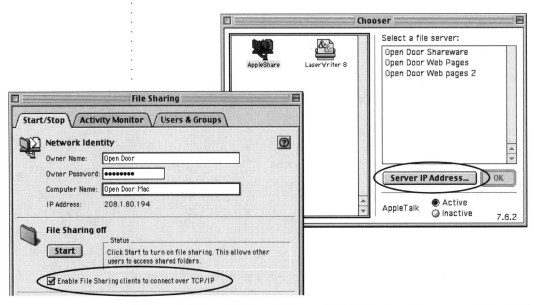

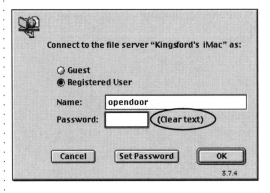

Figure 14.5a and b The AFP over TCP/IP client and server are integrated directly into the Mac OS.

AFP is extensible in terms of login security—that is, the random-number exchange implemented in the Macintosh Apple-Share client, AppleShare IP, and Mac OS 9 File Sharing can be replaced by other options. A few less-secure, non-Apple servers implement a clear-text password exchange as part of the AFP login process. You'll notice this security risk if you see the phrase *Clear Text* in the AppleShare client (**Figure 14.6**). Clear-text password exchange through AFP is no more secure than it is through FTP.

Figure 14.6 Certain less-secure AFP servers may not implement AFP's advanced login security. If you see the words Clear Text, the system is no more secure than FTP.

Other AFP servers, including Mac OS X and the iDisk server, implement an alternative password exchange process through an advanced encryption technique called Diffie-Hellman Exchange (DHX). DHX is in some ways more secure than AFP's built-in random-number exchange. Its use is indicated in the AppleShare client by the phrase *Encrypted Password Transport* (**Figure 14.7**).

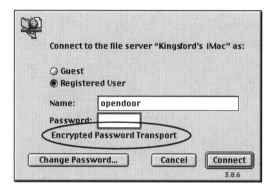

Figure 14.7 iDisk and Mac OS X servers use an alternative AFP login process called DHX. Like AFP's standard login process, DHX is much more secure than FTP.

AFP, being a more modern protocol, also works better with firewalls than FTP does. Like FTP (and most other alternatives described in this chapter), AFP does not encrypt the files for transfer, however. If you want to make sure that no one spies on the files as they're sent over the Internet, you'll need to encrypt them before transfer. One method is to use Apple's encryption application, described in Chapter 9.

AFP clients and servers are available for most other operating systems. If you transfer files mainly between Macs but need to do so with another type of machine every so often, looking at an AFP client or server for that machine may make sense. Windows AFP implementations have been available for years, and they work well, although Windows NT servers' default password exchange uses clear text (see Chapter 17). Most Unix platforms can also run AFP servers. Because Unix is the most popular platform for Web servers, ISPs and Web-hosting services can provide AFP access for their Mac users.

Windows alternatives

If you need to access a Mac AFP server from a Windows PC or exchange files through a Mac's built-in File Sharing, running an AFP client on a Windows machine may make sense. Adding any software to a Windows machine can be difficult, however, especially when you're adding network software. If a procedure is difficult, the odds of opening a security hole increase. Windows has its own built-in file-sharing system, and using this system for transfer makes sense if you don't want to install new software on the Windows machine or if your Mac often exchanges files with several Windows machines. Just as you can add software that enables Windows machines to use the Mac's native File Sharing, you can add software that enables Macs to use a Windows machine's native file-sharing system.

The native Windows file-sharing protocol is Server Message Block (SMB), sometimes called NETBIOS or CIFS (Common Internet File System). SMB uses a verification process similar to AFP's random-number exchange; this algorithm is called NTLM (NT LAN Manager) authentication. Due to the popularity of Windows machines, several highly advanced SMB-targeting sniffers are available. These applications go beyond looking for clear-text passwords; they attempt to recover the password used in NTLM authentication (by trying every word in the dictionary to see whether it matches the observed exchange, for example). Some of these sniffers work quite well, so Microsoft developed an enhanced version called NTLMv2. For maximum safety, you should use NTLMv2 wherever it's available.

Both AppleShare IP and Mac OS X Server provide implementations of SMB. Windows machines can transfer files to these servers via the built-in Windows SMB client and you can copy these files from the servers through AFP (or vice versa). If you want to transfer files from a Windows SMB server (such as one running Windows NT or 2000) to a Mac, or to let a Mac act as a Windows SMB server, you can install third-party software such as DAVE from Thursby (see Chapter 17). Many versions of Unix also provide SMB file-transfer capability, usually through an application called Samba Companies.

Other alternatives

In almost all cases, you should be able to use AFP or SMB to transfer files over the Internet. Your Mac has built-in AFP support, and you can add a third-party application to provide SMB support as well. Most machines with which you want to exchange files should support one or both of these options, enabling you to transfer files without the security risks associated with FTP.

You also can use the HTTP protocol to transfer files (for instance through Personal Web Sharing), but HTTP's built-in password-exchange mechanism is not significantly more secure than FTP's. Although the password is not sent in clear text, it is encoded in such a trivial fashion that it can be recovered with essentially no work on the part of the hacker; a sniffer can detect and decode HTTP passwords automatically. HTTP file transfers can be made highly secure, however, if they're made with SSL. Your password is encrypted during the transfer, and so is the data within the file. SSL-based HTTP file transfer is the most secure method possible if you're concerned about the security of your password and the security of the file's data. Unfortunately, not many servers support SSL-based HTTP file transfer.

If you need to upload a Web site to a server, you should see whether that server supports WebDAV (Web-based Distributed Authoring and Versioning). WebDAV is a rapidly evolving standard that makes developing and maintaining Web sites significantly easier. One issue that WebDAV is designed to address is the lack of security in uploading Web sites through FTP. WebDAV is based on HTTP, but it uses an algorithm similar to AFP's random-number exchange to ensure the security of the passwords.

WebDAV clients are available for Mac OS 9, and a client is integrated directly into Mac OS X; you can mount a WebDAV volume directly on the Mac OS X desktop just as you can an AFP volume. WebDAV is also being integrated into Web-site development software, such as Adobe's GoLive, which previously included direct integration with FTP only for site uploading (**Figure 14.8**). The server part of WebDAV is included with Mac OS X Server.

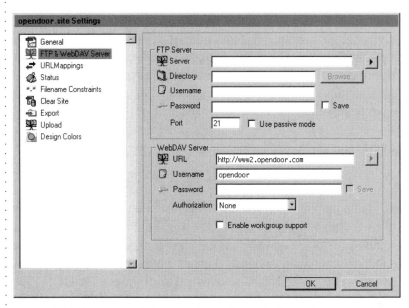

Figure 14.8 Due to much-improved security and other advanced features, WebDAV is being integrated into Web-site development software to help in uploading sites to servers.

If you must use FTP

With all the alternatives available, you should rarely need to use password-based FTP. But many ISPs and Web-hosting services have not gotten the security message and still provide only FTP for uploading Web sites or transferring certain files. If your provider supports only FTP, you should ask it to support AFP as well, or you should consider finding another provider.

If you feel that you need to use password-based FTP, you should take a couple steps to minimize the potential damage. You can at least make sure that any compromise does not affect your other services. We've made this recommendation previously, but it's important enough to repeat:

 Do not reuse your FTP password, or any password similar to it, for any other service.

Hackers who find out your FTP password may attempt to use it to try to get into your other services. They also may use that password as a hint about how you might construct your passwords for those services. If your FTP password is an English word combined with a couple of numbers, for example, a hacker could use that format to implement a dictionary attack. The possibility that your FTP password may provide a clue about the format of your other, more-secure passwords has a somewhat surprising consequence: using an otherwise unsafe FTP password (such as a common word or your initials) may increase the security of the passwords that you use for other services. FTP's negative security means that the less data you put in your FTP password, the better. FTP passwords should also be very low on the levels-of-protection scale detailed in Chapter 4.

If you use password-based FTP, be sure to monitor the FTP server that you use for signs that it has been hacked. If you use the server to upload a Web site, defacement of that Web site usually is obvious. But other hackers want to conceal their dirty work, so they can use the server for other things. They may upload pirated or otherwise-illegal files to hacked FTP sites as a way to distribute those files without the risk of getting caught with the files on their machines. So periodically check all the files in any FTP directory to which have write access. Also examine your Web pages carefully to make sure that they have not been subtly hacked (a link changed, for example).

Minimizing your use of password-based FTP and checking for signs of password compromise can help keep the risk of that use low. By far the best alternative, however, is to just say no. FTP use should diminish as more and more people understand the security risks involved, making the Internet safer for all of us.

Home Networking

Owning a computer once was considered to be a luxury. Now owning a computer is considered to be almost as essential as owning a telephone, and more and more households have two, three, or more machines. Some surveys suggest that sales of new computers to households that already have at least one machine is the fastest-growing segment of the computer market.

If your home has more than one computer, you may want to share resources, such as disks and printers, between your computers. You can create a home network to implement this sharing. An even bigger reason for a home network, however, is to share a single cable or DSL Internet connection among your home machines. Because these connections are high-speed and always on, they can be shared in such a way that each of your home computers can use the connection at the same time. This arrangement differs from phone-based Internet connections, in which one computer has to initiate the connection. Those connections are so slow that only one computer at a time can use them effectively anyway.

All new Macs have a built-in high-speed Ethernet port. Ethernet has traditionally been used for local-area networking in work and school environments, but the technology can also be used to create nearly free home networks, which most cable and DSL modems can connect directly to. Apple's AirPort and related wireless technologies are quite popular for home networking as well; we cover them in Chapter 16. Options for using phone and power lines within a house for home networking are also available.

When a home network is used to share an Internet connection, every machine on that network is effectively connected to the Internet. Regardless of the wiring technology used, home networks sharing Internet connections introduce security issues beyond those associated with stand-alone Internet-connected computers.

Network Address Translation

Each machine that accesses the Internet using a home network must have its own Internet address. Internet addresses, like phone numbers, are somewhat limited. Most ISPs either do not provide multiple Internet addresses per household or charge extra for each Internet address beyond the first one. For this reason, home networks can use a technology called Network Address Translation (NAT) to share a single Internet address.

NAT is implemented using a NAT gateway, which is either a dedicated network-attached device or software running on one of the computers on the network. The NAT gateway is assigned the single address provided by the ISP; the machines on the home network talk to the NAT gateway to use that address to access the Internet.

How NAT works

The NAT gateway (**Figure 15.1**) assigns a private IP address to each computer on the home network (usually, through the Dynamic Host Configuration Protocol, or DHCP). These private addresses, which have the same form as public Internet addresses, are used internally on the home network and do not have to be unique throughout the Internet (see "Public Versus Private IP Addresses" in Chapter 6). When a machine on the home network wants to access the Internet, it does so through the NAT gateway, which sits between the home network and the Internet connection. From the accessing machine's point of view, the connection looks just as though that machine were accessing the Internet directly by using its private address, with the NAT gateway serving as the router that connects the accessing machine to the Internet. In reality, the NAT gateway changes the access request so that the request uses the public IP address assigned to the NAT gateway, which is the only IP address the ISP is going to accept from the user's network, and then sends that request out to the Internet via the ISP. When a response comes back from the Net, the NAT gateway routes that response to the machine that made the original request.

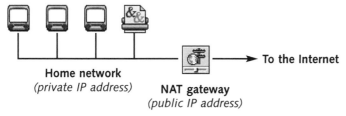

Figure 15.1 A NAT gateway can be used to share a single Internet connection, and a single Internet address, among multiple machines on a home network.

The details of NAT are tricky, because NAT needs to do two difficult tasks at the same time. First, it needs to fool the machines on its network into thinking that they're talking directly on the Internet, so that those machines (and users) can keep doing things the way they're used to. Second, the NAT gateway has to manage multiple Internet requests and responses in parallel, determining which machines on the home network are involved.

A NAT gateway can be implemented in hardware, as a dedicated, network-based device, or in software running on one of the machines on the home network (which must be kept on for any machine to access the Internet). NAT gateways usually have two ports for network connections (**Figure 15.2a**). One port is connected to the Internet, usually through a cable or DSL modem although sometimes through a phone modem. The other port is connected to the home network. In some cases, the gateway has only one physical port (**Figure 15.2b**). In such cases, the modem and home network are connected to each other and to the gateway, usually through Ethernet. Either way, all conversations between machines on the home network and the Internet go through the gateway. **Figure 15.3** shows an example of a Macintosh running Sustainable Softworks' IPNetRouter NAT gateway software, configured for a single port.

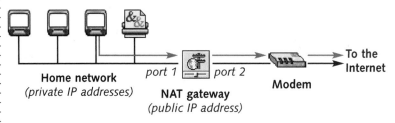

Figure 15.2a A typical NAT gateway with two network ports, one for the Internet and one for the home network.

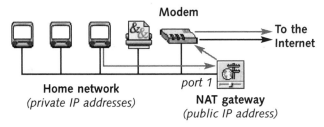

Figure 15.2b A NAT gateway configuration with only one network port. The port is used for both the Internet and the home network, which are physically the same network but logically separated by the gateway, which routes between the two.

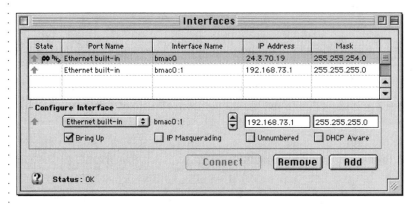

Figure 15.3 The IPNetRouter NAT gateway software can turn a Macintosh into a NAT gateway, eliminating the need for a dedicated hardware gateway.

Concerns about NAT gateways

NAT gateways are complicated, don't work right in some applications, and introduce new security concerns. If your ISP provides multiple Internet addresses, you should consider taking advantage of that option rather than using a NAT gateway.

NAT was designed after the Internet started to get popular, when it became apparent that IP addresses were going to be limited commodities. Due to its late design and its complexity, NAT does not work with all Internet protocols. A couple of Macintosh technologies that haven't worked well with NAT are QuickTime streaming and USB printer sharing. NAT's complexity also makes NAT gateways subject to bugs that can introduce security holes or create hard-to-diagnose problems in accessing the Internet. NAT gateways also can slow high-speed Internet connections due to the amount of work they have to do.

While enabling Internet access from machines on the home network, NAT usually prevents services on that network from being accessed from the Internet. Because machines on the home network don't have their own public IP addresses, access to those machines can't be initiated from the Internet. Only services on the NAT gateway's machine can be accessed directly from the Net. In general, the gateway's blocking of Internet access to services on the home network is desirable. The gateway acts, in many ways, like a network-global firewall for the home network (see Chapter 12).

A NAT gateway is a limited firewall however. If you wanted to provide Internet access to a service on your home network (such as a Mac's built-in File Sharing, for example), you would have to use a NAT feature called port mapping to enable that access through the gateway. Configuring port mapping is somewhat complex; if set up incorrectly, port mapping can open other machines on the home network to undesired access. NAT gateways usually do not have the advanced logging and monitoring features of firewalls, so it's also harder to notice unauthorized accesses and access attempts to machines on your network.

If you're going to use a NAT gateway as a network-global firewall, you should be sure to use a two-port NAT gateway. A one-port NAT gateway does not provide any isolation between the home network and the Internet (refer to Figure 15.2b earlier in this chapter). Although all access from the Internet is still supposed to go through the NAT gateway, nothing physically prevents communication from the Internet to machines on the home network. A poorly designed cable or DSL modem, for example, could be used to bypass a one-port NAT gateway and access machines on the home network, to which the modem is connected directly in a one-port system.

Additionally, a hardware-based NAT gateway usually is more secure as a firewall than a software-based gateway. Hardware gateways are much less likely to be infected with viruses that could compromise the security of the home network. Also, the machine running the software-based gateway can be accessed directly through the Internet; therefore, it is less secure than it would be behind a hardware NAT gateway or network-global firewall.

If you want to use a NAT gateway as a network-global firewall, the best one to use should have two ports and should be hardware-based.

All-in-One Home Networking Devices

Building a home network, especially one used for sharing an Internet connection, is a new experience for most people. You'll need many pieces to put one together, although these pieces are now being merged into all-in-one appliance-like devices —Apple's AirPort base station, for example. The base station serves as a wireless access point, a NAT gateway, and a dial-up modem for phone-based Internet access. Other combination devices offer features such as the capability to act as an Ethernet hub (a piece of hardware for connecting multiple devices through Ethernet cabling), a network-global firewall, a cable or DSL modem, and even a content filter for limiting the Web sites that specific home-network users (such as children) can access.

Most all-in-one home networking devices are dedicated pieces of hardware that are set up remotely and monitored through your home network. As a result, they introduce several security risks that you should take into account.

All-in-one devices need to be administered from your home network, but that network usually is connected to the Internet. Carefully managing the passwords used by these devices is important (see Chapter 4). These devices also introduce a serious security complication: many of them come with a default password. You use the default password to access the device the first time it's installed, as documented in the user's guide.

> *Because a default password is involved, for security reasons you must connect to the all-in-one device and change the password before connecting the device to the Internet.*

Hackers can find default passwords for popular all-in-one devices easily on the Net, and they are out there scanning the Net for devices that still use those default passwords. If a hacker finds such a device, he can take control of it and of your home network as well. Hackers can change the device's configuration and possibly even upload new software to it to change what it does and how it interacts with your home network. And they can do all this in such a way that you'll never even know.

Even after you change your all-in-one device's default password, never enter the new password over the Internet, because you don't know how good the device might be at encrypting that password. As a general rule, even though the device is hooked up to the Internet, you should do all your administration and monitoring of that device from your home network, not from the Net. Administration from your home network ensures that no one on the Net is spying on your conversation with that device.

Due to the need for remote administration, some all-in-one devices use a cryptic, command-line based interface, often through the popular Telnet protocol. In addition to passing cryptic commands, Telnet sends all its data in clear text, making the security risk much worse. In selecting home-networking hardware devices, look for ones that you can administer through a standard Macintosh application or through a Web-based interface. Mac-friendly administration will make these devices easier for you to set up and use and also minimize the likelihood that you will misconfigure the device and cause a security hole. Farallon's NetLINE Broadband Gateway is a good example of such a product (**Figure 15.4**).

Figure 15.4 The Web-based interface and Macintosh focus of the NetLINE Broadband Gateway make it much less likely that you'll misconfigure it and create a security hole in your home network.

All-in-one devices may have additional network-accessible features beyond configuration. If possible, you should disable the capability for these features to be accessed from the Internet and make them accessible only from the home network. If a device supports remote monitoring, or SNMP (see Chapter 9), you should disable this support or ensure that it's accessible only from the home network. By eliminating accessibility to the device from the Internet, you make it much less likely that a hacker will obtain access to that device and, through it, to machines on your home network.

General Security Precautions for Home Networks

Home networks mean more machines. More machines mean more opportunities for hackers. Although you should look over the security precautions we recommend throughout this book before setting up a home network and connecting it to the Internet, we'd like to point out a few especially important precautions in this section.

If you're going to set up a home network that will be connected to the Internet, be sure to secure each machine on the network. In particular, turn off Internet services that are not needed and properly secure those services that are needed. (We cover securing Internet services in chapters 7 through 10.) If possible, use AppleTalk protocols rather than TCP/IP to share resources, because those resources' vulnerability to attack will be less if TCP/IP is not used to share them. For instance, if you're sharing files among machines through Mac OS 9's built-in File Sharing, do not check the checkbox for enabling File Sharing through TCP/IP (**Figure 15.5**). AppleTalk will work just as well and with better security.

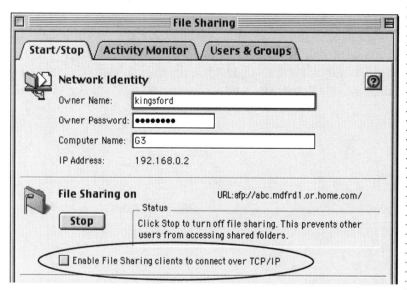

Figure 15.5 Use AppleTalk and disable TCP/IP for sharing resources, such as files, on home networks.

Although home networking devices such as NAT gateways may attempt to provide firewall functions, you shouldn't rely on their capability to do so. Personal firewalls are inexpensive and almost always provide greater flexibility and more advanced monitoring and analysis capabilities. Installing a personal fire-wall on each machine on your home network is the safest procedure. Likewise, install antivirus applications on each machine, even if you don't intend to download software to a particular machine. You run too great a risk that all machines on the network will be compromised if one machine is. (See chapters 11 and 12 for more information on viruses and personal firewalls.)

If your home network includes more than 2 or 3 machines, it's beginning to approach the complexity of some office networks. Real computer fanatics may even have home networks that are bigger and more complex than our work networks. If you have more than a couple machines on your home network, be sure to read Chapter 17 on Internet security at work. Particularly relevant to large home networks are the sections on network-global firewalls, Windows machines (if you have any on your home networks), and the ongoing transition from AppleTalk to Internet protocols.

Finally, look at Chapter 18 if you plan to run Mac OS X. Due to its Unix base, Mac OS X introduces a new set of security issues that can affect not just the machines running Mac OS X but also the other machines on your home network.

Wireless Networking

16

Every few years, Apple invents, creates, or popularizes an amazing technology. In the late 1970s, that technology was the Apple II. In the mid 1980s, it was the Macintosh and desktop publishing. In the early 1990s, it was QuickTime and the PowerBook. In 1999, after a bit of a drought, Apple did it again with AirPort wireless networking.

AirPort technology lets Macs communicate through networks created without wires. More important for the rest of us, AirPort lets Macs access the Internet without wires. If you have AirPort installed at home, you can roam around your house and yard with your PowerBook or iBook while staying connected to the Internet the whole time. You can also share your Internet connection among your home Macs without running wires all over your house. Like most networking technologies, AirPort introduces new security issues that you need to be aware of as you take advantage of its amazing capabilities.

How AirPort Works

AirPort is based on a computer networking standard called 802.11b. The 802.11b specification describes how a wireless network sends data through radio waves, in a way similar to how a cordless phone sends voices (cordless, as in the kind you use in your house, not cellular, as in the kind you use around town or in your car).

Macs shipping today are AirPort-ready, meaning that they've got the necessary antenna and special AirPort card slot built in. You can order Macs with that card installed, or you can add it later. If you have an older PowerBook that isn't AirPort-capable, you can purchase an 802.11b card for its standard PC Card slot. You won't have the built-in antenna, however, so your wireless communication probably won't go as far. (The nominal distance that Apple claims for AirPort is 150 feet.) Windows notebooks with PC Card slots can add 802.11b cards to talk on AirPort networks as well.

You can use AirPort to create peer-to-peer wireless networks of Macs—to share files on a home network, for example. But like a cordless phone, AirPort is most useful when you use it to talk to machines on a traditional wired network. Cordless phones talk wirelessly to the phone network, and AirPort machines talk wirelessly to the Internet. In both cases, the conversation goes through a base station that's connected physically to the wired network (**Figure 16.1**). The base station converts the radio waves to wired signals; it also converts the wired signals to radio waves, enabling full two-way conversation between the wireless machine and the wired network.

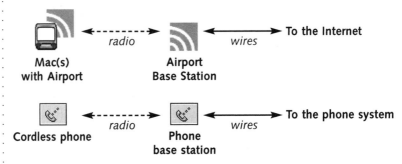

Figure 16.1 You use AirPort to talk through a base station to the wired Internet just like you use a cordless phone to talk through a base station to the wired phone network.

AirPort works at 11 Mbps, which is faster than just about all home Internet connection technologies, so this translation doesn't even slow your Internet connection. One important difference between an AirPort base station and a cordless-phone base station is that as many as 10 computers can talk through one AirPort base station at the same time.

The base station is the key to AirPort's functionality and ease of use, along with being the central point for its security. You can use a Macintosh running Apple's AirPort base-station software as a base station, but most people use Apple's flying-saucer-like hardware base station (**Figure 16.2**).

Figure 16.2
Apple's uniquely designed AirPort base station is a convenient all-in-one home networking device.

Apple's hardware base station is a Mac-focused all-in-one home networking device (see Chapter 15) that includes many useful features. It contains a built-in phone modem for talking to an ISP through a dial-up connection. It also contains an Ethernet port, which connects it to most high-speed Internet connections, such as DSL and cable. The base station can act as a NAT (network address translation) gateway for sharing a single Internet address among multiple computers on a home network. Or it can work in bridging mode, making the computers on the AirPort network appear as though they were on the Ethernet network.

You can administer the base station remotely, from either the AirPort or the Ethernet network, through an easy-to-use Macintosh application (**Figure 16.3**).

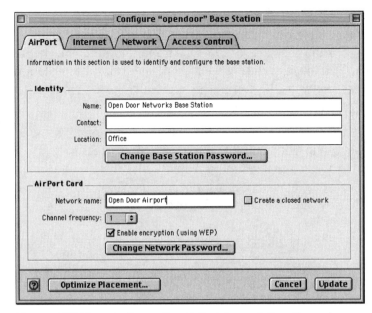

Figure 16.3 You configure the AirPort base station through an easy-to-use Macintosh application.

How AirPort Is Used

Because AirPort is versatile, you can use it in several ways.

AirPort machines can talk directly to one another, even without a base station, which permits sharing of files and other resources on those machines through a home network without wires (**Figure 16.4a**). In many cases, however, you'll simply enable wireless Internet access for a single home machine with AirPort (**Figure 16.4b**). Instead of connecting a DSL or cable modem to your machine, you connect that modem to the base station through its Ethernet port. (If you're using a dial-up connection, the phone modem is built in to the base station, so you don't have to connect one.) When the base station is connected to the Internet, you can roam anywhere within 150 feet of the base station with your PowerBook or iBook and have Internet access just as though you were connected directly. Often, if a lot of walls aren't in the way, you can go even farther than 150 feet.

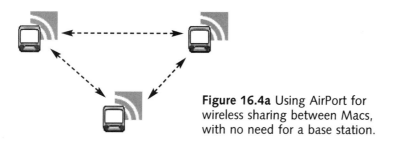

Figure 16.4a Using AirPort for wireless sharing between Macs, with no need for a base station.

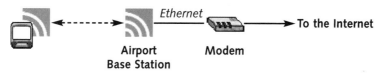

Figure 16.4b Using AirPort through a base station to provide a single Mac with wireless Internet access. Multiple wireless machines can connect at the same time.

If you already have a home network (see Chapter 15), you can use AirPort to add machines to that network wirelessly. You also can share your Internet connection among all the machines, both wired and wireless, on your network (**Figure 16.4c**). Simply connect the AirPort base station to the wired part of your home network through the base station's Ethernet port. You can then roam with your notebook machines and add new computers anywhere in your house easily without having to string wires.

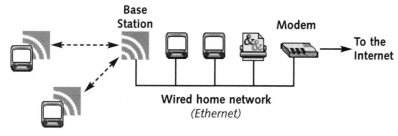

Figure 16.4c Using AirPort and a base station to add Macs to a home network wirelessly.

AirPort technology is starting to be available in public places through setups similar to Figure 16.4b but with the capability to connect multiple machines wirelessly at the same time. Coffee shops and other businesses in Ashland, Oregon, for example, make AirPort-based Internet connections available free to patrons who bring in their own notebook computers. Many other cities are following suit, and 802.11b networks are even popping up in hotels and, well, airports. Larger AirPort networks are being set up at colleges and private businesses, enabling campuswide and buildingwide wireless intranet and Internet access.

Securing AirPort

AirPort and 802.11b provide a degree of freedom that the rest of us have never had before. With AirPort, you're no longer tied to your desk if you want to access the Internet. You can roam around your house, yard, or office and still maintain your Internet connection. You can also connect wirelessly to public high-speed Internet access sites without having to plug in a single cable. With AirPort's additional freedom comes additional security risks, however.

Too much freedom

Networks based on radio waves provide too much freedom from a security point of view. Traditional wired networks can be accessed only through a physical connection to that network. Someone has to have a cable running physically from the network to do anything on that network. But radio-based networks do not require physical linkage. Anyone within range of the base station can, in theory, access that network as an active participant or as a passive spy. Unless you take special precautions, someone sitting out on the street with a Power-Book, or at your neighbor's house with an iMac, can be as much a member of your AirPort network as your own machines are.

Even if your home network is just your Mac and an AirPort base station, it's still a network. Anyone who has access to that network can see all your Internet communications. We've talked elsewhere in the book about spying on the Internet. Most Internet spies still need to tap into the Internet backbone physically, which is not easy to do. But someone on your home network doesn't need Internet access at all. A hacker can see all your wireless communications from right outside your house by running a common Mac program such as WildPacket's EtherPeek (**Figure 16.5**). If it's not configured correctly, AirPort makes it just too easy for anyone who's even a little bit curious to check out everything you're doing on the Net.

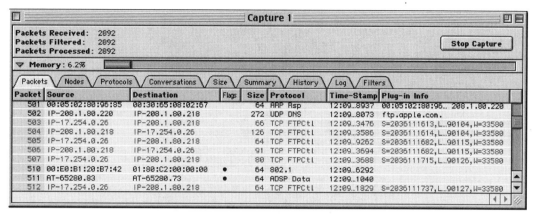

Figure 16.5 Unless you're careful, anyone with a program such as EtherPeek can sit outside your house with a PowerBook and see all your wireless communication.

The designers of 802.11b learned from similar security problems with wireless telephones (both cordless and cellular) and built antispying features into the technology. The principal antispying feature of 802.11b and AirPort is called wired-equivalent privacy, or WEP. WEP is an encryption technique that makes it difficult for someone listening in on 802.11b data to figure out what the data actually says. WEP doesn't make spying on wireless networks impossible (the encryption used is basic); it just makes wireless networks pretty much as secure as wired ones—hence, the *wired-equivalent* part of the name. With WEP enabled, you still need to take actions to prevent Internet-based spying (such as ensuring that Web sites are secure before you enter confidential information), but no more than you would on any other Internet connection.

To enable WEP on your AirPort network, you use the AirPort Admin utility to turn on WEP in your AirPort base station (**Figure 16.6**). WEP encrypts data before sending it out on the wireless network. Because any machine that's on the network legitimately (including the base station) needs to be able to decrypt that data, you choose a password for the network and tell the base station that password at the same time that you enable WEP. The password is used as the key to encrypt and decrypt the data. All users of the network must enter the password before connecting to the network (**Figure 16.7**).

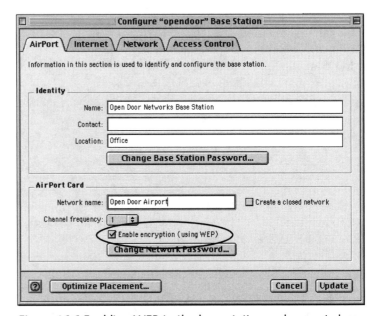

Figure 16.6 Enabling WEP in the base station makes a wireless network effectively as secure as a wired one.

Figure 16.7 When WEP is enabled, all users of the wireless network must enter the password before they can access the network.

Multiple levels of defense

WEP passwords not only prevent spying on your wireless network but also make it much harder for someone to become a member of that network without authorization. As described in chapter 7, you want to maintain as many levels of defense as you can. If a person gets on your network, he or she has bypassed some of your levels of defense, such as your network-global firewall or your use of AppleTalk instead of TCP/IP. By requiring AirPort network users to enter the WEP password, you prevent unauthorized users from getting on the network and bypassing key levels of defense.

AirPort provides levels of protection besides the WEP password. When you set up an AirPort network through the base station, you can make it a closed network (**Figure 16.8**). Users of closed networks must go through additional steps to access the network. Most important, potential users can't see the network in their list of available AirPort networks. Someone who's going around looking for accessible AirPort networks won't even know that your network exists. Someone who knows the network exists through other means still must enable access to closed networks through their AirPort application and type in the password *and* exact name of that network to gain access.

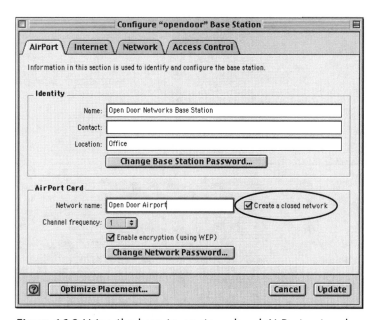

Figure 16.8 Using the base to create a closed AirPort network, which requires users to type the exact name of that network before gaining access.

An additional security measure we recommend for home AirPort networks is enabling access control in the base station (**Figure 16.9**). Access control lets you specify exactly which machines can connect through the base station to your Internet connection and wired home network. You specify a machine that's allowed to connect by its AirPort ID. A machine's *AirPort ID* is a 12-character indicator unique to the machine's AirPort card. You can find the ID on the card itself or by running the AirPort application on the machine with the AirPort card installed (**Figure 16.10**).

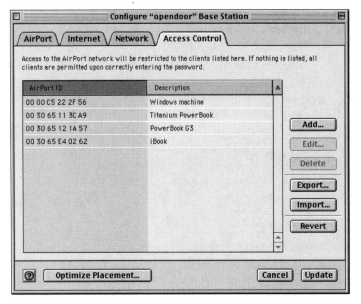

Figure 16.9 You can limit access through your AirPort base station to a specific set of machines by typing those machines' AirPort IDs in an access-control list.

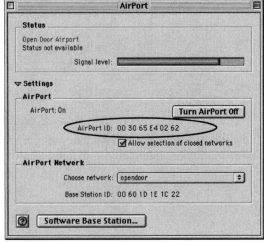

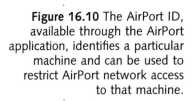

Figure 16.10 The AirPort ID, available through the AirPort application, identifies a particular machine and can be used to restrict AirPort network access to that machine.

Access-control lists are a safe way to restrict access through the base station. AirPort's access-control system, however, has one confusing aspect:

> *Access controls restrict access only from machines on the AirPort network, through the AirPort base station, to devices on the wired network (such as the modem that connects to the Internet). They do not restrict access to the AirPort network itself.*

Machines not listed in the base station's access-control list can still connect to your AirPort home network, which means that they could access any machines on that network (**Figure 16.11**). Machines that are not in the access-control list can't connect through the base station to any wired machines you might have or to your Internet connection. But you'll still want to use other security measures, such as WEP passwords, to keep unauthorized machines off your AirPort network.

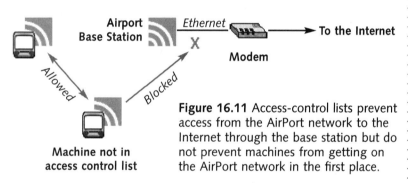

Figure 16.11 Access-control lists prevent access from the AirPort network to the Internet through the base station but do not prevent machines from getting on the AirPort network in the first place.

A final level of defense in the AirPort base station is its capability to function as a NAT gateway—a feature that you must configure through the AirPort Admin utility. As described in Chapter 15, NAT is a way of sharing a single Internet address among multiple computers on a home network. NAT can also provide some of the features of a network-global firewall (see Chapter 12), making it difficult for machines on the Internet to access devices supported by the gateway. When the base station is acting as a NAT gateway, however, it does not provide any protection from machines already on the AirPort network, and it does nothing to prevent machines from getting on that network.

A down side of AirPort's security measures is that they don't prevent a stolen machine from getting on your network if it was on the network before. When you use WEP passwords, for example, the password is saved on your Macintosh after you first type it. Saving the password makes network access more convenient at the expense of security. In the absence of additional security measures, anyone who gets hold of your Macintosh can get on your wireless network. Even the name of a closed network is saved on the machine, so closed networks don't help either. And, of course, the stolen machine will have the correct AirPort ID, so it will be authorized through the access-control list. If your machine does get lost or stolen, be sure to remove its ID from the access-control list as well as change the password for your AirPort network.

Securing the base station

The AirPort base station controls all the security aspects of your AirPort network, so you should protect it carefully. Like many all-in-one home networking devices (see Chapter 15), the base station ships with a default password.

Changing the AirPort base station's default password as soon as you hook up that base station is critical. Otherwise, someone else can change it for you and take control of the base station—and of your network. They don't even need physical access to do so.

Because all base stations ship with the same default password, that information is readily available to every potential AirPort hacker. That default password is easy to guess: public. You should change it to something much better (see Chapter 4) by running the AirPort Admin utility and choosing Change Base Station Password (**Figure 16.12**).

A second important precaution is to restrict physical access to your AirPort base station. Beyond issues of theft, anyone who knows what he's doing can reset an AirPort base station if he has physical access to that base station, and the process will take about five seconds. Resetting the base station causes the password to be reset to the default. So someone who has even temporary physical access could reset the password and connect to the base station later, without physical access, through the wireless network and the default password. For these reasons, you should put the AirPort base station somewhere that other people can't access easily.

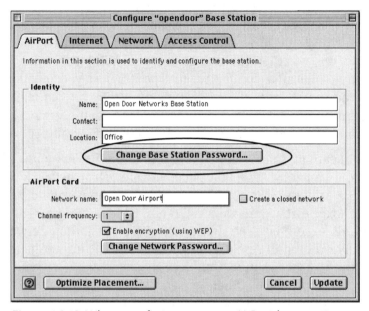

Figure 16.12 When you first set up your AirPort base station, be sure to change its password, which is the same for all base stations by default.

Apple's base station is designed for home use, in which security is not as great a concern as it is in business use. But 802.11b is becoming popular in the business world, and many companies are offering alternative base stations (sometimes called access points) that include additional security measures, such as network-global firewalls. The alternatives may be much harder to configure than Apple's base station, however. If you're considering a third-party product, follow the advice about all-in-one devices in Chapter 15, and find one that's as easy to use and as Mac-friendly as possible. Otherwise, you could compromise the security of your wireless network by mis-configuring the base station's security options.

Public access

Through careful use of AirPort's security features, you can set up a home AirPort network that's as secure as any wired network. AirPort access through public sites is another story. If you're using AirPort at a coffee shop, hotel, or airport, check the security measures that the site has put in place. You can easily tell whether the site is using a WEP password, for example, because you'll have to type it before you're granted any access. If the site is not using WEP, be particularly careful about anything you type; anyone in the area who's curious or bored could see your Internet conversations.

Also keep in mind that you're on a public network that anyone can join. The Internet itself is such a network, but access through AirPort is much more open and harder to track. The local AirPort network will not have a network-global firewall to protect you from other users on that network. It will also support AppleTalk as well as TCP/IP, further increasing the risk of unauthorized access. (Any Mac user will see your machine's File Sharing setup in the Chooser, if File Sharing is enabled, for instance.) Be sure that you're running a personal firewall (see Chapter 12) before surfing the Net through a public wireless connection. Also make sure that all your machine's services are disabled or well protected (see chapters 7 through 10). You may want to turn off AppleTalk as well (through the AppleTalk Control Panel), because most personal firewalls don't block AppleTalk access.

Internet Security at Work 17

Most of this book has focused on Internet security from an individual's point of view. Although many of us go online only using a Macintosh at home, many of us also are online when we get to work or school, and some of us go online only from there. Everything you've read so far continues to apply to online security at work, but outside the home, you need to keep additional issues in mind. In this chapter, we'll go into the nuts and bolts of protecting a group of networked users such as in a school or office.

Security Goes Both Ways

Internet security at work is integrally related to Internet security at home. Assuming that you're online both at home and work, if your home environment is secure, it's easier to keep your work environment secure, and vice versa. More important, if your home environment is not secure, you risk not only your own online safety at home but also your own and your colleagues' online safety at work.

In some rare situations, your home and work environments are totally unrelated —if you never take work files home or home files to work, maintain independent e-mail accounts and don't send anything between the two, and don't telecommute. In most cases, however, your home and work security are linked in many ways. For example:

Telecommuting. You use your home machine as your work machine too.

Dialing in to your work network from home or getting on through a VPN (virtual private network). You're not telecommuting but need occasional access to your machine or network at work.

Sharing an e-mail account between work and home. Many people use their work e-mail address as their personal e-mail address.

Bringing files home from the office on a floppy disk or other removable media.

In all these cases, your home and office security are linked directly. In most cases, your work security is at greater risk due to a compromise in home security than the other way around. Work environments tend to be more secure, so your home environment often offers the path of least resistance for an attack. Additionally, security breaches in office environments generally have more severe ramifications: A breach in security can affect more machines on your work network, and the amount of potentially exposed material usually is much greater at work than at home.

Despite the risks, many organizations provide a way to access their networks from outside. Perhaps you dial in to work through a modem or access it through a VPN. (We describe both these options later in this chapter). If so, when you're connected to your work network, you often have access to the same confidential information that you can access when you're physically at work. So if your home machine is poorly protected, a hacker could break into it (or a thief could steal it), connect to your work network, and access all sorts of stuff that they shouldn't. Usually, such access is password-protected, but if you save those passwords on your home machine or don't choose good passwords, those passwords won't be much good in keeping hackers (or industrial spies) from damaging access to anything on your entire network at work.

Even if you don't connect to your work network from home, if you take work home with you, that information will be vulnerable to any security holes you may have at home. A hacker could access work files off your home machine over the Internet, or the files could be infected with any virus that's infected your home machine. If you then took, e-mailed, or transferred those files back to the office, you could infect machines in the office. Your work environment should have adequate virus protection and other such precautions (which we'll discuss in the following section), but you don't want to test those precautions if you can avoid doing so.

Security can go the other way, too. Your work environment may have fewer security precautions than you do at home, especially if you've read this book. So don't assume that work is a completely secure environment. Your work network probably is not as wide open as the Internet as a whole, but security breaches could occur.

Centralizing Security

Most organizations provide several centralized services. In an office, purchasing is done through one department (or by one person, in a small office) and payroll through another. In a school, registration and administration are centralized. In larger organizations, computer services are centralized through an IS (information services) or IT (information technology) department, and network-specific issues are addressed by a specific network administrator. Smaller organizations may have no IS department or network administrator. Despite a lack of network training, you may be your organization's network administrator. Due to the Mac's ease of use, in a small office or department, just about anyone can be the network administrator.

If you're in the IS department, or if you've assumed the role of network administrator, the information in this chapter probably is of critical importance to you. But even if you're just a user of network services, you should understand the basics of how things should be set up so that you know as much as possible about the security environment in which you should be operating. Some of the details may seem fairly technical, but you still should be able to get a good overall picture.

Network-global firewalls

Many organizations use a network-global firewall to connect their internal network, or *intranet,* to the Internet. As opposed to a personal or machine-specific firewall (see Chapter 12), which protects the machine on which it's running, a network-global firewall protects an entire network of machines against malicious access from the Internet. Like a personal firewall, a network-global firewall allows outgoing access to the Net while offering that incoming protection.

As shown in **Figure 17.1**, a network-global firewall sits between the Internet and your intranet. If someone tries to access any of the machines or services on your intranet from the Internet, the firewall checks the access against a set of rules that have been programmed into it by the network administrator and allows the access only if it's authorized. For outgoing access attempts from your network to the Internet, the firewall usually does not get in the way; it lets the access attempt pass unchecked. (The firewall can be set up to limit outgoing as well as incoming access, however.)

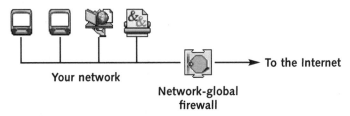

Figure 17.1 A network-global firewall protects a network against unauthorized access from the Internet.

A network-global firewall's rules use the same parameters as personal firewalls: the IP address of the machine attempting the access and the service to which that machine is trying to get access, indicated by the destination port number. A network-global firewall also uses at least one additional parameter in its rules: the IP address of the machine to which access is being attempted. Personal firewalls usually don't need to use this parameter, because the machine they're protecting almost always has only one IP address. But a network-global firewall protects several machines, each of which has a different IP address. To offer different forms or protection (via a different set of rules) to different machines, the firewall rules must include the IP addresses of those machines. Here is an example of a set of network-global firewall rules:

1. Allow access from any IP address to port 80 (the Web-server port) on the machine at IP address 10.0.0.2 (the Web server).

2. Allow access from any IP address starting with 208.1.80 (the address range of a particular business partner) to port 548 (the AppleShare file server port) on the machine at IP address 10.0.0.3 (the company-wide file server).

3. Allow no outside access to any port on any other machine.

In this example, the rules offer unlimited access to your company's Web server (so anyone can see your Web site), limited access to your company's file server to only your business partner, and no outside access to your and your colleague's machines.

Network-global firewalls are implemented several ways. Some network-global firewalls are pieces of hardware specifically designed for that purpose; they have one connection for the Internet and one or more connections for your intranet. Other network-global firewalls are processes running within your organization's Internet router. Your organization's Internet router connects your internal network to the Internet and enables your Internet access. It is a natural place to run a firewall, because all Internet traffic goes through it. The router, too, has one connection for the Internet and one or more connections for your intranet.

Another type of network-global firewall is implemented in software; it runs on a computer with multiple network connections, such as a Mac with a built-in Ethernet port and an Ethernet port added through a plug-in card. **Figure 17.2** shows an example of such a firewall implemented through IPNetRouter. As in a dedicated or router-based firewall, one port is hooked up to the Internet and the other ports are hooked up to your intranet. Software firewalls can act as routers as well. Finally, a NAT gateway (see Chapter 15) can provide many of the features of a network-global firewall.

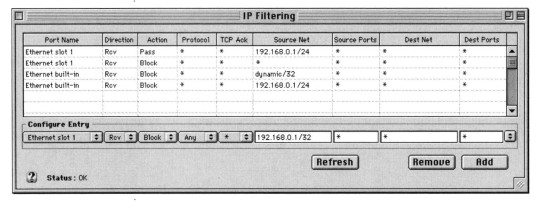

Figure 17.2 A network-global firewall implemented through IPNetRouter software.

In addition to allowing more complex rules and running on a dedicated box (as opposed to on the computer they're protecting), network-global firewalls are different from personal firewalls in several ways:

- Network-global firewalls usually are much more difficult to configure. Their rule sets are more complex, and they often don't have a keyboard or screen attached and must be configured remotely from a computer on the network. Even worse, remote firewall configuration can sometimes be done through a series of complicated keyboard commands as opposed to a graphical user interface.

- Usually, only the network administrator has access to an organization's network-global firewall, so if someone needs a rule changed, he or she has to ask the administrator.

- Network-global firewalls can be quite expensive, although less-expensive ones have been coming on the market recently.

- Network-global firewalls present a single point of failure. If your network-global firewall fails, you might not be able to access (or be accessed from) the Internet, or the firewall might provide no protection at all.

- Network-global firewalls present a single target for attack. Hackers can concentrate significant efforts on your firewall, knowing that if they break through, they can gain access to your whole network.

- The logging and monitoring capabilities of network-global firewalls are often limited or difficult to figure out.

One important final difference between a network-global and a personal firewall is that network-global firewalls don't protect against internal access. If someone on your internal network tries to access your machine, that person won't go through the network-global firewall, so none of the firewall rules will apply. This lack of internal protection of network-global firewalls has two important ramifications:

- Many attacks and thefts are made from within the organization. Network-global firewalls offer no protection against internal attacks.

- If any machine on your internal network is compromised— due to an incorrectly set rule in your network-global firewall that allows a particular attack to succeed from the Internet, for example—that machine can be used as a relay to attack any of the other machines on the network. These attacks will appear to be coming from within the organization and won't be defeated by the network-global firewall.

You should never assume that your work organization has a network-global firewall installed. Check with your network administrator to be sure. If you are your organization's network administrator, this chapter should be useful to you in determining whether to install a network-global firewall. Based on the limitations of network-global firewalls, however, everyone should consider the following advice:

Regardless of whether your organization is running a network-global firewall, you should install a personal firewall on your work machine. If the organization has no network-global firewall, the personal firewall will offer critical protection. If the organization has a network-global firewall, the personal firewall will offer additional flexibility and ease of use; more immediately accessible logging and monitoring features; and additional forms of protection, especially against unauthorized internal access.

Remote network access

Computers and internal networks, coupled with the power and omnipresence of the Internet, have become critical parts of many businesses. Most organizations find it desirable to allow employees to connect to their internal networks from outside the organization. Such remote connections can enable telecommuting, after-hours work, and access when traveling and can result in a significant decrease in costs and increase in productivity.

Remote network access presents significant challenges from a security perspective, however. Because the remote machine is not under direct control of the centralizing organization, that machine may be less secure than internal machines. Additionally, the mechanism used for remote network access is in theory accessible by anyone who has the appropriate software and information; thus, remote access presents a potential avenue of attack. In general, remote network access can be one of the biggest chinks in the armor of any well-designed security system.

By far the safest way to address this security challenge is to ban remote access to your network. If the benefits of remote network access don't outweigh the risks, then you shouldn't have such a system. But in most cases, the benefits do outweigh the risks, especially if the system is implemented carefully, with security as a primary focus.

The two principal types of remote-network-access systems are traditional phone-based dial-in services and Internet-based virtual private networks (VPNs).

Dial-in remote access

We talked about dial-in remote-access servers from an end-user perspective in Chapter 9. From a network-administrator perspective, you have to decide what type of dial-in server to implement at work. A dial-in server (**Figure 17.3**) accepts phone calls via modem, verifies the identity of the caller, and connects that caller in such a way that the caller appears to be physically connected to the network on which the dial-in server resides (albeit usually at a much slower speed than through a local connection). The decision on what dial-in server to use should take into account the security aspects of that server. Mac OS 9 has a built-in single connection server, which may be all you need for a small office. Through careful use of Users & Groups and management of passwords, the Mac OS 9 dial-in server may provide all the functionality and security necessary for a small office.

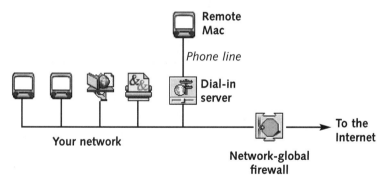

Figure 17.3 Schematic of a dial-in system.

The Mac OS 9 built-in remote-access server presents a challenge to administrators of both small and big networks, however. Because the server is built into the OS and is so easy to set up and use, others on your work network may be tempted to set up their own remote-access servers, and they may not address the major security risks associated with remote access. If you are a network administrator, you should try to prevent unauthorized dial-in servers through your security policy (see the section below on policies and procedures) and by limiting the availability of outside phone lines to network users.

In many cases, you may want to provide dial-in access through a dedicated dial-in server. Dedicated dial-in servers support multiple dial-in lines simultaneously, often with built-in modems, and provide centralized control and advanced security options. Users can be authenticated through a token-based system (detailed later in this section) or through an organizationwide directory system (see "Directory services" later in this chapter). A large number of companies manufacture and sell dial-in servers, many of which have specific Macintosh support.

A significant security risk of dial-in access is password compromise. If a user chooses an easy-to-guess dial-in password or saves that password on a laptop machine that is then lost or stolen—a likely scenario, because dial-in access is commonly used during traveling—another person easily can impersonate that user and connect to your network. Ideally, you're using good passwords for all your network services so unauthorized users can't access those services, but you never know.

Both you and network users should understand the importance of choosing good passwords and not saving them on machines used for remote access. A good security policy will help. Also, several third-party security products offer dial-in-access protection beyond passwords. Although biometric solutions (see Chapter 4) are not yet widely available, token-based systems work well with dial-in access.

Figure 17.4 A token-based system like SecurID can provide greatly increased security for networks that require remote access.

The most popular token-based system is SecurID from RSA Security (**Figure 17.4**). A token-based system is similar to a bank ATM, requiring both a physical token (the ATM card), and a password (the PIN number). In the case of SecurID, the token is a wallet-size card with a number that changes every 60 seconds. Users dialing in must enter both the currently displayed number and a password to get connected. The number and password are verified by a SecurID server back on the network being dialed in to to confirm the identity of the person dialing in.

Virtual private networks

A more flexible and often faster approach to remote network access is a virtual private network, or VPN. A VPN system works in a manner similar to a dial-in system but is somewhat more complex (**Figure 17.5**).

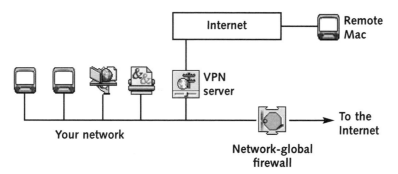

Figure 17.5 A VPN system provides a more flexible, faster remote-network-access connection by using the Internet in place of a phone line.

A VPN uses the Internet rather than dedicated phone lines for communications. Instead of connecting via phone line and modem, a remote user first establishes a normal connection to the Internet through an ISP. The user then uses that Internet connection to establish a virtual connection (often called a tunnel) through the Internet to a VPN server, which is both on the Internet and connected to the work network. The virtual tunneled connection is essentially the same as a phone connection but usually much faster, assuming that the original Internet connection is faster than a dial-in connection. As in a dial-in connection, the VPN server accepts the connection, verifies the identity of the connecting user, and connects that user so that the user appears to be physically connected to the server's network.

Unlike dial-in systems that operate through dedicated phone lines, VPNs use the public resources of the Internet. The Internet offers significantly greater flexibility and speed than the phone system, usually at much lower cost. VPNs, however, present significantly more complex security issues than dial-in systems do. VPN servers must be publicly available Internet resources, theoretically accessible to anyone. Also, all data sent through a VPN tunnel passes over the Internet and is vulnerable to spying. Therefore, VPN servers must implement significant additional security measures to address these concerns.

Like other types of Internet services, VPN service is subject to the type of attack in which a hacker uses a program to scan a series of IP addresses, looking for the service. Looking for dial-in servers in this way is much less practical, because the hacker would have to dial every phone number. If the hacker finds a VPN server, he could begin trying various user names and passwords to obtain access, such as through a dictionary attack. If the hacker obtained access, he would be able to get onto the VPN server's network, usually in such a way as to bypass any network-global firewall that might be in place. Although machines on a company's internal networks should implement their own security measures, such as good passwords and machine-specific firewalls, if attackers get on that internal network, they've gone a long way toward breaching the security of the overall system.

Due to both the significant potential for attack and the major ramifications involved with a successful attack, VPN servers usually implement advanced security measures based on an Internet standard known as IPSec. IPSec specifies three aspects of security: authentication; data scrambling (encryption); and key exchange, which is the exchange of passwords or other more advanced tools for authentication. The authentication part of IPSec is intended to thwart unauthorized attempts to connect to the server.

IPSec is flexible in allowing any of several authentication methods. One of the most secure IPSec authentication methods is based on the concept of the public-key infrastructure (PKI). Similar to SSL and the PGP secure e-mail system (see Chapter 5), PKI uses a combination of public and private keys based on digital certificates to authenticate users who attempt to connect to the system. Depending on the length of the keys used, the system can be made as cryptographically secure as desired.

PKI is a complex system, requiring significant resources on the part of the implementer. The administrator must create, manage, and distribute keys and certificates and must understand the system before it is rolled out as part of the VPN. When implemented, however, a PKI system provides the advanced level of security needed for VPN and is available for use in securing other services (such as e-mail) and for digital-signature service within the organization. In the future, new services may be based on PKI, so the system is well worth investigating if you're considering a VPN.

Simpler authentication and encryption options are available for use with VPN, but these options may be less secure. VPNs can use simple password exchange, a token-based system, or an organizationwide directory system. Some VPNs are based on standards other than IPSec and provide additional features such as the routing of AppleTalk in addition to TCP/IP. Such standards include PPTP (point-to-point tunneling protocol) and L2TP (level-2 tunneling protocol). You need to evaluate the cost versus the risk before deciding on the details of any VPN system.

After users have been authenticated to the VPN system, they usually can perform operations as though they were connected to the VPN server's network directly. The VPN tunnel simply serves as a long cord. But the data sent over this cord must travel across the Internet, from the user's machine to the ISP to the VPN server and out onto the server's network. This data can be insecure and vulnerable to spying as it travels on the Internet, just like data sent through an insecure Web page or over standard e-mail. IPSec and other VPN solutions provide options for scrambling the data as that data is transmitted, just like secure Web pages or e-mail. In fact, the mechanisms used may be the same, involving digital certificates.

Just as a digital certificate is used with SSL to authenticate the Web site and encrypt the data, digital certificates are used with VPN for both authentication and data encryption. First, the user is authenticated through the digital certificate; then data sent to and from that user is encrypted based on information in that certificate, thereby securing that data against spying. Other forms of encryption that do not require digital certificates are also available.

Even the most secure VPN systems can be compromised without user and administrator vigilance. After a machine is authenticated and connected through a VPN, that machine is an integral part of the VPN server's network. The machine can obtain access to network resources without verification through any network-global firewall that connects the network to the rest of the Internet, because the firewall cannot check the encrypted traffic passing through the secure VPN tunnel between the user and the VPN server. Although the VPN server can limit user access to specific areas, these limits are not always implemented so that VPN-connected users have the same degree of access that they do when they're physically connected. If you can place limits on access, however, you may want to do so.

To minimize vulnerabilities caused by VPN-connected machines, you should consider any VPN-authorized machine to be part of the work network any time it is connected. Users of machines that connect through VPNs need to be aware of the risks involved. Whenever VPN users are connected to the work network, they have effectively extended that work network to wherever their machines reside. Thus, any security precautions implemented at work should also be implemented at home.

All users should understand one key rule of VPNs:

> *When you're not using your home machine, you should disconnected it from the VPN.*

A worst-case scenario involves someone leaving a machine connected and going on vacation. At any time while that user is gone, someone could break into the house (a much easier proposition than entering a secure place of business) and obtain access to the work network through the VPN-connected machine. Even leaving the house to go to lunch entails unneeded risk if the VPN connection is left in place.

To minimize the risk involved with unauthorized physical access to a VPN-connected machine, both sides of the VPN connection should implement automatic disconnection. An automatic-disconnection mechanism terminates the connection after a period of inactivity (and often after other events occur). Reestablishing the connection will require reauthentication on the part of the user. Combined with emphasizing to VPN users the importance of terminating the connection whenever they're away from their machines, automatic disconnection will greatly increase the security of any VPN system.

Directory services

A centralized service for larger networks that is rapidly becoming popular is the directory service. Directory service potentially provides enhanced security and enhanced convenience. This type of service began as a simple way of determining and maintaining users' e-mail addresses. Recently, however, directory services have been used for many additional functions, such as maintaining users' digital certificates and serving as organizationwide control points.

Most directory services are based on the Lightweight Directory Access Protocol (LDAP), an evolving Internet standard for directory clients and servers. The two major directories are Novell's NDS (Novell Directory Services) and Microsoft's Active Directory. Although both systems provide only limited Macintosh support, with Mac OS X's Unix base, additional Mac support is forthcoming.

The principal convenience advantage of directory services is single sign-on. In a directory system configured this way, a network user (either local or remote) can authenticate one time with the system; from that time on, he or she is granted the appropriate levels of access to network services without needing to sign on for each one.

Single sign-on is not just a convenience advantage of directory services; it can be a security advantage as well. By eliminating or minimizing the need for users to manage multiple passwords, single sign-on allows users to concentrate on maintaining a single password. Because users have a single password to maintain, they will be more likely to adhere to recommended password-management practices (see Chapter 4). Also, because users have to sign on through the directory system only one time, the system can use advanced forms of authentication that otherwise would be impractical, such as biometrics.

Directory servers act as centralized points of control within an organization. By centralizing control, directory systems can provide security advantages beyond single sign-on. These features include:

Centralized authentication and authorization. Instead of leaving it up to individual services to implement their own, possibly flawed security schemes, a centralized authentication and authorization system can make these functions consistent across services. Concentrating these features in one system also makes much more efficient use of the developer's and the network manager's resources, because they need to implement these functions only once.

Centralized monitoring point. As we indicated in Chapter 13, logging and monitoring are crucial security aspects. Directory services can provide a centralized point for these functions. Although logging and monitoring on the individual services remain important, network managers can concentrate much of their monitoring efforts on the directory servers.

Centralized software distribution. A directory system can be used as a centralized source of software distribution, making it more likely that only security-approved, virus-checked applications will be used on the network.

Integration point. The directory system can serve as a centralized integration point, allowing the administrator to add new and improved services to the system with minimum overall disruption. The overall authentication scheme can be upgraded from simple passwords to digital certificates, for example, largely through changes in the directory servers.

Focal point of a security policy. A security policy is a crucial aspect of any organization's security effort. An organization's directory can be a focal point for developing and implementing such a policy.

Network administration

In larger organizations, having a central place for many of the administrative functions needed for the computers and for the network makes sense. Centralizing these services ensures that these functions are performed and may also reduce expenses. Important network-administration functions include monitoring machines and devices through SNMP, machine backup, and remote machine control.

SNMP (Simple Network Management Protocol) provides a way for the network manager to monitor individual machines for potential security and reliability problems. As a network manager, you may want to install the Mac SNMP client as part of the OS installation and to obtain an SNMP console for monitoring. Chapter 9 provides details on security issues relating to SNMP.

Backing up user data is critical to the reliability and security of any machine on your network. You may want to perform this function on an organizationwide basis. In other cases, you may want to implement a redundant backup strategy, in which users are responsible for backing up their own machines but an additional networkwide backup is also made. The network-wide backup can be an additional fail-safe procedure and include remote backup. Chapter 3 describes many of the security aspects associated with backup systems from an individual perspective. Most backup systems also have several advanced features for performing networkwide backup.

If you're acting as network manager, users may ask you for assistance with machine-specific problems. Alternatively, companywide support personnel may provide such help. In either case, you may want to install remote-control software, such as Apple Network Assistant or Timbuktu, on users' machines. As mentioned in chapters 9 and 10, significant security risks are associated with remote-control software, so consider whether installing it is really necessary. In smaller organizations, providing assistance where the user is working may be a better idea.

Windows Machines

If you use a network of any significant size at work, that network probably includes machines running the Microsoft Windows operating system. These machines present a variety of security challenges.

Interacting with Windows machines

You can share files with Windows machines in two ways: the Macintosh way and the Windows way. As a general rule, if your network has more Macs than Windows machines, you'll probably share files the Mac way. If the network has more Windows machines than Macs, you'll probably share the Windows way. In some cases, you may use both methods.

Macintosh file sharing normally is handled through AppleShare and the Apple Filing Protocol (AFP). Every Mac has a built-in AppleShare client (through the Chooser or Mac OS X's Connect to Server option) and a limited AppleShare server (through File Sharing). Windows file sharing is normally done through the Network Neighborhood and a protocol called Server Message Block (SMB). Windows machines also have both built-in clients and basic servers. AppleShare clients cannot talk to SMB servers (either those built into Windows or other dedicated ones), and SMB clients cannot talk to AFP servers (either those built into the Mac or other dedicated ones, such as AppleShare IP).

If you're on a network that consists mainly of Macintoshes, to do file sharing the Macintosh way, you'll need to install an AppleShare client on your Windows machines. Such a client will allow those machines to copy files to and from AFP servers. You may also want to install an AFP server on the Windows machines if you want them to provide files for Macs. Likewise, if you're on a network that consists mainly of Windows machines, you'll need to install an SMB client and possibly an SMB server on your Mac to share files the Windows way. In both cases, multiple options are available. **Figure 17.6** shows the TSSTalk AppleShare client for Windows, and **Figure 17.7** shows the DAVE SMB client for Macintosh.

Figure 17.6 You'll need to install an AppleShare client (such as TSSTalk) on your Windows machines if you want them to access the Mac's built-in file sharing or any other AFP servers.

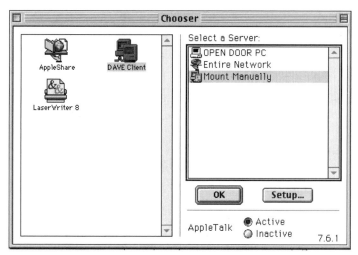

Figure 17.7 To enable Macs to access Windows machines' files, install an SMB client (such as DAVE) on the Macs.

Both AFP and SMB are relatively secure protocols. Especially if files are being exchanged over the local network, cross-platform use of either protocol to share files should present no additional security issues. You should be cautious about cross-platform exchange of files over the Internet, however, because nonnative protocol implementations (implementations of the protocol on an OS other than the one it was developed for) may not fully include all the security options of the particular protocol or may not be as well tested as native implementations. A Windows NT server can serve files to Macs through AFP, for example, but it does so without AFP's random number exchange during log in, often sending passwords across the network in clear text instead.

If you have a choice between using AFP and SMB, you should choose AFP. We recommend AFP not because this book is for Mac users; we recommend it because this book is about Internet security, and AFP is more secure than SMB. A machine running an SMB server is much more likely to be attacked than one running an AFP server. As mentioned in Chapter 2, this increased likelihood is a side effect of the fact that Windows machines are more popular than Macs. Another reason to choose AFP is that if you are running AFP internally and have no need to share files over the Internet, you can use the more secure AppleTalk protocol on both the Macs and Windows machines, rather than IP.

An additional area of Mac/Windows interaction is remote control. The popular Timbuktu application can run on either a Mac or a Windows machine and can control either a Mac or a Windows machine. If you're going to use Timbuktu from Windows to control Macs, however, be especially careful that the Timbuktu Windows machine is protected from a security perspective. Timbuktu is a powerful application, and if the Windows machine were compromised, it could wreak havoc on the Macs that it controls.

Preventing cross-platform contamination

The principal problem with using Windows machines on Macintosh networks is cross-platform contamination. Because Windows machines are much more often targets of network and virus attacks, their use on the same networks as Macs can decrease the overall security of the network. Windows machines are more likely to be compromised, possibly exposing the whole network to attack, and are more likely to spread cross-platform viruses, usually through macroviruses in documents created in cross-platform products such as Microsoft Word and Excel.

Any Windows machines on Macintosh networks must be as well protected as the Macs on that network—if not better protected. Luckily, many Windows protection options are available. As a Mac user or network administrator, you should ensure that any Windows machines on your network have antivirus and personal firewall applications installed and that their virus-definition files are kept up to date. (New Windows viruses appear at a much greater rate than new Mac viruses do.) If you use Symantec's popular Norton Antivirus and Personal Firewall applications on your Macs, you may want to consider them for your Windows machines as well (**Figure 17.8**). Symantec's Web site also can scan your Windows machines for security vulnerabilities.

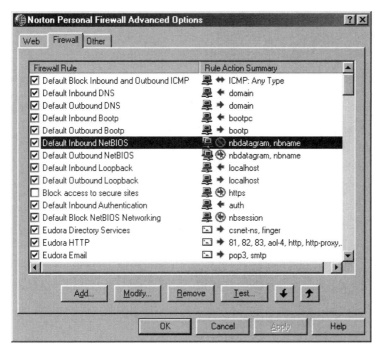

Figure 17.8 A personal firewall such as Norton Personal Firewall for Windows is critical on all Windows machines connected to Macintosh networks.

Securing Macintosh Servers

Many network administrators are server administrators as well. In addition to being responsible for maintaining the overall functionality and security of the network itself, network administrators may be responsible for maintaining the dedicated servers that are key to the functioning and safety of that network. Many server applications for the Mac OS turn Macs into dedicated servers that provide services and information within an organization and to the Internet at large. Apple even ships machines that are preconfigured as servers.

Ensuring the security of dedicated Macintosh servers could be the topic of an entire book. We cover securing the services provided by end-user Macs in chapters 7 through 10. In this section, we cover the high points of protecting your dedicated servers, from the perspective of ensuring the overall security of your network and the individual users connected to that network.

General server security

The security of your dedicated server machines and applications is critical to the security of your network, which in turn is critical to the security of individual network users. If your network is not secure, you risk the safety of the individual machines, files, and data on that network, as well as the security of each user who uses the network. Securing your servers is critical to the security of your overall network for two reasons:

1. Your servers are the key repositories of most of your important applications, documents, and other data. If a server is compromised, you risk losing significantly more information that you do if an individual machine is compromised.

2. Your servers are the front line of defense for your network, protecting the individual machines on the network. Servers may be the only machines to which the world is given access through your network-global firewall or the only machines on which applications or documents are made available to individual users. If the servers were compromised, the attacker could gain access to machines on the network that they would not have access to otherwise. These machines should have additional forms of protection (such as personal firewalls and well-managed passwords), but a successful hacker attack on your server would be a big step toward compromising those individual machines.

Server security has one simple rule:

Do everything we've been recommending so far, but do it to an even greater extent.

Consider putting your server machines in a locked room and giving keys to only a few people. You may believe a locked room to be overkill, and in some cases, it may be. But think about what would happen if visitors or disgruntled employees gained access to your servers; they could steal the servers or destroy the data. A more devious-minded hacker could install a Trojan horse or virus that could harm the server and the entire network. Most servers' security mechanisms protect against network access under the assumption that physical access to the server is controlled as well. The AppleShare IP documentation suggests that a locked room is needed for full security. In addition to being locked, the room should be as earthquake-, fire-, and floodproof as possible, and all power should be surged-protected and battery-backed-up through a UPS (uninterruptible power supply).

Perform backups of the server frequently. Consider backing up daily, if not more often. Your employees probably depend on your servers for much of what they do, and the loss of even a day's worth of data could be devastating to your business. You may use your servers to accept orders and other information from outside vendors and customers, the loss of which would have a significant impact. The automated backup applications discussed in Chapter 3 make frequent backups easy. In addition to making frequent local backups, make remote backups weekly, if possible.

Make server-administration passwords especially long and hard to guess, and follow all the other password-management rules to the extreme. Memorize server passwords, because they're so critical, and consider placing written copies of the passwords (along with keys to the locked rooms) in a safe-deposit box or other highly secure form of storage with very limited access, in case you're not around when critical server access is needed.

Monitor and analyze server use closely, looking for unauthorized accesses and access attempts. If a potential problem occurs, you want to catch it as early as possible, before an implanted Trojan horse or virus can begin to spread throughout your network, for example. Likewise, install an antivirus application on the server, and set it to scan the server daily for new viruses—probably late at night, because the scan will have a performance impact on the server. Update virus-definition files at whatever rate they are usually updated by your antivirus software vendor. You may want to check for updates even more often, just in case a major new virus is discovered between scheduled updates.

Do not allow FTP uploads to the server over the Internet. Even if users are willing to compromise their own security by using

FTP, you should not be willing to do so on your server. In general, such a compromise might affect only a particular user account, but you cannot be sure. Uploading a CGI, for example, could compromise the security of your server. Safer and more convenient upload methods are available and should be used (see Chapter 14).

The importance of your servers may mandate additional security measures. If a server is critical to your business, you may want to maintain various levels of redundancy for that server in case of a security breach or a hardware failure. The ultimate server backup would be maintaining a complete image copy of the server's disk on a daily basis. If you discovered that a security breach occurred at a particular date, you could roll the server back to before that date.

A RAID (redundant array of inexpensive disks) is another good way to add redundancy to a server, but RAIDs usually are used in case one of the disks fails. RAID disks back up one another, so a security breach would end up corrupting all disks involved. Maintaining a redundant server machine also is a good idea, but it increases only the availability of the server, not its security (although the two are closely related from your users' and customers' points of view).

Macintosh servers can crash for several reasons, including hardware and software failure, virus infection, or a denial-of-service attack. Several hardware add-ons for Mac servers can reboot the Macintosh automatically if they detect that the Mac has crashed. Devices such as Rebound and Kickoff! (**Figure 17.9**) from Sophisticated Circuits can even integrate with specific Mac servers, such as WebSTAR and AppleShare IP, to reboot the Mac if that server software stops working. These devices can also maintain log files that help you understand what went wrong and caused the reboot. By rebooting the server automatically, these devices increase both reliability and security. The log files can alert you to attacks and viruses that may cause crashes and shutdowns, and the automatic-rebooting feature may prevent the need to grant additional access to the servers' locked rooms if you're unavailable.

Figure 17.9 The Kickoff! device automatically restarts a Macintosh server that has crashed or otherwise stopped working.

As we mentioned in Chapter 7, a key way to minimize the likelihood of unauthorized access to Macintosh services is to implement those services over AppleTalk instead of TCP/IP. If your servers are internal-only and support AppleTalk, using AppleTalk and disabling TCP/IP access will generally make it impossible for those servers to be accessed from the Internet, even in the event of a firewall or VPN breach. You must be sure, however, that AppleTalk is fully routed throughout your organization, because some networks are moving away from proprietary protocols such as AppleTalk and toward the routing of only TCP/IP (see "Macintosh Networking in Transition" later in this chapter).

A final measure for increasing the overall security of any Macintosh server is to minimize the number of services that it is running. This point is key:

> *A server should run only those services that are absolutely essential to its purpose.*

Any additional services present additional opportunities for hackers and viruses, as you'll see in the following section. In a related vein, don't run end-user applications such as Web browsers and e-mail readers on the server machine.

WebSTAR security

WebSTAR (**Figure 17.10**) is one of the most popular Macintosh servers. Shipping since 1995, WebSTAR has evolved from a simple Web server to a full-fledged Internet server suite. WebSTAR is centered on its highly advanced Web server but includes such services as SSL, e-mail, FTP, and a proxy server. It offers easy integration with Macintosh databases such as FileMaker and 4D, and a highly functional interface for extending the server through CGIs (common gateway interface modules) and plug-ins.

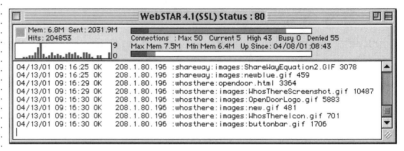

Figure 17.10 WebSTAR is a highly functional and secure Macintosh Internet server.

StarNine, the original developer of WebSTAR, has always considered security to be of paramount importance. (StarNine and WebSTAR became part of database developer 4D Inc. in 2000.) Even in 1995, the glaring security holes of Unix-based servers highlighted a growing opportunity. StarNine realized that the security advantages of the Mac OS could be leveraged to provide an incredibly secure server. By focusing on security throughout WebSTAR's development, StarNine has been proved right on many occasions. As indicated in Chapter 2, the ultimate validation of this strategy was provided by the U.S. Army when it selected WebSTAR as the server for its incredibly popular (and previously hacked) home page in 1999. No reports of break-ins to that server have been made since that time.

WebSTAR includes several built-in security features, most of which are user-configurable. Additionally, WebSTAR includes an excellent array of logging features that let you capture details of accesses and access attempts for real-time monitoring (through applications such as those mentioned in Chapter 13) and detailed postprocessing.

Crack-a-Mac

As a further test of WebSTAR's security, several "Crack-a-Mac" contests have been held. The sponsors of these contests ran WebSTAR servers on the Internet solely for the purpose of having people try to break into those servers. The sponsors also put up significant rewards ($10,000 and more) for anyone who could break into the server and do something like change its home page or obtain a credit-card number from it. Despite hundreds of thousands of recorded accesses, only one such server was ever breached, and the breaching of that server provided a key lesson in server security.

The first Crack-a-Mac challenge featured a bare-bones Macintosh running only the WebSTAR server. No additional services, CGIs, or plug-ins were run on the server. Based on the success of that challenge (no one broke in), the sponsors got a little cocky—or, as they would say, wanted to push the envelope on security a bit more. The second challenge involved a more advanced server system. The sponsors added several plug-ins to WebSTAR, including one that integrated with a FileMaker database and one that allowed users to upload their Web pages to the site. Through a combination of security holes in these plug-ins, a contestant was able to break into the server, change the home page, and collect the $10,000 prize. But the cost of that prize was well worth it to the Macintosh security community. The holes in the plug-ins were fixed, and more important, the critical lesson of service minimization was portrayed in the process. Only those services that are absolutely necessary should be run on any server. The less a server does, the safer it is.

WebSTAR serves only files within its hierarchy (that is, within the folder in which the WebSTAR application resides), which prevents it from accidentally serving other files on the machine. WebSTAR also implements a key security feature that prevents it from serving out its own internal files, regardless of where those files reside. This extra safeguard is important, because internal files include configuration details, user names and passwords, and even private digital-certificate data.

In addition to implementing only those services that are absolutely needed on your WebSTAR server, you should take other security precautions on any WebSTAR server. Keep in mind that many of WebSTAR's security features apply only to its Web-server component. FTP, for example, is intrinsically insecure (see Chapter 14), and neither StarNine nor anyone else can do anything about that situation.

Following are some of WebSTAR's security features that you should consider:

Users, passwords and realms. WebSTAR lets you define realms for different Web sites or pages. A *realm* is an area on the Web server that can be accessed by a limited set of users. When users attempt to access a realm-protected page, their browsers presents a dialog box, in which they must enter a user name and password before they can access the page. As noted in Chapter 14, however, this type of password is insecure and can easily be read over the Internet unless the page in question uses SSL. WebSTAR also supports third-party plug-ins that provide advanced access security.

Allow/deny. WebSTAR implements an allow/deny feature similar to the one implemented in most firewalls. Allow/deny lets you specify the IP addresses of users who should and should not have access to the server. Because WebSTAR's allow/deny feature is specific to its services, this feature is more flexible and fine-grained than the equivalent feature in a machine-specific or network-global firewall. You can allow or deny access within a particular realm, by host name, or by IP address (**Figure 17.11**). Allow/deny works with Web-STAR's mail server as well as its Web server.

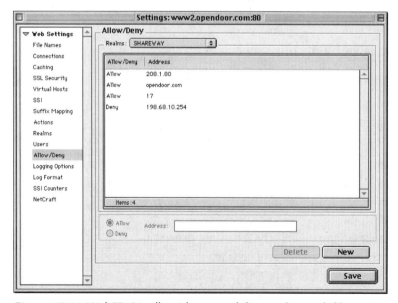

Figure 17.11 WebSTAR's allow/deny capability works much like a firewall but provides additional features specific to its services.

Remote administration. WebSTAR includes two methods for remote administration of its settings. One method is through a Web browser. Web-based administration is insecure (unless done through SSL) and not recommended in most cases. For this reason, WebSTAR alternatively makes available a custom Admin application that provides full-featured, encrypted, password-protected remote administration. You can use this application across the Internet to administer the server, although you should administer the server from your local intranet if at all possible. Doing so is faster, and you shouldn't send data over the Internet if you don't need to, even if it is encrypted.

Limiting CGIs and other executables. CGIs (common gateway interface modules) are a Web standard for extending the functionality of Web sites. CGIs are little applications that run on the server and add functionality to a site. This functionally can include processing the data entered in a form; providing a hit counter on a Web page; or interfacing with a more advanced application, such as a database. CGIs are powerful but also risky.

Being applications, CGIs have full access to anything an application on their server can access. For this reason, WebSTAR can require CGIs to be run only from a specific folder on the server. This highly recommended feature prevents users (or hackers who have obtained users' passwords) from uploading CGIs to the server and then executing those CGIs by invoking them through a custom-written Web page. Any users executing their own CGIs on a server running Mac OS 9 or earlier would have full access to that server and possibly to the server's network. (Mac OS X, being Unix-based, can limit the damage caused by such rogue CGIs.) By restricting CGIs to running from a specific folder on the server and limiting access to that folder, you can ensure that only authorized users (or better yet, no one) can upload and execute CGIs (**Figure 17.12**).

Other executables can present the same sort of risk on the server. Server plug-ins are like CGIs, but they execute through an API proprietary to WebSTAR. Plug-ins cannot be uploaded to the server by users, so they do not present the same risk as CGIs. SSI (server-side includes) executables, however, are similar to CGIs in this regard and should be limited to their own folder through an equivalent option provided with WebSTAR.

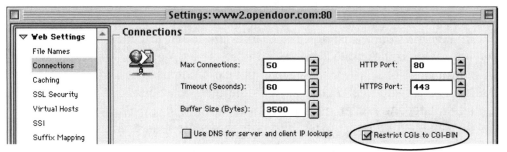

Figure 17.12 WebSTAR's option for limiting CGIs to a specific folder is critical to preventing rogue CGIs from being uploaded and executed.

AppleShare IP security

AppleShare IP (**Figure 17.13**) is Apple's Mac OS 9-based Internet server suite. In many ways, AppleShare IP is similar to WebSTAR, but it has some additional features and lacks others. Like WebSTAR, it includes Web, FTP, and e-mail servers.

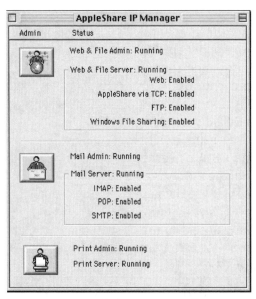

Figure 17.13 AppleShare IP is Apple's Mac OS 9-based Internet and file-sharing server. It provides several advanced features but lacks an SSL server.

Additionally, it includes a print server; an advanced AFP (Apple Filing Protocol, or AppleShare) file server; an SMB server for easy file sharing with Windows machines, which use this protocol the same way that Macs use AFP; and the Apple Network Assistant Administrator (see Chapter 9). It also includes a basic machine-specific firewall and DNS (domain name server). Despite this wide variety of applications, AppleShare IP does not include an SSL server, which is a key omission from a security perspective.

One main difference between Apple-Share IP and WebSTAR is the security model. WebSTAR bases its model on realms and an allow/deny metaphor. AppleShare IP bases its model on an extended version of the Macintosh standard Users & Groups (see Chapter 7). As is true of much of AppleShare IP, this model results in easier setup and use at the expense of a minor sacrifice in certain security areas. The main security problem with the Users & Groups model is that a user's password must be the same for all services provided by AppleShare IP. Secure services such as AppleShare file service (AFP) and e-mail (assuming that APOP is used) must share the same password with insecure services such as FTP and non-SSL HTTP (Hypertext Transfer Protocol).

Due to the security limitations in AppleShare's Users & Groups model, if the server is accessed over the Internet, you should consider the following precautions:

Do not use password-based FTP (see Chapter 14). If a user were to use password-based FTP, he or she could compromise not just the FTP service but also all other services to which he or she has access.

Try to avoid using password-based HTTP, which, without SSL, is only slightly more secure than FTP.

Require the use of APOP for e-mail. AppleShare IP has the capability to enforce APOP use, which we highly recommend.

If users must use password-based FTP or HTTP, you should give those users different user names for those services than for the secure services, such as AFP and e-mail.

AppleShare IP provides for separate guest accounts for each service, so you can let anyone access the Web sites served by AppleShare IP without necessarily giving them access to files through AFP, for example.

AppleShare IP's Users & Groups information can be shared across AppleShare servers on an intranet, so if you have multiple AppleShare servers, you need to set up the Users & Groups information only once. This ease-of-use feature also presents a security risk, because someone could use the protocol used for Users & Group sharing to obtain details about the Users & Groups file over the Internet. You should disable this feature unless you need it, and if you do use it, you should block Users & Groups exchange over the Internet through your firewalls.

Perhaps to compensate for the security shortcomings in its Users & Groups model, AppleShare IP implements advanced security features for passwords (**Figure 17.14**). These features help you and your users implement many of the recommendations in Chapter 4. As an AppleShare IP administrator, you can require that users' passwords be a certain minimum length, and you can disable a user's capability to save a password through the AppleShare client (not shown in the figure). You can also have a password expire after a certain amount of time, requiring the user to change the password the next time they log in. Another excellent security feature is the capability to disable a user's account after too many failed login attempts. This feature goes a long way toward preventing the repetitive password attacks described in Chapter 4.

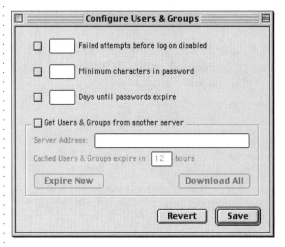

Figure 17.14
AppleShare IP implements a number of advanced password security features.

One novel password feature of AppleShare IP has been the subject of much debate. Any AppleShare administrator can log in to the file server as any other user simply by specifying that user's name and the administrator's password. This ease-of-use feature is intended to give the administrator the ability to see the server the way a particular user does. The theory is that the administrator has full access to the server anyway, so looking at it from the limited point of view of a user is not a security compromise. This feature makes it even more important that administrators' passwords be chosen carefully, because if that password were to be compromised, the person who acquired it would be able to log in and act as any user (assuming that this person knew the other users' login names).

AppleShare IP's Web server supports the same CGIs and plug-ins as WebSTAR. It does not, however, provide the capability to limit a CGI's execution to a particular folder. A malicious user who obtained a legitimate user's password could upload a CGI and execute that CGI from a Web page. So keeping users' passwords secure is even more important in this case.

Another security limitation of AppleShare's Web server is that it may display a list of any directory inside the folder designated as the Web folder. Like the Mac's built-in Web Sharing feature (see Chapter 8), this ease-of-use feature is a security risk, because it allows users to browse for and potentially access files that they wouldn't otherwise know existed. The feature can be disabled through the Server Admin application, and disabling it is recommended (**Figure 17.15**).

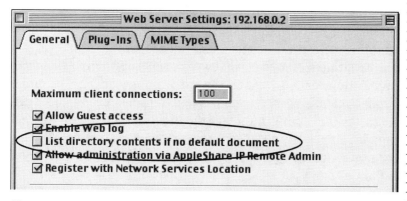

Figure 17.15 For security purposes, you should disable AppleShare IP's directory listing option.

AppleShare IP's file server is a much-enhanced version of the Mac's built-in File Sharing service, supporting many more users and groups and including advanced security features. The file server supports an API called User Authentication Modules (UAMs) that enables developers to replace or supplement AppleShare's security scheme with one of their own or with an existing scheme such as a directory service. UAMs are available from third parties.

The file server also has an advanced feature that can disconnect any user who has been idle for a specified period. This feature minimizes the security risk of a user's connecting to the server and then leaving his or her machine accessible with the server mounted. Although not as potentially devastating as leaving a machine connected through a VPN, leaving a server mounted this way still enables a malicious user who has physical access to the machine to implant a Trojan horse or virus on the server through the user's account or to delete or modify the user's files on the server.

AppleShare IP's UAM and automatic-disconnection features do not work through its SMB file server, which is intended for access by Windows machines without requiring any modifications to those machines.

Like WebSTAR, AppleShare IP includes two forms of remote administration: a custom application and a Web-based interface. As is the case with WebSTAR, AppleShare IP's Web-based administration is insecure. Apple does use a custom Java applet to encrypt the admin password, so using AppleShare's Web Admin across the Internet for limited operations that do not send confidential data is somewhat safe. Apple's remote admin application, called Mac OS Server Admin, can be run either locally on the server or across an intranet or the Internet. Running this application across the Internet is not recommended, however, because Apple does not make available any data on whether, or how, data sent to and from Mac OS Server Admin is encrypted.

Finally, AppleShare IP includes a basic machine-specific firewall called TCP Filter. The firewall can block access attempts based on the sender's IP address and the destination port number, which specifies the service to which access is being attempted. TCP Filter does not include any logging capabilities, however.

Security suites for WebSTAR and AppleShare IP

Many third-party add-on products are available for WebSTAR and AppleShare IP. But because most of these products will provide another application in which security flaws can be exploited, you should not install most of these unless you need them. Some add-on products, however, are designed to enhance the security of the server. Two of these are Open Door Networks' Security Suites for WebSTAR and AppleShare IP (we mention these not because we helped Open Door create them but because we feel what they do is critical to the security of your servers).

Both security suites attempt to present an integrated approach to server security and include documentation, templates, and examples targeted at enhancing the security of the server machine on which the components are installed.

The central product in both suites is DoorStop Server Edition (**Figure 17.16**). DoorStop, a machine-specific firewall (see Chapter 12), is an advanced version of the TCP Filter application included with AppleShare IP. DoorStop includes logging, which is a central feature of any security system (see Chapter 13). It also can specify firewall rules based not only on the sender's IP address and the destination port but also on the receiver's IP address. This capability, called multihoming support, is useful on servers that provide Web or other services on multiple IP addresses from the same Macintosh. (Multihoming is useful for creating multiple virtual Web sites, each with its own domain name, on the same machine.) Templates included with the suites provide examples of ways to configure DoorStop to maximize security on both servers.

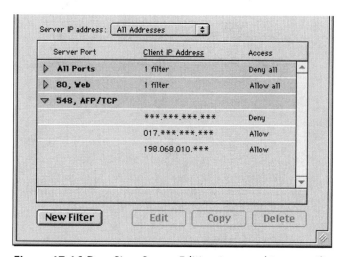

Figure 17.16 DoorStop Server Edition is a machine-specific firewall for use with servers such as WebSTAR and AppleShare IP.

Both suites also include the LogDoor real-time server monitor (**Figure 17.17**). LogDoor adds key monitoring and analysis capabilities to the server, enabling administrators to monitor access attempts in real time, thereby increasing the likelihood that security violations or violation attempts will be detected as early as possible. LogDoor can monitor and analyze the log files created by the Web server and by DoorStop. It also can monitor and analyze AFP log files, such as the ones created by AFP Logger and ShareWay IP. AFP Logger is the third component of the security suite for AppleShare IP, and ShareWay IP Personal Edition is the third component of the security suite for WebSTAR. Suite templates include examples of ways to configure LogDoor to monitor server accesses.

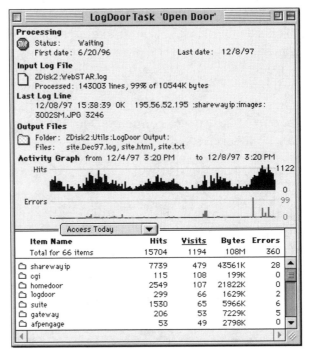

Figure 17.17 LogDoor adds critical real-time monitoring and analysis capabilities to WebSTAR and AppleShare IP.

AFP Logger (**Figure 17.18**) adds logging capabilities to the file-server (AFP) component of AppleShare IP. Without AFP Logger, the only record of users connecting to the file server would be through the DoorStop log, and then only if they connected via TCP/IP. (DoorStop does not log or block AppleTalk accesses.) The DoorStop log is also service-independent and thus limited to basic TCP/IP information for each access or access attempt. AFP Logger provides the AppleShare administrator a detailed log of all AFP accesses and access attempts. The log includes such information as the user name under which the access was attempted, whether the access succeeded, and the file or folder that was accessed. Combined with real-time analysis and monitoring through LogDoor, AFP Logger significantly increases the overall security of the server by providing details about access of what is often its most heavily used service.

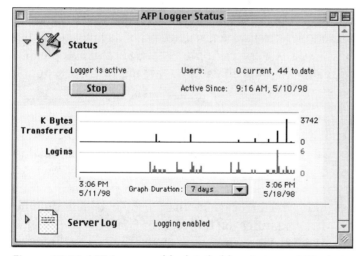

Figure 17.18 AFP Logger adds detailed logging capability to the file-sharing (AFP) component of AppleShare IP.

WebSTAR does not include an AFP server. AFP capability is essential to the security of the server; otherwise, FTP might need to be used to upload Web sites or otherwise copy files to the server. WebSTAR can take advantage of the Mac's built-in File Sharing to provide AFP serving capability. Before Mac OS 9, however, File Sharing worked only over AppleTalk, not over TCP/IP. The addition of ShareWay IP Personal Edition (see chapters 8 and 10) was required to provide AFP over TCP/IP capability. Even under Mac OS 9, the version of ShareWay IP included with the OS to implement File Sharing over TCP/IP is limited from a security perspective and does not provide logging. For these reasons, the security suite for WebSTAR includes the latest version of ShareWay IP Personal, adding File Sharing over TCP/IP to WebSTAR machines running Mac OS 8, and critical logging and other security features to WebSTAR machines using Mac OS 9's TCP/IP File Sharing feature.

Mac OS X Server

With the introduction of Mac OS X, Apple created a platform on which it can leverage the popularity of the Unix operating system for running Internet servers. Although the reasons for Unix's popularity for servers are open to debate, Unix has traditionally provided greater functionality and better performance at the high end of the server spectrum than desktop computer operating systems such as the Mac OS and Windows. With Mac OS X Server, Apple is migrating its AppleShare IP functionality to Unix to take advantage of Unix's popularity in the server arena.

Keep in mind that the current version of Mac OS X Server is the second one by that name. The first Mac OS X Server, which shipped in early 1999, was based directly on Unix technology acquired in Apple's purchase of Next. Although some attempts were made to add a Mac-like user interface to the product, it was more a Unix system than a Mac OS. It did include many of the features of the current Mac OS X Server, such as an Apache Web server, a QuickTime streaming server, WebObjects middleware, and an AppleShare-like AFP server. It also included NetBoot support for network-based booting of Macs and Macintosh Manager for further controlling the environment and access rights of Macs on internal networks. (Macintosh Manager replaced a similar product called At Ease.) The first Mac OS X Server was the first Apple product to be based on the Darwin open-source model; much of its source code was available for public inspection and even modification.

The current Mac OS X Server (**Figure 17.19**) is based on Mac OS X and is a full-fledged Macintosh product. It includes all the features of the preceding Mac OS X Server and of AppleShare IP and it is highly functional and easy to use. Because Mac OS X Server—and Mac OS X itself—are new products and have not yet had significant security analysis, we can only cover a few of the security issues that you should watch out for. Be sure to read Chapter 18 for more information.

Figure 17.19 Mac OS X Server is a full-fledged Macintosh server that takes advantage of Mac OS X's Unix base.

Mac OS X Server addresses several security shortcomings of AppleShare IP. Most important, it includes a complete SSL server, enabling the publishing of secure Web pages for both internal and external use. Additionally, Mac OS X Server's Unix base significantly limits any exposure to rogue CGIs or other applications, because CGIs and applications in general are run in a much more limited environment. One advantage of Unix over the traditional Mac OS is that it can run applications such as CGIs in walled-off environments, where they don't have access to the other applications or to the OS. Mac OS X Server also includes an implementation of the emerging WebDAV (Web-based distributed authoring and versioning) standard. WebDAV includes a wide variety of features for shared development and uploading of Web sites; ideally, it will replace the insecure FTP as the method of choice for Web-site upload.

Mac OS X Server's NetBoot and Macintosh Manager features give network administrators significant control of machines on their networks. Administrators have centralized control of the

OS configuration that users see, what network resources they can access, and even which applications they can run. In general, more control means more security. Before these features, enforcing any sort of security policy was difficult (see "Policies and Procedures" later in this chapter). With NetBoot and Macintosh Manager, an organization's security policy can be made much more meaningful.

Mac OS X includes full support for the LDAP directory system as well as a simple directory system called NetInfo (see "Directory services" earlier in this chapter). NetInfo, developed by Next before it was acquired by Apple, provides many of the features of other directory systems without requiring the same level of management and infrastructure. It is, however, proprietary to Mac OS X (and Next) networks. Finally, Mac OS X includes a machine-specific firewall, based on Unix's built-in firewall functionality.

Mac OS X Server's Unix base can be both a good and a bad thing from a security perspective. Its open-source code enables worldwide scrutiny and speedy repair of security holes, making Unix by far the most-analyzed and most-tested OS in the world. On the other hand, open source enables an expert hacker to find holes that he might not have been able to find otherwise. Additionally, Unix is most hackers' OS of choice, so many scripts are available for hacking Unix. In the SANS Institute's January 2001 list of the Ten Most Critical Internet Security Threats, five applied only to Unix; one applied to Microsoft Windows, and four were general. Only one of the four general threats mentioned the Mac OS.

Unix also has an incredibly large base of tempting Internet applications. Before adding any new application to a server, however, analyze that application carefully from a security perspective.

Policies and Procedures

To some people, the concepts of policy and procedure are very un-Mac-like. The Macintosh is in some ways a statement that we're not going to toe the party line when that line asks us to do things the difficult and painful way. Remember the "1984" commercial? Policies and procedures remind us of Big Brother; the Mac reminds us of the woman throwing the hammer.

Nonetheless, policies and procedures are necessary in any medium-size or large environment if security is of any concern. The trick is to manage those policies and procedures in such a way that they are accepted, understood, and even embraced by everyone involved.

Inside jobs

Just as in the physical world, many crimes in the virtual world are inside jobs, committed or abetted by someone within the victim organization. Sometimes, participation by the organization member is intentional; at other times, an outsider simply takes advantage of that person. Statistics vary, but almost all businesses have lost significantly more money due to insider attacks than due to external hacking from the Internet.

Organizations are especially vulnerable to insider attack if they are using a network-global firewall as their principal form of Internet security. Almost all trusted members of an organization are provided a computer with a network connection inside the firewall. These users' access to services on the company network is direct and does not pass through a network-global firewall, because the firewall is meant to protect against threats coming in from the Internet. If a trusted member's machine is compromised in any way (either intentionally or through a Trojan horse), a critical level of protection is bypassed (**Figure 17.20**). Other levels of protection should remain active, but the overall security of the network clearly has been degraded.

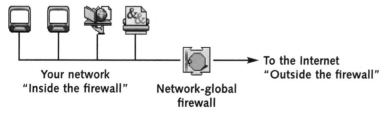

Figure 17.20 Machines inside the firewall provide a significant additional security risk if they are compromised.

An important way to combat attacks initiated inside the firewall is to implement multiple levels of security on all services and machines. The more levels of security you have, the harder it is for any attacker to breach that security. Your organization should implement as many of the security measures described in this book as possible. Well-managed passwords, personal firewalls, and antivirus applications are critical security measures, in addition to a network-global firewall.

Another way to combat attacks initiated inside the firewall (and insider attacks in general) is to implement a *level-of-trust system*. A level-of-trust system assigns degrees of trust to users within the organization and maps trust levels to access levels. The president of an organization might have access to all services on the organization's network, but a college intern might have limited access. All affiliates of an organization are implicitly trusted to some extent. Just providing an affiliate access to the organization implies some trust, and providing a computer and network access inside the firewall implies a good deal more trust. But what users can access on the network is where level of trust really matters. The more users can access, the more they can affect, intentionally or unintentionally. If someone can't access a particular file server, for example, he or she can't introduce a virus onto that server.

People should have access only to what they really need to do their jobs and only to what they can be trusted to use. Anything else compromises the security of the whole organization. On the other hand, productivity can be hurt if employees don't have access to the resources they need to do their jobs or if they feel mistrusted. So an administrator must walk a fine line in determining and implementing levels of trust. Trusting everyone fully is tempting but probably the worst security policy possible.

Formal security policy

In the small organizations in which Macs are popular, formal policies and procedures may not be needed. If you own your own company or run a family business, you generally can manage things as they come up. The overhead of developing and maintaining formal policies and procedures may not be worth the cost.

In the case of security, however, all organizations can benefit from at least thinking about the need for a security policy, and most can benefit from creating one. A security policy documents, in a clear and concise way, how the organization addresses the myriad security issues that it may encounter in day-to-day business.

Security policies serve several goals:

- They help an organization think about and address security issues.
- They provide guidelines for how employees and the organization as a whole should react to security threats and incidents.
- They help propagate awareness of security issues throughout the organization.
- They provide an easy way to educate new employees about security issues.
- They prevent misunderstandings by documenting security rules.
- They serve as important documents should legal issues arise concerning an organization's security implementation.

Security policies should always be written. They should be developed with input from across the organization, so that all personnel feel that they have been involved in the process. Policies should also be maintained in that way, so that everyone continues to feel involved and continues to keep the security policy in mind. A security policy is not static, because the Internet and technology in general are not static. An important part of any security policy is its provision for change.

As is the case with levels of trust, most security policies must strike a balance between being too strict and too lax. If a policy is too strict, it will prevent organization members from doing their jobs and get in the way of progress. If the policy is too lax, it won't serve much purpose. Each organization will be different in this respect.

All organization members must know about the security policy and understand its purpose. They should understand that the policy exists for the benefit of the organization and for its individual members. If anyone has concerns about the policy, those concerns should be discussed and addressed throughout the organization. If people resent a security policy, they will not follow it to as great a degree as they would if they accepted the policy.

A formal security policy should include several items. A large organization with many employees and affiliates has more risk than a small organization, so its security policy should be longer and more detailed. Following are some aspects of a security policy that your organization should consider:

Level of trust. A security policy should include a clear explanation of the need for a level-of-trust scheme, as well as the details. Defining levels of trust probably is the most important part of the policy.

Acceptable use. This part of the policy states what uses of the internal network and the Internet are considered to be acceptable. Clearly specifying unacceptable use may prevent employees from using the network in ways that could affect overall security.

Adding new machines. If organization members want to add a new end-user machine or server to the network, how do they go about doing so? Often, they should go through a central organization that can make sure that security issues are addressed adequately.

Backups. Users should know to what degree they are expected to maintain their own local and remote backups and to what degree the organization performs backups for them.

Software use. One of the most important parts of a software policy is a list of those applications that should always be run, such as an antivirus application and a personal firewall. The policy should also document what applications should not be run and how a user determines whether a particular application may be run or not.

Passwords. The policy should state password requirements, such as minimum length, disallowed password types (such as names or initials), and the rate at which passwords should be changed. Some services, such as

AppleShare IP, can enforce a password policy directly by rejecting disallowed passwords automatically and requiring periodic password changes.

Remote access. The policy should state how and whether users can access the organization network remotely. The "Centralizing Security" section of this chapter points out the serious risks involved with remote access. If remote access is not allowed, the policy should clearly explain why.

Taking work home. The policy should state what, if any, company documents (physical and electronic) and equipment can be removed from the premises or accessed from home or the road. Working from home can significantly increase an employee's productivity and overall satisfaction, but the policy needs to address security risks.

Information protection. The policy should state how an employee handles company information so as to maintain its confidentiality. A critical part of an information-protection policy states what information should and should not be sent via e-mail, both within the organization and outside it, and should emphasize the insecure aspects of e-mail (see Chapter 5).

Incident-escalation procedures. The policy should state what employees should do if they discover a potential security problem. Incidents usually should be brought to the attention of an individual or group responsible for dealing with the incident. The policy should also state how that individual or group should escalate the incident up the management chain as needed.

Exceptions. No policy should be so rigid that there can never be an exception to it. But the exact method through which exceptions are suggested, approved, and documented needs to be clearly spelled out.

Expect the unexpected

The only constant is change. This maxim applies to an incredible extent on the Internet. Organizations' security policies and procedures need to expect constant and rapid change—new hardware and software; new hacker attacks, viruses, and other threats; new security options; and new management and company ownership. Your policies and procedures need to expect and react to change. As a particularly relevant example, the Macintosh is going through two overlapping changes that affect network security: a migration from AppleTalk to Internet protocols, and a move from Mac OS 8/9 to Mac OS X. Because these changes are so significant, we'll devote the rest of the chapter to them.

Macintosh Networking in Transition

Macintosh networking is in the middle of what can be considered to be the biggest transition of any computer network system. Until recently, Macintosh networking had two underpinnings. The first was the Mac OS itself, which, despite continuous evolution and enhancement, has remained fundamentally the same since the Mac first shipped in 1984. The second was the Mac's built-in AppleTalk protocols, which have provided innovative, easy-to-use, and secure network services for the Mac OS since 1985.

Mac OS X and its Unix base represent a significant set of changes in the way that the OS provides services to applications, such as network systems. Apple has done an excellent job of shielding the internals of Unix from its users and making Mac OS X look much like previous versions of the Mac OS. The internal workings of Mac OS X become much more apparent at the network level, however, especially in terms of security.

AppleTalk served the Apple community well for its first 15 years or so and pushed the envelope in networking ease of use (just as the Mac did in computer ease of use). But with the tremendous popularity of the Internet and Internet protocols, Apple came to realize that it needed to phase out use of AppleTalk on Macintosh networks in favor of IP. Apple only had so many resources, and it needed to concentrate on IP to have the Mac continue as the Internet machine of choice. This transition, under way since 1997, accelerated recently with the shipping of Mac OS 9 in 1999 and Mac OS X in early 2001.

Even with both of these major changes occurring simultaneously, if you use a single Macintosh and simply surf the Internet through a dial-up, DSL, or cable-modem connection, these ongoing changes should not affect you in a big way. (Be sure to read Chapter 18 if you're using Mac OS X, however.) If you use or run a Macintosh network at work, you need to consider the effects of these ongoing changes, especially in terms of security.

Macintosh network security in transition

You should focus on one simple, critical issue when you think about the Macintosh networking transitions:

> *Unless they are carefully implemented, the transitions from Mac OS 9 to Mac OS X and from AppleTalk to IP can result in a significant decrease in the overall security of your Macintosh network.*

Any transition involves risk, because administrators and users are learning about and adopting new technologies and services. Many factors are unknown, and mistakes can be made. When two transitions are made in parallel, the unknowns and risks are even greater. But the reason why these Macintosh networking transitions involve so much security risk is more fundamental:

> *Without specific and focused attention on security issues, each transition, from Mac OS 9 to Mac OS X, and from AppleTalk to IP, will result in a less-secure network.*

The transitions would be risky enough if the systems being adopted were *more* secure than the ones they are replacing. In this case, however, both systems are *less* secure.

From AppleTalk to IP

Several factors contribute to the potential decrease in security in moving from AppleTalk to IP. The Internet was designed and originally used principally by engineers and educators; no one expected that the Internet would be used by millions of people worldwide or that Internet protocols would be used on internal networks as well as on the Internet. Therefore, fundamentally insecure protocols arose, such as FTP and Telnet. Although Internet designers now realize that security is a paramount issue in the Internet's evolution, they continue to struggle to get overall security up to the level needed for the Internet to be the main worldwide telecommunications system for the 21st century.

AppleTalk, on the other hand, was designed for use on internal networks in which security was going to be a concern. Apple wanted to sell the Mac to businesses, schools, and other large organizations, all of which required not only functionality and ease of use but also security. Learning from the mistakes of the early Internet, Apple designed a system that could grow into large-scale use while remaining secure at the same time.

Another reason why moving from AppleTalk to IP can result in a decrease in overall security is popularity. AppleTalk protocols are less popular than Internet ones. Just as the popularity of Windows machines has resulted in significantly more Windows-specific hacking attacks and viruses, the popularity of the Internet has resulted in many more attempts to hack IP-based systems than AppleTalk ones. Hackers are much more familiar with IP, and many more tools exist for hacking IP than for hacking AppleTalk.

A final major reason for the security of AppleTalk systems is that AppleTalk is not routed over the Internet. IP-based internal networks (intranets) speak the same language as the rest of the Internet. When an intranet is connected to the Internet (through a router and, ideally, a network-global firewall), it becomes possible for its machines to talk to machines anywhere on the Internet. It also becomes possible for machines anywhere on the Internet to talk to—and conceivably hack—machines on the intranet. Macs speaking AppleTalk on networks also connected to the Internet do not have this risk (**Figure 17.21**), because the Internet does not pass AppleTalk between machines and networks connected to it (other than, sometimes, within a particular ISP's local network). Even if one Mac needs to speak TCP/IP to access resources on the Internet, other Macs and servers on the AppleTalk network are not at risk.

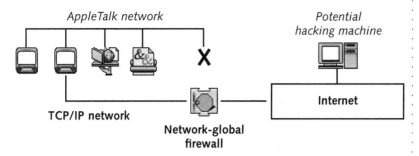

Figure 17.21 AppleTalk is not routed over the Internet, resulting in significantly higher security for networks that use AppleTalk protocols internally.

From Mac OS 9 to Mac OS X

The transition from Mac OS 9 and earlier to Mac OS X is just starting, so less is known about the security issues involved than about the transition from AppleTalk to IP. Unix, on which Mac OS X is based, has been around for almost as long as the Internet has, however, and its networking security issues are well understood. Whole books have been written on the subject of Unix security, and we discuss many Macintosh-related Unix security issues in Chapter 18. Mac OS 9 and earlier do not include many of the features that cause Unix systems to be at high risk:

- The design of Mac OS 9 and earlier is proprietary. Apple has kept secret most of the source code that provides details of how the Mac OS works, making it much more difficult for hackers to look for flaws. Unix source code is publicly available.

- Mac OS 9 and earlier evolved as a single-user OS. The OS has little support for multiple users accessing a specific machine at the same time, either from the keyboard of that machine or over the network. Unix's multiple-user and remote-control features are some of the easiest features to exploit over networks.

- Most Mac OS networks were not accessible over the Internet until recently and thus were secure from Internet hacking. Because Macs could not be hacked over the Net, hackers concentrated on other systems (mainly Unix) and didn't learn how to hack Macs. Thus, the state of the art in Mac hacking is years behind Unix hacking.

Although the Mac OS has a much higher installed base than Unix, Unix still evolved as the operating system of choice for many hackers.

The transition from Mac OS 9 to Mac OS X involves one additional security complication: Mac OS X includes a virtual Mac OS 9 machine (**Figure 17.22**). So that Mac OS X could run applications written for Mac OS 9 and earlier, Apple implemented a Mac OS X process called "Classic" that essentially is a complete copy of Mac OS 9. Because pre-Mac OS X applications, including many networking applications, run in the Mac OS 9 environment, you need to continue to worry about Mac OS 9 security issues even on machines that you migrate to Mac OS X.

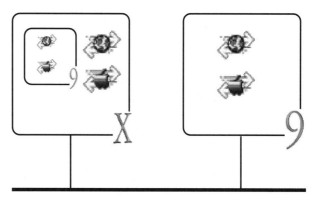

Figure 17.22 Mac OS X includes a virtual Mac OS 9 environment.

Transition management

When you face the daunting task of managing these two major transitions, keep in mind that both transitions have been designed to be implemented gradually and more or less independently. You can migrate your network from AppleTalk to IP without moving a single machine to Mac OS X, because most applications and services will support Mac OS 9 and earlier for some time to come. In fact, we recommend migrating from AppleTalk to IP first in many cases. The longer you can hold off on the Mac OS X migration, the better it will be understood. Additionally, the functionality of Mac OS X should increase rapidly as Apple fills in some missing pieces and third parties port their applications to the new OS.

In theory, you can migrate machines on your network from Mac OS 9 and earlier to Mac OS X without moving your network from AppleTalk to IP. The first release of Mac OS X lacks full support for certain AppleTalk services, however. Most significant is the lack of support for AppleTalk-based file sharing, making a purely Mac OS X transition (without a concurrent AppleTalk to IP transition) somewhat problematic. If you use Mac File Sharing at all (and most of us do), before beginning the transition to Mac OS X, you may want to migrate partially from AppleTalk to IP by getting any Mac sharing files to support both protocols (through products such as Apple-Share IP and ShareWay IP). Later releases of Mac OS X may well have more complete support for AppleTalk, eliminating any immediate need for the AppleTalk-to-IP migration.

Migrating slowly is a good idea and pretty much a requirement. Many applications will not support Mac OS X for some time, and some never will. Although most of these applications can run in the Mac OS 9 environment in Mac OS X, others will not. Additionally, many Macs cannot run Mac OS X, which will run only on the PowerPC G3 or later processors with at least 128 MB of RAM.

Your network may also be running some old AppleTalk applications that don't work over TCP/IP, especially if you've had any custom application development done. So as part of your transition strategy, you should plan for the coexistence on the same network of Mac OS 9 and earlier and Mac OS X machines, as well as machines running AppleTalk, TCP/IP, and both (**Figure 17.23**).

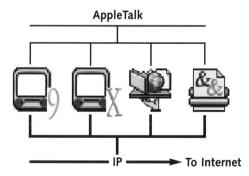

Figure 17.23 Macintosh networks in transition will consist of a mix of Mac OS 9 and Mac OS X machines as well as AppleTalk and TCP/IP protocols.

By migrating slowly, you will minimize the upheaval due to any loss of services or ease of use that Mac users have come to expect. Most important, you will be able to combat more thoroughly the loss of security that the migration could cause. As long as you consider security issues at every step of the migration, the overall security of your network should not suffer, despite the mixture of machine types and the potential decreased security of TCP/IP and Mac OS X. Only if you take security for granted or rush the implementation will your risk increase.

While migrating, focus on the security measures detailed throughout this book. If you have a large network, you may want to make someone specifically responsible for security as the network migrates. This person can act as a central point and knowledge source for security issues and can help maintain security consciousness throughout the organization.

Even after your network has migrated, having a security person may be a good idea. A completely migrated network is not necessarily one with all machines running Mac OS X and TCP/IP. More likely, it will have a mixture of Mac OS 9 and Mac OS X and of AppleTalk and TCP/IP. A completely migrated network is simply one that has all the changes that you wanted to make. Most migrated networks will continue to look like Figure 17.23 for some time to come. Whether or not the migrated network is mixed, the increased security risks of the migrated network warrant increased security resources.

For the latest on Mac OS X networking security, check out our book's companion website at *www.peachpit.com/macsecurity/*.

Securing Mac OS X

In 1984, Apple began a transition from the computer that got the company started, the Apple II, to the computer the rest of us use today, the Macintosh. In 2001, with the shipping of Mac OS X, Apple began the most significant transition since 1984. Although one of the main goals of Mac OS X is to ensure that a Mac running it looks and feels much like any Mac that came before, the advances in Mac OS X required radical changes in the underlying operating system. Operating system changes, particularly to networking components, combined with the fact that Mac OS X is based on the security-challenged Unix operating system make ensuring the safety of any Mac OS X machine connected to the Internet even more important than it was with previous versions of the Mac OS.

The Mac in Transition

Any transition involving a large installed base should be as smooth as possible. Users should be able to upgrade gradually and without loss of functionality. New digital television sets, for example, need to continue to be able to receive standard analog signals, just as the color TVs of the 1960s needed to receive black-and-white signals. Likewise, Mac OS X needs to continue to support applications and services that ran on Mac OS 8 and 9.

Apple had to solve many problems to make the Mac OS X transition a smooth one. Mac OS X had to continue to run on as many of the installed Macs as possible (which ended up being any PowerPC G3 or G4 machine). The Mac OS X user interface had to remain familiar and easy to use. And almost all of a user's applications and services had to continue to work on the new OS.

At the same time, Apple had to advance the state of the art not only in user interface but also in reliability and functionality. Apple chose to accomplish this goal by yanking the guts out of the 17-year-old Mac OS and replacing them with those of the Unix operating system (see the following section). But almost none of the applications that run on Mac OS 8 and 9 can run unmodified on Unix. Although Apple has minimized the number of changes application developers need to make to get applications to run on Mac OS X, developers still need to make some changes. Few users would move to Mac OS X if they had to get all new applications, even if those applications appeared quickly. For this reason, Apple implemented the Classic compatibility layer in Mac OS X.

Classic is essentially a large Mac OS X application (**Figure 18.1**). The Classic application creates a Mac OS 9 environment within Mac OS X. When a Mac OS 8 or 9 application is run under Mac OS X, Classic runs that application within the Mac OS 9 environment that it has created. The application is, for all intents and purposes, running under Mac OS 9. But Mac OS 9 is running under Mac OS X rather than directly on the Macintosh hardware.

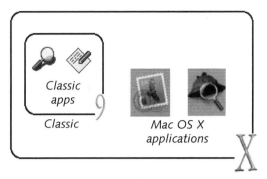

Figure 18.1 Classic is a large Mac OS X application that creates a Mac OS 9 environment
for apps that haven't been upgraded to
support Mac OS X.

Classic is the key to making the transition to Mac OS X seam-
less for applications. But it creates some interesting security
challenges, because services can exist in both environments
at the same time. Sometimes, protecting a service just under
Mac OS X will protect it in Classic; at other times, it won't.

Another transition accelerated by Mac OS X presents additional
security challenges. As we indicated in Chapter 17, Apple has
been moving Macintosh networking protocols from AppleTalk
to IP (Internet Protocol). Mac OS X puts heavy emphasis on
IP while continuing the gradual phaseout of AppleTalk. But
both protocols continue to exist within both Mac OS X and
Classic.

As you proceed through this chapter, keep in mind the additional
security issues introduced by these three key factors:

- The use of Unix in the Mac OS core
- The transition from Mac OS 8/9 to Mac OS X, especially
  its use of the Classic compatibility layer
- The ongoing transition from AppleTalk to IP

Also keep in mind that Mac OS X is new. Mac OS 9 has nearly
two decades of history behind it, so it is slow-changing and relatively well understood from a security perspective. Although
Mac OS X maintains a bit of this history, it is evolving rapidly
and is not well understood yet. New information comes out daily
and will continue to for some time. Use the rest of this chapter

as a guide to enhancing the security of your Mac OS X machine, but also check the Web and other sources to make sure that you have the most up-to-date information. The Web site for this book, at *www.peachpit.com/macsecurity/*, is another particularly good source of information on Mac OS X security.

Mac OS X General Overview

To understand and implement Mac OS X security, it is important to understand how Mac OS X works internally, which means learning about Unix as well as the Apple-added parts of the OS.

Unix

By far the biggest change between Mac OS 9 and Mac OS X is the new operating system's Unix base. Mac OS 9 was built on a home-grown foundation that evolved over nearly two decades. That base, however, was not designed for today's computer, which is capable of running multiple large programs simultaneously, taking advantage of myriad hardware options and peripherals, and interacting on a high-speed worldwide Internet. Apple has done a good job of maintaining the evolving Mac OS and keeping it up with the times, but it could go only so far without replacing its engine. Unix is Mac OS X's new engine.

Unix provides the Mac OS a new level of robustness. Each process (application) in Unix runs in its own walled-off memory space and can't interfere with other processes or with the OS. If a process crashes, it can't hurt other processes or bring down the whole machine. Unix also provides preemptive multitasking, making sure that each process gets its fair share of CPU time and that one process doesn't hog everything. Before Mac OS X, a malfunctioning Macintosh application could prevent all others from running.

Unix was designed as a multiple-user operating system, unlike Mac OS 9, which added multiple users on top of an inherently single-user OS. Getting around user restrictions is much harder in Unix than in Mac OS 9. Unix is also much harder to use, because its multiple-user design resulted in a complex command-line user interface.

Older Than Macs

Unix has been around longer than the Mac OS has. It was developed at AT&T's Bell Labs in the early 1970s, not coincidentally at about the same time that the Internet was getting started. Like the Internet, many of Unix's goals were academic. The original Unix developers were not burdened with the commercial pressures of bringing a product to market quickly (AT&T could sell only phones), so they built a scalable, forward-looking framework on which a major operating system could evolve. Also, Unix was developed for the larger minicomputers of its day, so it was ready when the speed and power of the personal computer advanced beyond those early machines.

Unix's design as a multiple-user operating system is also the principal reason for many of its security issues. Almost all its features were built to be accessed locally (from the keyboard) or remotely (over a network). Unix includes many network services, and its networking strengths are one reason why it has been growing in popularity in this Internet era and why Apple chose it as the basis of Mac OS X. These functional strengths, however, result in security weaknesses. You can do so many things to a Unix machine over a network that its designers and implementers have never been able to protect all its functions adequately.

Unix's networking features and security weaknesses have had a snowball effect. From the early days of the Internet, Unix's networking features made it the most popular operating system for providing Internet services. But this popularity, combined with its security weaknesses, encouraged early hackers, well before many Windows machines or Macs were on the Net. This security snowball gained momentum and size as the Internet developed.

> *Although Windows machines and Macs are now much more numerous on the Net than Unix machines, Unix machines are still the most common targets of hackers.*

Unix is *open-source*, which means that the detailed operating instructions (or source code) for the OS are available to anyone who is interested. An outgrowth of Unix's academic roots, open source helped Unix evolve and grow and was instrumental in such phenomena as Linux. On the other hand, Unix's open source has helped hackers search for and exploit vulnerabilities (although it's also helped security experts search for and plug security holes).

Unix is a highly functional, reliable, mature operating system, and it is an excellent choice for Apple to use as the guts of the Mac OS for years to come. But keep this telling fact in mind:

> *In the SANS Institute's list of the Ten Most Critical Internet Security Threats from January 2001, five apply only to Unix.*

Any security advantage that earlier versions of the Mac OS enjoyed due to its secure design and its lack of popularity with hackers is gone. The Unix security snowball is about to hit the Macintosh.

Unix for the rest of us

Mac OS X is Unix for the rest of us. Apple has done an amazing job of taking advantage of the good parts of Unix while shielding users from most (but not all) of its problems. The main Unix feature that Apple shields from users is Unix's command-line interface. After setting the standard for user interface for most of its existence, Apple wasn't going to settle for an interface that is a step 30 years backward. The Mac OS X interface is completely a Mac OS interface. It looks like a Mac, it feels like a Mac, it even talks like a Mac. As always, Apple is pushing the interface envelope in a few places, so things aren't exactly the same as they are in Mac OS 9. But if you've used a Mac before, you can use Mac OS X, whereas most of us wouldn't have a clue where to start with the Unix command line.

The Classic compatibility layer overcomes Unix's inability to run pre-Mac OS X Macintosh applications and facilitates the smooth transition that will encourage users to move to Mac OS X. Almost any application that runs on Mac OS 9 runs under Classic on Mac OS X without modification. The principal exceptions are applications that access the Macintosh hardware directly; Classic does not run on that hardware but on a virtual machine running on Mac OS X on that hardware. An additional limitation is that all applications running under Classic are part of a single Mac OS X application, so if any Classic application crashes or misbehaves, it can affect all the others.

But due to Unix's design, a crash can't affect any of the native Mac OS X applications or Mac OS X itself. Classic's limitations are a small price to pay for the amazing level of backward compatibility that it provides.

Another area in which Apple has done a good job of shielding Unix peculiarities is networking. Unix uses a significantly different internal networking model than the traditional Mac OS did and does not always include AppleTalk support. Apple had to adapt Mac OS networking features to this new model while continuing to support the old model for Classic. Despite the large amount of work involved, Apple managed to make Mac OS X's networking features almost as easy to use as those of Mac OS 9. Certain AppleTalk features are lacking in Mac OS X's first releases, but AppleTalk is not used for Internet access, and Mac OS X remains the Internet OS for the rest of us.

Finally, Apple has shielded users from many of Unix's security issues. By shipping the OS with most networking services disabled, enabling those services in their most secure mode by default, and making them as easy as possible to under-stand and use, Apple has gone a long way toward securing Mac OS X. Unfortunately, Apple could do only so much. Mac OS X is fundamentally Unix at its core, and Unix has many security problems. Add to these problems Apple's making Unix easy to use and more popular and thus increasing the number of hackers focusing on it, and security issues become even more significant.

This chapter will help you understand security in Mac OS X networking so that you can begin to feel as safe under Mac OS X as you have under past versions of the Mac OS.

Mac OS X Networking Overview

Before we get into specific issues relating to securing Mac OS X on the Internet, let's look at the networking support it offers, both from a client and a services point of view.

Client overview

Most users will use Mac OS X only as an Internet client, not to provide Internet services. When you install it, Mac OS X asks you a series of questions and sets up most of your Internet client information automatically. If you want to change that information or just see how your Mac is configured on the Internet, you can use the Network (**Figure 18.2**) and Internet System Preferences windows.

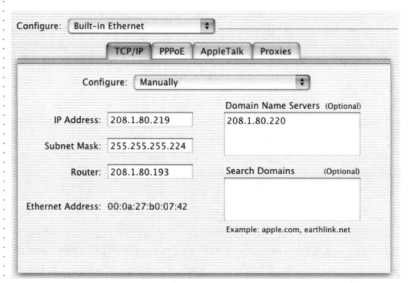

Figure 18.2 Mac OS X's Network System Preferences window allows you to view and change your machine's network configuration.

One new networking feature you may notice is that Mac OS X supports PPPoE (Point-to-Point Protocol over Ethernet) for DSL connections that require this Internet login technology.

The two most-used Mac OS X Internet clients are likely to be e-mail applications and Web browsers. Mac OS X can run Mac OS 9 e-mail applications and Web browsers through the Classic compatibility layer. But to take advantage of all of Mac OS X's features, check to see whether your preferred e-mail application and Web browser are available in Mac OS X versions.

Early versions of Mac OS X ship with a preview release of Microsoft Internet Explorer and include Apple's new e-mail application, simply called Mail. Mail is a highly functional and well-thought-out application and is integrated with Mac OS X, managing your password via the Mac OS keychain (see Chapter 4). It is also security-conscious in other ways, especially with regard to viruses (see "Safe Surfing" later in this chapter).

Mac OS X includes new clients for printing and accessing Apple-Share file servers. You choose printers and manage the print queue through the Print Center utility. You can connect printers to your machine directly through the USB (universal serial bus) port, through a local AppleTalk network, or via an intranet or the Internet through the LPR (line printer) protocol.

You access AppleShare servers through the Finder's Connect to Server command, which displays a dialog box similar to Mac OS 9's Network Browser dialog box (**Figure 18.3**). The first releases of Mac OS X do not support AppleTalk for accessing file servers; neither do they support User Authentication Modules (UAMs), which we mention in Chapter 17. You can connect only to servers that are accessible over TCP/IP. Even the Classic Chooser can access AppleShare servers only via TCP/IP. To illustrate the clash in the concurrent transitions from Mac OS 9 to Mac OS X and from AppleTalk to IP, the Classic Chooser shows AppleShare servers in its AppleTalk window but then tries to switch to TCP/IP to access them (which works only if the server supports TCP/IP as well as AppleTalk). The Classic Chooser does support UAMs.

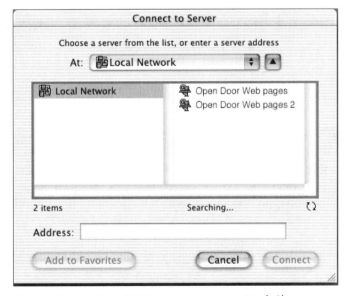

Figure 18.3 In Mac OS X, you connect to AppleShare servers through a dialog box much like the Mac OS 9 Network Browser dialog box.

The Connect to Server command also provides direct access to WebDAV servers. As described in Chapter 14, WebDAV is a secure alternative to FTP for use in developing and maintaining Web sites on external servers. WebDAV servers mount on the desktop just like AppleShare servers, making them more secure than those accessed through FTP and easier to use. You access Web-DAV servers by typing their URL (starting with http://) in the Address text box of the Connect to Server dialog box.

An interesting networking addition in Mac OS X is the Network Utility, which lets you perform various tests on your local TCP/IP network or on the Internet itself. You can send a ping to any machine on the Internet to see whether that machine is reachable, for example, or you can trace the full route to that machine. The inclusion of the Network Utility in Mac OS X is questionable, however. Some users will find it helpful for performing some simple diagnostics, but most users will not be able to understand much of it. Worse, the Network Utility can be misused in such a way that it affects the security of other machines on the Internet.

As mentioned in chapters 12 and 13, an important aspect of securing any machine on the Internet is installing a personal firewall on that machine, monitoring its log, and analyzing and reacting to apparent attacks. The Network Utility makes it easy to "attack" any machine on the Internet unintentionally. The attacks, which really are just diagnostic tests that you're trying to run from your machine, usually won't cause any direct harm to the machine you're testing, but they may appear in that machine's firewall's log file, sometimes flooding that log file so that real attacks are much harder to notice (**Figure 18.4**). Although the utility is just running a diagnostic test, that machine's user and analysis software may interpret it as an attack, especially because many hackers use two of the Network Utility's features (ping and port scan) extensively. As a general rule, you should not use these two features unless you know what you're doing, and then only in a limited manner. If you're port-scanning a machine over the Internet, for example, you should always scan a limited range of ports to minimize the effect of the test (**Figure 18.5**).

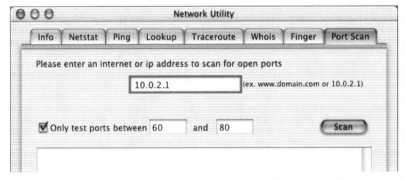

Date and time	Action	Service	Port	Mode	IP address
5/7/01 3:54:54 PM	Allow	unknown	60	TCP	208.1.80.218
5/7/01 3:54:54 PM	Allow	Dynamic Host Configuration Protocol	68	TCP	208.1.80.218
5/7/01 3:54:54 PM	Allow	unknown	67	TCP	208.1.80.218
5/7/01 3:54:54 PM	Allow	unknown	61	TCP	208.1.80.218
5/7/01 3:54:54 PM	Allow	Gopher	70	TCP	208.1.80.218
5/7/01 3:54:54 PM	Allow	unknown	62	TCP	208.1.80.218
5/7/01 3:54:54 PM	Allow	unknown	65	TCP	208.1.80.218
5/7/01 3:54:54 PM	Allow	unknown	63	TCP	208.1.80.218
5/7/01 3:54:54 PM	Allow	unknown	66	TCP	208.1.80.218
5/7/01 3:54:54 PM	Allow	Trivial File Transfer Protocol (TFTP)	69	TCP	208.1.80.218
5/7/01 3:54:54 PM	Allow	unknown	72	TCP	208.1.80.218
5/7/01 3:54:54 PM	Allow	Web Sharing	80	TCP	208.1.80.218
5/7/01 3:54:54 PM	Allow	Finger	79	TCP	208.1.80.218
5/7/01 3:54:54 PM	Allow	unknown	78	TCP	208.1.80.218
5/7/01 3:54:54 PM	Allow	unknown	77	TCP	208.1.80.218
5/7/01 3:54:54 PM	Allow	unknown	76	TCP	208.1.80.218
5/7/01 3:54:54 PM	Allow	unknown	75	TCP	208.1.80.218
5/7/01 3:54:54 PM	Allow	unknown	74	TCP	208.1.80.218

Figure 18.4 Certain features of Network Utility can flood another machine's firewall log with information, potentially causing real attack data to be missed.

Figure 18.5 If you need to do a port scan over the Internet, be sure to scan a small number of ports.

Services overview

Mac OS X's Unix base makes it possible for a Mac OS X machine to provide a wide range of Internet services. Apple included several of these services with Mac OS X, although they are turned off by default. Due to Unix's security vulnerabilities, you should leave Mac OS X services turned off unless you really need them (which should be rarely, if at all).

You access most of Mac OS X's built-in services through the Sharing option in the System Preferences window (**Figure 18.6**). Just as you can in Mac OS 9, you can use File Sharing to share files via AFP (Apple Filing Protocol) and AppleShare. In the first releases of Mac OS X, however, this sharing is possible only through TCP/IP, not through AppleTalk. To aid in the ongoing migration from AppleTalk to IP, if you have File Sharing on and enable AppleTalk (through the Network System Preferences window), your machine will show up in the Chooser of other machines on the same AppleTalk network as yours. When those machines try to communicate with yours, however, they will switch over to TCP/IP (unless they don't support it, in which case they'll indicate an error).

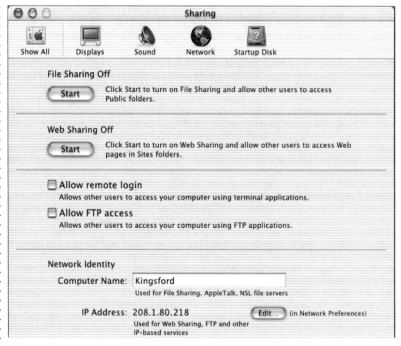

Figure 18.6 You enable most Mac OS X services through the Sharing System Preferences window.

Mac OS X's Web Sharing is much like it is in Mac OS 9. You enable this feature through a checkbox in the Sharing System Preferences dialog box, not through a control panel. Apple takes advantage of Mac OS X's Unix base to provide Web Sharing through Apache, the world's most popular Web server. Apache is incredibly powerful, but Apple provides no user interface for any of its wide range of features.

The Sharing System Preferences window provides checkboxes for two new services in Mac OS X: remote login and FTP (File Transfer Protocol). These features are standard Unix services and are powerful but risky in security terms (see the following section). Remote login allows a network user on your intranet or the Internet to log in to your machine and access its underlying Unix command-line interface as though he or she were at your machine. Remote login is useful for power users (and hackers) but not for most other users, because the command line requires detailed knowledge of commands and of the workings of the Unix operating system.

FTP (which we talk about throughout this book and especially in Chapter 14) is an old and insecure way to share files. Having been around a long time, FTP is available on almost all computer platforms and acts as a least-common-denominator method of sharing files. If you have a Windows machine on your home network and want to exchange a file with it, FTP may be the easiest way to do so. Most users, however, will have little need to enable this service.

One service that is missing from the Network System Preferences window, at least in the early releases of Mac OS X, is Program Linking. Although Mac OS X fully supports Apple Events and AppleScript, it does not include the capability to send these events to other machines via either AppleTalk or TCP/IP, which is how Program Linking is implemented. Program Linking is supported in the Classic layer, however.

In addition to the services in the Network System Preferences window, Mac OS X provides NetInfo, which is a central directory for storage of service information. NetInfo in its most general sense is a distributed database, with portions of the database being stored on different machines on a local network. Because most users do not run Mac OS X networks, NetInfo is simply a local database that they can access through the NetInfo Manager utility. You may want to look at the large set of information available in NetInfo, but you shouldn't change anything unless you know what you're doing. You may prevent a service from working or turn off some of its security settings accidentally.

Also in the "look but don't touch" category, Mac OS X provides access to the Unix command-line interface through the Terminal application (**Figure 18.7**). After running Terminal, you see a standard Unix prompt and can type any Unix command you want. Due to the number and complexity of its commands, Unix provides access to a detailed online manual through the command line. Type **man man** and then press Return to get the manual pages.

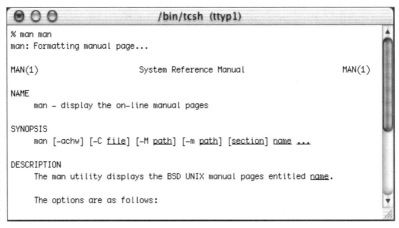

Figure 18.7 The Terminal application can provide full access to the Unix command line.

You can enable any of a large variety of Unix services through the command-line interface, including the Unix standard for file sharing, NFS (Network File System). Getting command-line-based services to work is well beyond most users' abilities, however, and using those services securely is a full-time job for many network administrators. In the future, Apple and third parties probably will provide graphical user interfaces for many of these services, at which time using them may become more practical. But you'll always need to keep security issues in mind.

Mac OS X Internet Security

This entire book is about securing your Macintosh on the Internet. Throughout it, we have tried to address security issues holistically and without regard to a particular version of the Mac OS. Everything we have said so far applies to Mac OS X.

Certain details are somewhat different, however. These details are also more critical, due to the new security issues that a Unix base brings to the Mac OS. In this section, we describe Mac OS X's security differences and what you can do about them.

What, me worry?

We started this book by asking this question. Mac users have long enjoyed a more secure Internet environment than other computer users. If you've read this far in this chapter, however, you understand that this advantage no longer exists with Mac OS X.

Yes, you worry!

Physical security

As part of their multiple-user heritage, all Unix machines require a password. This password provides an additional level of physical security, because you have to know the password to turn a machine on and use it. The Mac OS, however, has never required a password, other than in Mac OS 9's multiple-user feature. Apple felt that most users would want to continue to use Mac OS X machines without entering a password every time they started those machines. For this reason, Mac OS X enters your name and password automatically whenever you start your machine, using the name and password that you gave it when you installed it. If you want to require Unix's standard manual login to enhance the physical security of your machine, you turn off the automatic-login option in the Login System Preferences window (**Figure 18.8**).

The Login System Preferences window also includes a checkbox that lets you turn off the Shut Down and Restart buttons that normally appear in the login window. When these buttons are inactive, a user who has physical access but not the password cannot easily restart the machine from Mac OS 9 (by holding down the Option key while restarting) or from a CD-ROM. This checkbox provides a false sense of security, however, because the user could always turn your machine off and back on and restart it that way.

The Login System Preferences window includes the option to select a custom authenticator. This option is used on company networks to allow login through custom-authentication systems and directory services such as those described in Chapter 17.

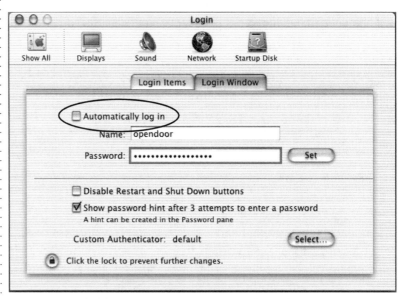

Figure 18.8 Disabling Mac OS X's automatic-login feature will enhance the physical security of your machine.

To provide further physical protection for your machine (**Figure 18.9**), an option in the Mac OS X Screen Saver System Preferences window requires you to enter your password after the screen saver starts. If you walk away from your machine and someone else walks in, that person will not be able to access your machine. To enable this feature, select "Use my user account password" and change the time for the screen saver to start from Never to a specific value. You can also use the Hot Corners feature to activate the screen saver right away before you leave.

Mac OS X provides direct integration with iDisk, no longer requiring you to go to the iDisk home page to mount your iDisk. Instead, you can mount it through the Finder's Go menu or even include an iDisk icon in the Finder's toolbars (**Figure 18.10**). As we mentioned in Chapter 3, iDisk provides an excellent backup option, especially for remote backup. Mac OS X's direct iDisk integration makes iDisk backup even easier to use, so you may back up more often, increasing the physical security of the data on your machine.

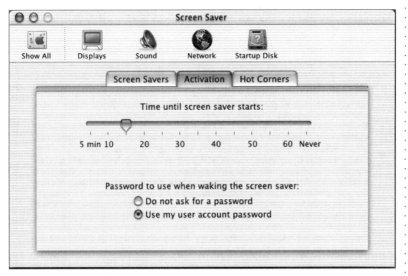

Figure 18.9 Mac OS X's screen saver can require you to enter your password after it's started.

Figure 18.10 Mac OS X's direct integration with iDisk makes iDisk even easier to use for backups.

Managing passwords

Unix passwords have at least one significant advantage over traditional Mac OS passwords: they can be more than eight characters long. The traditional Mac OS's Users and Groups control panel restricts passwords to eight or fewer characters. When few hackers existed and computers were much slower at guessing passwords, eight characters probably were sufficient for most services. But with the advanced password attacks we describe in Chapter 4, eight characters may not be enough.

Although Mac OS X allows much longer passwords than previous versions of the Mac OS, most of its services use only the first eight characters of a password. This arrangement creates a false sense of security, because hackers need to try only the first eight characters. Still, the ability to set longer passwords makes it less likely that people will use easy-to-guess passwords, because the first eight characters of longer words or phrases usually are hard to guess. In the future, Mac OS X services may take advantage of the full password.

Mac OS X also includes a password-hint feature. The password hint helps users remember their passwords, thereby allowing them to use passwords that are more difficult to remember (and harder to guess) without the fear of forgetting those passwords. When you set up a user account (see "Mac OS X's model for securing services" later in this chapter), you can enter a password hint for that user. If a user trying to log in enters an incorrect password three times, the hint for that password is displayed. Hints are optional, and if you use them, you should be sure that they provide significant information only to the user for whom they're intended. Hints work only for logging in to Mac OS X, not for accessing Mac OS X services.

The Mac OS X keychain works much like the same feature in Mac OS 9. It is better integrated with the system, however, and both the Mail application and your iDisk's passwords are included automatically. The keychain's password uses all the characters you enter, not just the first eight. One of the keychain's integration features can result in significantly decreased security, however. When you start your machine, your keychain is unlocked automatically if it uses the same password that you use to log in. Even if your machine is set up for automatic login, you still have a login password, and the keychain will be unlocked at startup if it uses that password (which it's set to do by default). This ease-of-use feature means that anyone who has physical access to your machine can access the services for which you have passwords on your keychain. They can also use the Keychain Access utility to look at the passwords you've saved for all those services, write those passwords down, and use them later without your ever knowing.

*After installing Mac OS X, run the Keychain Access utility, and change your keychain password to something other than your login password or set up the keychain to lock automatically after a specified period and when the system sleeps (**Figure 18.11**).*

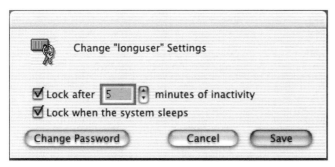

Figure 18.11 Immediately after installing Mac OS X, use Keychain Access to change the keychain's password or set the keychain to lock automatically.

Changing your keychain password, which prevents the system from unlocking your keychain automatically, is the preferred alternative; otherwise, a user could restart your system and obtain access to the keychain. A determined user will almost always be able to restart your system.

A final Mac OS X password issue to keep in mind: Anyone who has a Mac OS X CD can reset your Mac OS X machine's password. (Such a person could also reinstall the system, but reinstallation would take a long time, and you'd notice the changes.) The Mac OS X CD lets anyone change a Mac OS X machine's password (or change the password of the administrator of that machine, which usually is the same thing). This feature is intended to make sure that Mac OS X users are never locked out of their own machines, even if they forget their passwords. It is useful for that purpose but serves to further emphasize the importance of keeping your Mac OS X machine physically secure.

Safe surfing

Mac OS X includes Apple's new Mail application, which is integrated with the Mac OS keychain and is security-conscious in regard to viruses. Mail deletes attachments automatically whenever you delete the e-mails with which they're associated and warns you if you try to open an attachment that's an application, which usually is a bad idea (**Figure 18.12**).

Figure 18.12 The Mac OS X Mail application will warn you if you are opening an attachment that is an application, because doing so could infect your machine with a virus.

Mail and its companion Address Book application can access LDAP directory servers to help you find e-mail addresses (see Chapter 17). In its first release, however, Mail does not include secure e-mail features, such as the capability to send encrypted or authenticated e-mail.

Mac OS X's model for securing services

Mac OS X allows you to offer a wide range of Internet services from your machine. By default, these services are turned off, which is the way you should leave them for maximum security. If you do need to enable a service, Apple does a good job of making sure that the service is enabled in a limited, relatively secure way. But services on Mac OS X are implemented quite differently from previous versions of the Mac OS, and you need to understand how they work. If you understand a service before you enable it, you're much more likely to set it up correctly and securely.

Mac OS X uses the Unix model of service security simplified a bit for the rest of us. Even if you are the only one who will use the machine, it's always set up to allow multiple users. Different users on Unix have different levels of access. The user called root has full access to everything on the machine. Many Unix security attacks are based on a network user's logging into a machine as root or running a process on that machine that has root privileges. In Mac OS X, Apple disables the root account, decreasing the likelihood that many common Unix attacks will succeed. Disabling the root account also prevents a user from accidentally doing something that would severely damage his or her machine. Many Unix and core Mac OS X processes still run with root privileges to do their job, but users can't log in as root, either at the machine or over the network.

Instead of root, Mac OS X uses administrative users. Administrative (or admin) users have less power than root users but more than other users on the machine. If you are the only user of your machine, you are an admin user automatically. Admin users can do pretty much anything at the Mac OS level, such as change system preferences, install new system software, and create new users. They still can't do damaging things at the Unix level, however, such as delete key OS files.

Each user of a Mac OS X machine gets a home folder, stored within the Users folder on the hard disk (**Figure 18.13**). Users' home folders are where they keep all their private files, in addition to files and a Web site that they want to share with other people. Users of the machine can't see most files in the other home folders.

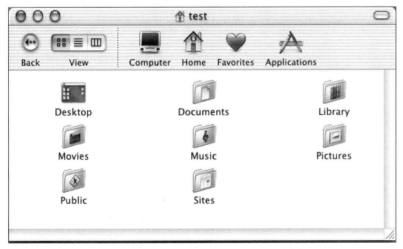

Figure 18.13 Each user of Mac OS X has a home folder.

You create authorized users for a machine in the Users System Preferences window (**Figure 18.14**). When you create a user, you give that user both a long name and a short one, although the system will derive a short name for you automatically, if you want. Most Unix services use the short name, which is limited to eight characters, is all lowercase, and cannot contain special characters (such as spaces). Passwords can be as long as you like, although most services use only the first eight characters. You can include a password hint in case a user forgets his or her password, although the hint is provided only when a user tries to log into the machine from the keyboard, not through other services. If you want the user to have full administrative privileges on the machine, you can check the appropriate checkbox.

Figure 18.14 You create Mac OS X user accounts in the Users System Preferences window.

Unix also uses groups, but Apple generally shields this concept in Mac OS X. Mac OS X admin users are placed in the admin group automatically, and Mac OS X defines a few other groups for its internal use (such as staff and wheel). But you can't create or assign users to specific groups easily.

Securing Mac OS X services

The four key Mac OS X services that you can make available through the Sharing System Preferences window are File Sharing, Web Sharing, Remote Login, and FTP (Figure 18.6). All these services give network users access to aspects of your machine that they otherwise could have only by sitting down at the machine itself. Each service provides a different form of access in a different way, but all the services use the same user name and password. As indicated in Chapter 4, this arrangement provides additional security exposure, because compromise of one service's password can lead to compromise of the other services and of the machine itself.

Of the four services, Remote Login is riskiest and also the least likely to be needed. Remote Login gives authorized network users the same level of access they would have at the machine itself, except through the Unix command line rather than through the Mac interface. Unless you are a Unix expert, follow a simple rule about Remote Login:

> *Do not enable Remote Login. The Unix command line is of little use to most Mac users but potentially of great use to hackers. Enabling Remote Login exposes your machine to network attacks that could take full control of the machine at the Unix level. Many Unix machines are compromised through Remote Login.*

If you feel that you need to use Remote Login, make sure that your version of Mac OS X is at least 10.0.1. To check, choose About This Mac from the Apple menu. The original release of Mac OS X, 10.0, shipped with a highly insecure implementation of Remote Login called Telnet. Telnet sends its entire session in clear text, including user name and password. Anyone listening in on the conversation between a Telnet client and your Mac OS X machine (usually through automated sniffer software) would be able to capture your name and password and log in to your machine as you.

In Mac OS X 10.0.1, Apple replaced Telnet with SSH (Secure Shell). SSH uses advanced encryption techniques to make the session much more secure. Regardless of this increased security, exposing the full command-line interface of your Mac

OS X machine over the network remains risky and is not very useful unless you're a Unix expert. The risk almost never justifies the reward. If you do take the risk, however, be sure to follow these guidelines:

- Use Mac OS X 10.0.1 or later.

- Verify that all users on the machine have well-chosen passwords.

- Install a personal firewall.

- Allow access to the SSH service only from IP addresses that really need it.

FTP is another Unix-based service with high security risks; generally, you should not enable it. (See Chapter 14 for details.) FTP gives authorized network users connecting to your machine the same level of access to files that they would have if they were logged in to the machine directly. FTP shows files and folders that generally are invisible in the Finder and are more difficult to access when a user is logged in directly.

Mac OS X does not support anonymous FTP, so users who access files from your machine with FTP must have a user name and password, even if you don't want them to be able to log in to your machine. Because FTP has a particularly high risk of password compromise, you should be sure that FTP users do not have administrative access to your machine. That way, if a password is compromised, the hacker will not be able to log into your machine as an administrator.

Mac OS X's File Sharing is a much more secure, easier-to-use alternative for sharing files, especially with other Macs. File Sharing is somewhat different from Remote Login and FTP in terms of the access it gives authorized network users. If an authorized network user is an admin user, that user has complete read-only access to all files and folders on the machine, in addition to any access that he or she normally would have at the machine. Non-admin users, on the other hand, have less access than they would have if they were at the machine. Specifically, a non-admin user has full access to only the files and folders within his or her home folder and not to other files, such as applications. Also, non-admin users, like guests, have read-only access to the public folders of other users of the machine. File Sharing does not display invisible files.

Mac OS X File Sharing supports guest users, just as Mac OS 9 does, so you don't need to create accounts for users with whom you want to share files—another significant advantage over FTP. By default, any guest user has read-only access to the public folders of all authorized users on the machine. A user who wants to share files with guests simply needs to place those files within his or her public folder, which is inside the home folder. Public folders also contain a drop box where guests can put (but not see) files that they want to transfer to authorized users.

Admin users can change the access privileges of files and folders on the machine, and all users can change the access privileges of files and folders within their home folders, although only public folders are actually shared to guests through File Sharing. To change an item's access privileges, choose that item in the Finder, and then the Finder's Show Info command from the File menu. In the dialog box that appears, choose Privileges from the Show pop-up menu and select the desired privileges (**Figure 18.15**). Even though you can assign sharing privileges to any file or folder, you can share only the folders that the Mac OS makes available for sharing— the whole hard disk for admin users, a user's home folder for nonadmin users, and public folders for guests.

Figure 18.15 Setting Mac OS X File Sharing privileges is much the same as under Mac OS 9 but somewhat more limited.

Mac OS X File Sharing uses a different AppleShare (AFP) authentication protocol than previous versions of Mac File Sharing. It uses Diffie-Hellman Exchange (DHX) rather than random-number exchange. DHX, described in Chapter 14, is highly secure and supports longer passwords than random-number exchange. (Mac OS X File Sharing currently uses only the first eight characters of the password however.) Most Macs support DHX for File Sharing, but some older ones may not. If an older Mac doesn't support DHX, it may send its user's password in clear text, which would be indicated in the Chooser (Figure 14.6). Most older Macs can be upgraded to use the latest AppleShare client, which supports DHX.

Mac OS X Web Sharing operates through the Unix-standard Apache Web server. Apache is extremely powerful, but Apple does not make its features available through the Mac OS X user interface. Experts can access these features through Apache's text-file and command-line interface, but the procedure is complex and not recommended.

When Web Sharing is enabled, specific folders are shared at specific URLs. Users of the machine can have their own Web sites, and the machine as a whole has a general Web site. Any files that users put in their Sites folders within their home folders will be available over the Web at *http://computers-IP-address/ ~ username/*, in which computers-IP-address is the IP address of the machine and username is the user's short name. The tilde (~) is an unfortunate Unix standard that Apple chose not to eliminate. Any files that you put in the Documents folder, which is inside the WebServer folder in the Library folder on your hard disk, will be available at your computer's main site at *http://computers-IP-address/*.

Mac OS X does not provide an easy way to apply privileges to files shared through Web Sharing. Web Sharing seems to be intended for Web sites that are accessible to the whole network to which the machine is connected. Apache does provide a high level of control in this area, but this control is available only through its text-file-based interface.

As you can see, each of the Mac OS X sharing services works a bit differently, which can be confusing and can lead to security holes if you assume that one service works the same way as another. **Table 18.1** summarizes the levels of access that these services grant to admin users, nonadmin users, and guests.

Table 18.1

Service	Type of Access	Admin-User Access	Nonadmin User Access	Guest Access
Remote Login	Unix command line	Same as at machine	Same as at machine	None
FTP	Files and folders via FTP client	Same as at machine	Same as at machine	None (no anonymous FTP)
File Sharing	Files and folders via AppleShare client	Same as at machine, plus read-only access to everything	User's home folder, other users' public folders	Public folders
Web Sharing	Web site via Web browser	Main and user sites	Main and user sites	Main and user sites

You can use the NetInfo Manager utility to set many advanced items associated with Mac OS X services (**Figure 18.16**). NetInfo is recommended only for expert users, however, because the risk of decreasing the security of a service far outweighs the potential benefits of tweaking that service. If you feel you know what you're doing, you can use NetInfo to put a user in a specific group, change the port used by File Sharing, or enable and set details of File Sharing's logging (see "Detecting and responding to security threats" later in this chapter). You can also use Net-Info to enable the root account, but doing so is asking for trouble.

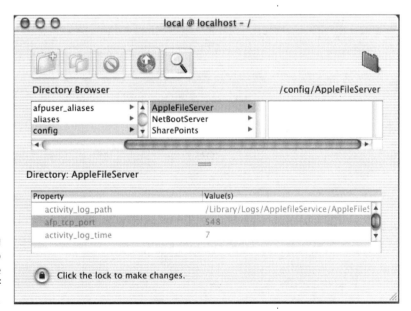

Figure 18.16 You can use the NetInfo Manager to change advanced features of Mac OS X services.

Remember that Mac OS X services run as Unix processes. Most Unix processes keep running even if you've logged out of your machine. Don't assume that a service is no longer accessible just because you've logged out. Either stop the service before you log out or shut down the machine rather than just log out of it.

You should also be sure that services that could run in the Classic compatibility layer are secure. See chapters 7 through 10 for details on securing these services, although all network services that run under Mac OS 9 do not necessarily run under Classic. To secure Classic services such as Program Linking, you need to run an older application that starts the Classic environment and then choose the service from the Classic Apple menu or the third-party user interface.

The Unix security community is an active one. Black hats (hackers) are always looking for new Unix security holes, and white hats (the good guys) are always working to fix them or to find them before the black hats do. Fixes are released in the form of patches that are applied to Unix-system files. Apple makes patches available through the Software Update System Preferences window. (Unix patches usually are applied through the command line.) It's important to run Software Update periodically or set it to check for updates automatically (**Figure 18.17**). Apple maintains a security Web site at *http://www.apple.com/support/security/* that provides details of the updates and related security issues.

Figure 18.17
Software Update will help you ensure that any security patches that Apple releases are applied to your system as soon as possible.

Viruses

Although Unix machines are popular for running Internet services, they have not been popular among the end-user community. End users tend to do things that spread viruses, such as installing applications and sending and receiving e-mail. Attacking a Unix machine could bring down a whole set of Internet services and is exciting to hackers. But infecting a Unix machine with a virus isn't very exciting to a hacker, because that virus wouldn't spread very quickly or to many machines. At least until Mac OS X, most virus creators weren't interested in Unix.

But Mac OS X's Unix base presents interesting opportunities for introducing viruses, and many hackers really understand that base. Ideally, most virus writers will continue to concentrate on Windows machines, but it's a safe bet that Mac OS X is causing at least some writers to consider Unix. New classes of viruses will be created, and new antivirus software will be needed. Mac OS X viruses will no doubt be a rapidly growing and changing area, so you should monitor it closely by checking the Web sites of the popular antivirus software manufacturers.

When you protect your Mac OS X machine against viruses, remember the Classic layer, because applications that run under Classic may not be protected by Mac OS X antivirus software. Check that software's documentation. You may need to install additional software to protect the Classic environment from viruses.

Personal firewalls

Due to Unix's significantly different networking implementation from that of previous versions of the Mac OS, personal firewalls that work under Mac OS 8 and 9 will not work under Mac OS X (except possibly to protect services running in the Classic environment). Because Unix machines have been especially vulnerable to Internet attacks, many firewalls have been developed for Unix. Most Unix implementations include some sort of built-in firewall. Like most Unix applications, however, these firewalls usually are configured through the Unix command line and are not appropriate for the rest of us. Nonetheless, you do need to understand a bit about Unix firewalls.

Even if you considered a personal firewall to be optional under Mac OS 9, Mac OS X's Unix base makes a personal firewall essential.

Mac OS X includes a Unix firewall feature called ipfirewall, which is accessible only from the command line. If you want to find out the details of ipfirewall, type **man ipfw** in the Terminal application and press the Return key. The information you get will show you why you don't want to consider using ipfirewall directly. Setting up ipfirewall is so complex that you're sure to make mistakes that open your machine to attack or prevent it from working on the Net (**Figure 18.18**). Also, ipfirewall requires root privileges, which you should never enable (see "Mac OS X's model for securing services" earlier in this chapter).

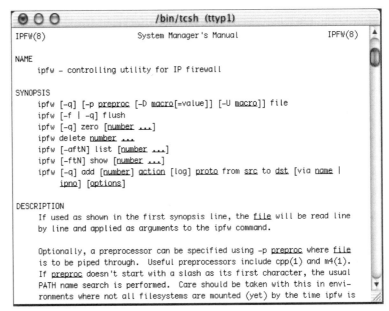

Figure 18.18 The firewall built into Mac OS X's Unix base requires a level of expertise that even most Unix users don't possess.

An early piece of Mac OS X shareware, Brickhouse, layers a Mac OS X user interface on top of ipfirewall (**Figure 18.19**). Brickhouse is highly functional, letting you access many ipfirewall features through a GUI and eliminating the need to know numeric details about many of the ports that common services use. Unfortunately, Brickhouse does not hide the underlying rules and logging model that ipfirewall uses and it is somewhat complex (although less complex than ipfirewall).

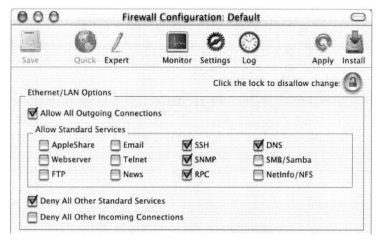

Figure 18.19 Brickhouse layers a Mac OS X user interface on top of ipfirewall.

Full-fledged versions of popular Mac OS 9 firewalls are available for Mac OS X, and you should consider installing one of them as soon as possible. Symantec's Norton Personal Firewall for Mac OS X, for example, is as easy to use as its Mac OS 9 product. It provides built-in support for key Mac OS X services such as FTP and Remote Login as well as logging and notification features (**Figure 18.20**).

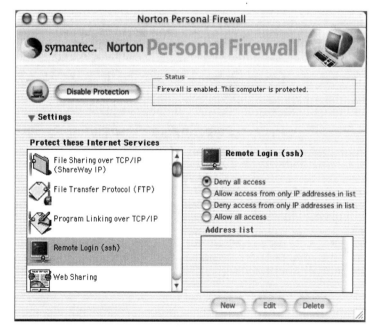

Figure 18.20 You should install a personal firewall on a Mac OS X machine as soon as possible.

Just as you do for antivirus software, you need to make sure that your Mac OS X personal firewall protects Classic as well as native Mac OS X services. The ipfirewall software included in early releases of Mac OS X did not protect Classic, so you have to install a Mac OS 9 firewall for Classic even if you use that software. Check your Mac OS X firewall's user guide to see whether it protects Classic.

As we mentioned in Chapter 12, personal firewalls may prevent you from downloading files via active-mode FTP. One way around this restriction is to enable passive-mode FTP. Under Mac OS X, you can enable passive-mode FTP in the Proxies tab of the Network System Preferences window (**Figure 18.21**).

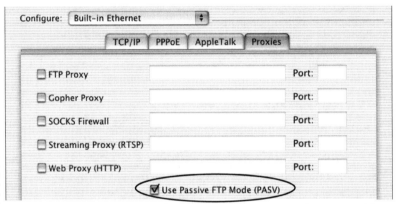

Figure 18.21 Use the Network System Preferences window to enable passive-mode FTP downloads through your personal firewall.

Detecting and responding to security threats

Because Mac OS X is Unix-based, common attacks that on previous versions of the Mac OS could be safely ignored (see Chapter 13) become much more significant. As long as you have installed and are running a personal firewall and have blocked access to the ports associated with these attacks, you should continue to be secure. When analyzing and responding to threats, however, pay additional attention to attacks against common Unix services such as RPC, DNS, LPR, and SMTP.

As we said in Chapter 13, one key security aspect of any service is its capability to log and monitor accesses and access attempts. The first releases of Mac OS X leave something to be desired in these areas. After you've enabled a Mac OS X service, it's difficult to determine whether that service is being accessed and by whom. Mac OS X has no equivalent of Mac OS 9's File Sharing Activity Monitor, for example. Most services can write log files, but the files are written in inconsistent formats and in different places on your machine's hard disk.

> *The difficulties in monitoring Mac OS X services make it even more important that you install a personal firewall with good logging and notification features and that you consider a firewall log-analysis application as well.*

Mac OS X's core Internet services have log files associated with them. Most of the services log to Unix-specific folders, which may not be visible in the Mac OS X Finder. To have the Finder display an invisible folder, you can type the full Unix path to that folder into the Finder's Go To Folder command, or use a shareware application such as TinkerTool, which causes the Finder to show all invisible files and folders.

Remote Login. All remote logins to your machine are logged to the general system log. Unfortunately, just about everything else that goes on is logged there as well, so you'll have to search this log carefully for logins. The system log is system.log in the log folder, which is inside the invisible var folder (or, in Unix parlance, /var/log/system.log). The format of the system log is the Unix standard syslog.

FTP. FTP logins and attempted logins are logged to /var/log/ftp.log in syslog format.

File Sharing. The File Sharing log is disabled by default. Turning it on is a bit tricky, because it requires the NetInfo Manager utility. If you use File Sharing, though, the File Sharing log can be quite important in tracking down details of successful or attempted accesses, so you may want to use NetInfo to enable the log. Run the NetInfo Manager from the Utilities folder, and choose config and then AppleFileServer (**Figure 18.22**). In the bottom list, you will see several attributes. Scroll down to near the bottom of the list, and set the activity_log attribute to 1. (You may need to authenticate as an admin user through the lock in the bottom-left corner to make changes.) Then close NetInfo Manager and confirm that you want to make the change. You'll need to restart your machine for logging to take effect.

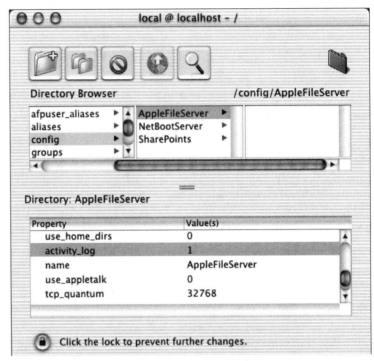

Figure 18.22 Turning on the File Sharing log is one of the few tasks for which you should consider using NetInfo Manager.

Unlike most other services, File Sharing does not store its logs in an invisible folder. Instead, those logs are in the Apple-FileService folder inside the Logs folder, which is inside the Library folder. The file name is AppleFileServiceAccess.log.

The File Sharing log is quite detailed, using a format similar to the one used by Web Sharing.

Web Sharing. The Web Sharing log is the standard Apache log, which comes in two parts. Both parts are stored at /var/log/httpd/, with the main log being named access_log and the error log being named error_log. These logs are in what has come to be known as common log format, or CLF. Many excellent log-file analyzers are available for CLF; the most popular is called Analog.

Some Unix services have automatic log archiving. Periodically, or when the log reaches a certain size, the log file is renamed and sometimes compressed, and a new log file is started. The system log is often renamed and compressed to a name such as system.log.1.gz. (gz indicates GZip compression.) Old log files are often automatically deleted.

Third-party services, especially firewalls, should also write log files. These files should be stored in the Logs or Preferences folder inside the Library folder, although if the service is Unix-derived, the log may be stored in /var/log/. Consult the service's user guide.

As indicated in the "Client overview" section earlier in this chapter, Mac OS X includes the Network Utility for diagnosing Internet problems. The Network Utility includes two features for investigating attacks detected by your firewall or other service: whois and traceroute. Chapter 13 describes both of these features.

Just say no to FTP

We cannot emphasize enough how risky it is to enable FTP on any Mac OS X system connected to the Internet. As indicated in Chapter 14 and the "Securing Mac OS X services" section earlier in this chapter, any access to your FTP server over the Internet could result in compromise of the user name and password associated with that access. Because you also have to create a Mac OS X user account on your machine to provide FTP access to that user, compromise of the FTP password also results in compromise of the login password and the File Sharing password. Even if you don't enable remote login, and even if the user is not an admin user, giving hackers access to a user password on a Unix system is asking for trouble.

Mac OS X provides more-secure file sharing services than FTP. File Sharing works well for sharing files with other Macs, and WebDAV (see Chapter 14) is also integrated into the Mac OS X Finder. (Only the client is included, however. You need Mac OS X Server to turn your machine into a WebDAV server.) Several Unix options are available for providing native Windows file service through SMB, although these features are not integrated into the OS and may be difficult to install and use. Still, the added security is worth the extra work.

The only situation in which using FTP may make sense is when you need to exchange files locally with a non-Macintosh platform, such as over a home network. As long as the exchange is local, the clear-text password will not be sent over the Internet and will not be subject to compromise. But make sure that you have enabled WEP in any wireless network you're using (see Chapter 16) and turn FTP off immediately after the exchange, because hackers commonly use dictionary attacks to look for available FTP servers.

Home networking

A Mac OS X machine can be a full participant in a home network. Follow the security measures in this chapter, however, because compromise of your Mac OS X machine is more likely than compromise of your other Macs, and your Mac OS X machine could serve as the weakest link in your network if you're not careful.

Due to the limited AppleTalk support in the first releases of Mac OS X, you need to use TCP/IP services within your home network—to share files with the Mac OS X machine, for example. AppleTalk is more secure than TCP/IP for home networking (see Chapter 15), because it's not routed over the Internet. If you do enable TCP/IP services on your home network, follow the recommendations in this book about how to do so securely.

Mac OS X's Unix base includes a command-line-based NAT gateway (see Chapter 15). gNAT, which is similar to Brickhouse, provides a Mac OS X interface on top of the built-in NAT gateway functionality. You can use gNAT to provide Internet access to machines on your home network with only a single IP address from your ISP and to act as a basic personal firewall (**Figure 18.23**).

Wireless networking

Mac OS X has full support for connecting to AirPort networks on machines that have AirPort cards. But you cannot administer the AirPort base station through the early releases of Mac OS X, even through Classic. You need to use a Mac OS 9 machine or restart your Mac OS X machine as Mac OS 9.

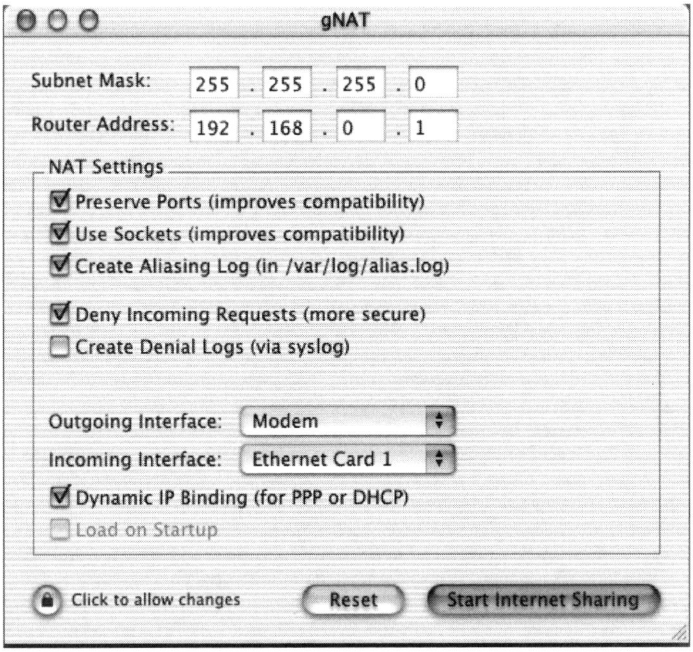

Figure 18.23 You can use gNAT to turn your Mac OS X machine into a NAT gateway.

You access AirPort networks through the Mac OS X Internet Connect application or the Signal Strength dock item (included in the Dock Extras folder in the Applications folder).

Internet security at work

Many issues are associated with Mac OS X security at work, especially with regard to the ongoing transitions from AppleTalk to IP and Mac OS 9 to Mac OS X. See Chapter 17 for all the details.

Index

Y

Z